PROFESSIONAL ETHICS IN EDUCATION SERIES
Kenneth A. Strike, EDITOR

"Real World" Ethics:
Frameworks for Educators and Human Service Professionals,
Second Edition
Robert J. Nash

Justice and Caring:
The Search for Common Ground in Education
Michael S. Katz, Nel Noddings, and Kenneth A. Strike, Editors

The Ethics of School Admnistration, Second Edition
Kenneth A. Strike, Emil J. Haller, and Jonas F. Soltis

Ethics in School Counseling
John M. Schulte and Donald B. Cochrane, Editors

The Moral Base for Teacher Professionalism
Hugh Sockett

Ethics for Professionals in Education:
Perspectives for Preparation and Practice
Kenneth A. Strike and P. Lance Ternasky, Editors

The Ethics of Multicultural and Bilingual Education
Barry L. Bull, Royal T. Fruehling, and Virgie Chattergy

The Ethics of Special Education
Kenneth R. Howe and Ofelia B. Miramontes

Classroom Life as Civic Education:
Individual Achievement and Student Cooperation in Schools
David C. Bricker

"REAL WORLD" ETHICS

∞

*Frameworks for Educators
and Human Service Professionals*

SECOND EDITION

Robert J. Nash

Foreword by Jonas F. Soltis

TEACHERS
COLLEGE
PRESS

Teachers College, Columbia University
New York and London

Published by Teachers College Press, 1234 Amsterdam Avenue, New York, NY 10027

Library of Congress Cataloging-in-Publication Data

Nash, Robert J.
  "Real world" ethics : frameworks for educators and human service professionals / Robert J. Nash ; foreword by Jonas F. Soltis. — 2nd ed.
      p. cm. — (Professional ethics in education series)
  Includes bibliographical references and index.
  ISBN 0-8077-4256-2 (pbk. : alk. paper).
      1. Applied ethics—Study and teaching. 2. Ethics—Study and teaching. 3. Professional ethics—Study and teaching.   I. Title. II. Series.
  BJ66 .N37   2002
  170'.71—dc21   2002024575

ISBN 0-8077-4256-2 (paper)

Printed on acid-free paper
Manufactured in the United States of America

09   08   07   8   7   6   5   4   3

To Madelyn, the most ethical person I have
ever known;

and to Cody James, my grandson:
May he strive to live the ethical life.

CONTENTS

FOREWORD

This is a book written for anyone who now teaches or who will be teaching applied ethics in education or such human service fields as counseling, social work, medicine and allied health services, clergy, law enforcement, journalism, and government. It demonstrates a keen sensitivity to the real world problems faced by such professionals, while also bringing genuine philosophical integrity to the process of applying ethics in the workplace.

It is also a book to be read profitably by anyone in any vocation who wants to make sense of the ethical dimensions of their work and understand where their ethical judgments come from. It is not an academic ethics text. It is one of the clearest renderings that I have ever seen of what an ethical life and ethical decision making by ordinary people in a pluralistic society is about.

Any individual who wonders if there can be any satisfactory basis for ethical judgment and behavior in the pluralistic, often nihilistic and relativistic society in which we all live will find much here to satisfy that need, without having to abandon their real feelings and intuitions about morality. This text speaks to real people in the real world of everyday life.

It is written by a highly successful and respected teacher of applied ethics, Robert Nash, who shares insights into his successes and failures of 34 years of teaching and listening to human service professionals in his courses, seminars, and workshops. He has been a pioneer in this rapidly developing field. His contributions neatly fit the current image of the good reflective practitioner, one who is continually developing his craft. He has moved from teaching the single dimension language of ethics dominant in philosophy today—that of moral principles, rules, ethical theories, and rational decision making—to include and describe what many students in ethics courses find missing in such a cool, thin, and detached approach. Taking on the "hot," "thick" problems of real life and encouraging reflective intuitive "involvement" by students, Nash develops a framework of three moral languages to serve professionals in the workplace.

The first moral language is one that helps students articulate their fundamental background beliefs and values about the work they do, why they do it, and what human good it serves. The second provides a means to explore and explicate their conceptions of moral character and professionally relevant virtues that define who they are and who they want to become as persons and professionals. The third is the abstract language of rules and principles, of ethical theories, but now it is related to the personal and communal contexts of the first two languages and provides a rich public tool for ethical justification. His text includes extended analyses of case studies using these languages, and he makes many excellent references to relevant contemporary books on the topics at hand. The point of this approach is to engage students in an extended and meaningful moral conversation, one that results in a richer command of these moral languages and serves professional purposes. This is not values clarification; it is the creation of moral understanding in the best sense of the term.

This second edition carries forward his earlier work with the addition of a lengthy Epilogue. In it, Nash practices his own principles of having meaningful moral conversations with students and critics who have raised probing questions about his approach to applied ethics as they read and used the first edition. It is a masterful job of adding layers of explanation and understanding to his earlier chapters as well as new ideas that will help anyone using the book to do so even more successfully. This is a book that will speak eloquently and practically to all human service professionals who know that they will constantly find themselves faced with critical ethical decisions in their work in the real world. It is a book that covers a lot of ground and does so with clarity, commitment, care, compassion, and common sense.

Jonas F. Soltis
William Heard Kilpatrick Professor Emeritus
Teachers College, Columbia University

ACKNOWLEDGMENTS

Blaise Pascal once remarked that ethics is basically simple: It is "thinking well" and doing the "kind, generous, and splendid thing." I agree. The following people have done the "kind, generous, and splendid thing" in helping me to write this book.

I am especially indebted to Madelyn, my wife, who has truly been a "splendid" model of love, support, and ethical inspiration throughout our 34 years of marriage. I hope the book's dedication to her accurately conveys the extent of my gratitude. I also wish to thank her for her professional advice on Chapter 4.

My daughters, Melissa Marie (Mika) and Kiersten Jennifer (Kayj), have listened patiently and lovingly to my ethical disquisitions through the years, and not once have they dismissed me as a mere "moralist." I am delighted to be the father of two such extraordinary young women, both of whom, I am proud to say, are following me into college teaching. For this project, I am indebted to Mika for her technical assistance with outlining and referencing.

I want to acknowledge Jonas Soltis, Professor Emeritus at Teachers College, Columbia University, a man I have never personally met but who, as a past editor of *Teachers College Record* and as a reviewer of my work in other venues, has been enthusiastically supportive of my ethics scholarship for years. I deeply appreciate his, and Professor Kenneth Strike's, assistance in getting this book published with Teachers College Press; and I am particularly thankful for Jonas's Foreword. At the Press, too, I thank Susan Liddicoat for her expert editorial advice.

At the University of Vermont, I am personally grateful to my colleague, friend, and past collaborator, Robert Griffin, for constantly encouraging me to write books as well as articles and for believing that I truly have something important to say about teaching. Because he himself is always working on a new book, Professor Griffin is that rare academician who inspires scholarly emulation.

I also wish to thank William C. McMurray, Jr., for help in developing, and thinking through, the admissions case in Chapter 5.

Finally, over a 34-year career, I have never once taken for granted the blessing it has been to teach ethics at the University of Vermont. I am surrounded by colleagues who are good friends, wise advisors, and worthy adversaries. If it is true that to teach is to learn twice, then I have learned countless lessons through the years, the most important being that I have the luxury of raising fundamental moral questions in a university classroom without always having to know the answers. The gifted, discerning students who come to my courses seem more than able, and willing, to find the answers themselves.

Chapter 1

TEACHING "REAL WORLD" ETHICS WITH COOL PASSION

"Passions unguided are for the most part mere madness."
Thomas Hobbes, *Leviathan*

Like most teachers, I have had my doubts about my effectiveness. In my darkest moments as an ethics professor, I often recall Oliver Wendell Holmes' dictum that, at best, science makes major contributions to minor needs. Pace Holmes, when things are not going very well, I believe, with only slight exaggeration, that professional ethics courses make minor contributions to major needs. Nevertheless, all of the pitfalls and struggles of teaching (and taking) ethics courses notwithstanding—and I will be describing some of these in the present chapter—what I wish to accomplish in the pages that follow is to write a very different kind of ethics textbook for both teachers *and* students of ethics.

For me, "real world" ethics is a complex admixture of personal, social, and professional morality, and ever since those initial years, starting in 1970, when I developed one of the first applied ethics courses ever offered in a college of education in the United States, I have scrupulously attempted to keep my ethics courses rooted in the real world of students' everyday lives. In keeping with this spirit, I have tried in the following chapters to write about applied ethics from the reality of my own everyday experience—as a college teacher who finds himself several times a year facing diverse groups of undergraduate and graduate students, each expecting to learn something useful about a huge and volatile subject matter called professional morality. Thus, my turn to the first-person singular in the pages to come is motivated less by arrogance and the need for self-revelation than by personal necessity: I find I can only write honestly and engagingly about a "real world" ethics by discussing in personal terms the *why* and the *how*, along with the *what*, of my ethics teaching.

Even though I have written a kind of hybrid ethics text that is somewhat personal and reflective, I have also written one that is mainly conceptual and practical—one meant to reach a very wide audience of both instructors and students in education and the human services. The book is calculated to serve two purposes: *One,* for teachers of professional ethics

1

courses in a number of professional and college venues, it emphasizes actual classroom pedagogy. Among other topics, the book includes: a code of ethics for teachers of applied ethics; the presentation and analysis of an ethics syllabus; an extensive applied ethics bibliography; accounts of how to help students construct an ethics case and do a case analysis; how to frame and carry out a "moral conversation" for talking ethically about ethics in the classroom; and how to teach technical moral languages in a down-to-earth way in order to help students resolve everyday ethical dilemmas.

Two, the book is directed to undergraduate and graduate students who are learning how to resolve ethical dilemmas in their respective professions. To this end, the book presents detailed problem-solving frameworks (what I call "moral scaffolding") that I have spent over a quarter of a century developing. The book demonstrates step by step for students: How to identify ethical dilemmas; how to use a number of technical languages to think through, and resolve, those dilemmas; how to read professional codes of ethics and to develop a personal code of ethics; and how to translate moral theory to professional practice in a way that is always concrete, applied, and very topical. Over the years, I have taught the content of this text to students who represent dozens of professions and disciplines.

Finally, in the pages to come, my working definition of the word *ethics* (*ethikos, ethos,* G., character, standards, custom, convention) is expansive, in that it has three parts. I will be employing the term in all three modes throughout the text. First, ethics has to do with the analysis of concepts such as ought, should, duty, right, wrong, obligation, and responsibility (Angeles, 1992). This *metaethical* dimension is not only concerned with a non-normative analysis of central terms, but it also deals with the logic of moral reasoning and the nature of moral justifications and inferences. I will be spending less time on this aspect of ethical investigation than on the following two modes. Second, a system of ethics provides a set of operational reference points (principles, rules, virtues, background beliefs) by which one can adjudicate conflicts of interest in order to make ethically justifiable decisions and judgments. In this sense, the purpose of *applied* ethics is to adapt general ethical background beliefs, virtues, and principles to the resolution of specific cases. This is sometimes called applied normative ethics or casuistic (*casus,* L., case) ethics, because it brings the content of ethics to bear on actual cases or dilemmas where two relatively equal choices (or goods) may be in conflict (Jonsen & Toulmin, 1988). And, third, ethics provides a set of ideals with which to build a coherent, moral life plan. In this usage, ethics furnishes a framework to judge the worth of one's life in order to declare it valuable, good, or right. I will be using the words *ethics* and *morals* (*mos, moris,* L., convention, custom, conduct) interchangeably, as do many leading ethicists (Frankena, 1973), because, etymologically, the root of each term is so similar in meaning.

THE EARLY YEARS

Because I teach in a professional college, my students represent a variety of helping professions: elementary and secondary education, higher education, counseling, social work, allied health, clergy, government, business and extension, and law enforcement, to name but a few. During my early years of teaching, this polyglot of professionals, frequently together in the same seminar, expressed similar concerns:

- How can a professional hope to be both competent and moral when, in some circumstances, the most effective course of action might have to be the most morally questionable one?
- Is it possible to know once and for all what is right and wrong in professional practice?
- Why is it important to do what is right as long as the job gets done well?
- Is it really possible to convincingly defend moral actions and beliefs to others who do not share similar ethical standpoints?
- Is there an objective basis for making moral decisions that everyone might agree on?
- Does there always have to be a consistency in ethical behavior, or is ad hoc ethical action the most realistic approach to moral practice?
- How can a professional believe in categorical, or universal, rights and wrongs when so many evidently successful people profess primary allegiance to their own subjective beliefs?
- Where should a professional's main ethical loyalty lie—to the self? to clients? to the profession? to the employer? to the society?
- What can a professional do when these loyalties appear to be in irreconcilable conflict?

What so many students many years ago wished to explore further in a systematic and helpful way was whether appropriate ethical behavior and problem-solving is a matter of feeling; whether it is blind; whether it is a matter of reasoned judgment; whether it is primarily a result of personal virtue; whether it is something learned in professional structures or personal communities; or whether it is a precarious mixture of all of these factors.

Since those early years, my ethics courses have undergone considerable modifications in content, goals, and procedures. I have developed four separate courses in applied ethics at my university, which means that, during a 27-year period, my offerings have probably been the first applied ethics exposure for hundreds of human service professionals in my state and region. This contact with student professionals has meant more to me than all the scholarship I have produced and all the ethics consultancies I have offered throughout the country. Unlike Oliver Wendell Holmes, who was pessimistic about science, I am optimistic that classroom instruction in ethics can touch professionals' lives in some very productive ways.

But I am not naive. While it is true that I have reaped many rewards from teaching applied ethics courses to professionals from a variety of fields, I hope I have also learned much from my failures.   I know full well the pitfalls of framing generalizations regarding the teaching of ethics to aspiring and practicing human service professionals. Indeed, if it is axiomatic that any kind of serious moral discourse is inherently hazardous, then certainly discourse on the teaching of ethics will compound those hazards. Professorial humility seems to be a prime requirement for successful ethics teaching and for writing about successful ethics teaching as well. In this regard, I remember wondering in those early days whether I was properly qualified to teach in this field. Because I did not have direct career experience in several of the professions represented in my classes, my applicative credibility felt quite tenuous. At that time, the scant literature on ethics training was of little help to me, because it usually specified rigorous grounding in moral philosophy coupled with, at least, minimal first-hand contact with a profession as a prerequisite for ethics instruction (D. Callahan & Bok, 1979).

And yet other criteria appeared to be important, too: a strongly developed social conscience, a life of personal probity, intellectual resilience, and clinical competence because, at times, class discussion grew intensely emotional and students became embarrassingly self-disclosing and, occasionally, even menacing and defensive. There were times when I found that students wanted me to be a kind of ethical polymath incorporating the best pedagogical qualities of a Lawrence Kohlberg, a Carl Rogers, and even a Phil Donahue. Was I an entertainer? a Socratic gadfly? a prophet? a values clarifier? a dispassionate scholar? Did I have the prudence to resist the temptation to moralize or to provide "ethical therapy" for the morally befuddled? These seductions intensified for me each semester as ethical investigation became more complex and problems appeared to grow more insoluble. I was not always confident of my ability to be acutely aware of those times when my classes were undergoing subtle shifts in direction, format, and tone.

Moreover, because I never had a monolithic professional group in my classes, my readings and applications had to be diverse in content and wide-ranging in practicability. In various semesters, I included study in such units as medical ethics, journalistic ethics, clinical/counseling ethics, educational ethics, business ethics, legal ethics, and even advertising ethics. (My more cynical students rarely missed an opportunity to inform me that the last three designations were oxymorons, so why bother!) Regardless of the profession, however, the unit on *educational* ethics had to remain constant because, in my college, it is assumed that *all* practitioners are engaged in helping relationships, and education is always a key component of helping others (Nash & Ducharme, 1976). Thus this professional diversity, coupled with an extremely latitudinarian definition of education, created a multitude of problems for me. While I diligently tried to identify cross-cutting moral themes common to all the professions, there were many times when I completely missed the mark. It seemed, at any given time, I was always out of sync with at least a few professional groups. To this day, I still struggle to find relevant readings, assignments, and activities that specify dramatically enough the ethical dilemmas pertinent to each of the professions represented in my classes. I want to recognize and respect the professional diversity in my classes while, at the same time, I wish to be scrupulously attentive to those moral issues, principles, and ideals that unify us in spite of our professional differences.

One other more strictly pedagogical problem plagued me in those early days. I was never really secure in my choice of teaching strategies. I had rarely been successful in using values clarification games (Raths, Harmin, & Simon, 1966) or a moral development approach (Kohlberg, 1981) because I had a built-in resistance to prepackaged ethical processes, stages, and outcomes. I had seen more than a few education professors become mere stockpilers of materials: films, tapes, games, case studies, overheads, grids, and handbooks. And yet I also knew that the pedagogical value of a problem-solving approach to teaching ethics to professionals was irrefutable. My students almost always responded enthusiastically. Two serious pedagogical pitfalls arose for me, however, whenever I tended to overuse problem-driven, game-based strategies. I found that my methodological paraphernalia sometimes overwhelmed the content of the course. Too often, the drama of my "dazzling" teaching techniques merely ended up blurring the important moral issues at hand. And such vaunted "nonjudgmental" strategies as values clarification and the use of moral development dilemmas were, in actuality, so loaded with the superiority of certain principles and ideals that their creators' claims of "value-neutral" inquiry seemed a sham. Whenever I used them, I sometimes ended a particular class session feeling more like a sneaky preacher than a Socratic provocateur.

STIMULATING THE MORAL IMAGINATION

As those early years unfolded, I discovered that as a teacher of ethics I needed to be unequivocally clear to myself and to my students about my purposes in teaching ethics courses. I knew vaguely at the outset that I wanted my course to be "applied," because the majority of my students were either preparing to be educators in a variety of human service settings, including schools and universities, or they were already full-fledged professionals operating mainly at middle-level management positions in a number of social service organizations. Although I have met very few students in my classes through the years whom I would call "anti-intellectual" (contrary to the ugly stereotype that colleges of education attract mainly students who are practical-minded dolts), it is true that undergraduate and professional students in a professional school often come to late afternoon and early evening classes with a set of more complex expectations than their counterparts in nonprofessional programs.

For one, my students demanded that, at some time during the course, philosophical theories had to be rigorously applied to the solution of definite problems. They also required a meticulous sensitivity on my part to the particular philosophical gaps in their previous educations. Undergraduates rarely took philosophy courses. And whenever I asked a graduate class of middle-aged professionals which ones had taken at least one philosophy course during their earlier years, only a few hands got raised; more alarming, not a single soul could remember even a scintilla of philosophical content from those courses. I realized that I could assume nothing philosophical regarding their prior intellectual training or else I risked—in spite of their best efforts to remain alert—losing the attention of a group of skeptical and confused students even before the first class hour had elapsed.

After the first few years, I decided, therefore, that simply "stimulating the moral imagination," as Daniel Callahan and Sissela Bok put it in an early essay (1979), was not a feasible goal in my teaching. Confusion seemed to arise constantly in my classes as to the relationship of moral beliefs to actual professional behaviors. Whenever I tried to emphasize what I thought was an exacting *philosophical* examination of their moral assumptions, calculated to stimulate the moral imagination, students would challenge me, at some point in the stimulation process, to help them resolve some very upsetting and very real ethical dilemmas they were facing in their workplaces. How should they deal, for example, with breaches of confidentiality, cheating, enticements to practice beyond their professional competence, corporal punishment, lying, whistle-blowing, disobedience, sexual harassment, the unfair distribution of scarce resources, favoritism, and conflicting professional/personal obligations and loyalties?

From my students' perspectives, these were truly concerns that cried out for exploration and resolution, but what was my response? I was clumsily, and contentedly, in the words of Daniel Callahan and Sissela Bok (1979), trying to cultivate a "moral imagination . . . that human beings live in a web of moral relationships, that a consequence of moral positions and rules can be actual suffering or happiness, and that moral conflicts are frequently inevitable and difficult" (p. 25). Such a standpoint is neither fallacious nor uninspiring, of course; at that time, however, I did not know how to connect it directly to the thorny and persistent ethical problems that plagued my students and that continued to come up in class, even during the most absorbing philosophical dialogues we had. With more than a modicum of self-pity and arrogance, I remember thinking during one class—in the midst of a very heated confrontation with a nurse who insisted loudly that I "put away the philosophy texts and get down to earth with me in the intensive care unit"—that I was perhaps destined to be an unappreciated, modern-day Plato soaring above a group of impatient pragmatists. I was damned if I was going to let a bunch of hard-boiled practitioners bully me into problem-solving every session!

Fortunately, my purposes for teaching an ethics course became clearer as my distinctions became sharper. Obviously, I wanted to encourage both moral perspective *and* ethical problem-solving, but how to do this was still a mystery to me. In searching the literature for some kind of help regarding applied ethics pedagogy in the 1970s, I happened upon four authors who themselves taught applied ethics courses. Although these authors were not concerned centrally with pedagogical problems, their early efforts to reconcile theory and practice in the classroom proved suggestive to me. Edward Stevens (1974) argued that the teaching of ethics should never freeze at the level of particular do's and don'ts, because this can lead to a "specious moralism" that degenerates into oversimplistic moral formulas, rules, and codes. Stevens contended that ethics instruction should take a broader view: It should help students to become less the "uncritical captives" to unstated moral assumptions they may already hold. Arthur Dyck (1977) went one step further: Effective ethics teaching should encourage "systematic reflection" upon the specific acts of individuals and groups, what they ought to do, and how they ought to behave. And Tom L. Beauchamp and James F. Childress (1979) argued that only when teachers undertake a systematic examination of moral principles in order to determine how they apply to specific cases would they be able to bring "some order and coherence" to a discussion of ethics. For Beauchamp and Childress, two bioethicists, applied ethics is "the application of general ethical theories, principles, and rules to problems of therapeutic practice, health care delivery, and medical and biological research" (p. 9). Beauchamp and Childress, in the 1970s, were among the first applied ethicists to employ actual case studies in their teaching and scholarship.

These authors helped me to understand that ethical study represented a modest yet effective way for me and my students to discover, before and after they acted, how they would best like to act—and then imaginatively test in advance some of the difficult choices that lay ahead. By trying to get students to look ahead *and* back, on the basis of a critical examination of their already present, deepest moral presuppositions, I managed to achieve some early success in clarifying my own goals for teaching ethics and in heading off a certain amount of unnecessary goal bewilderment (and resistance to philosophical concepts) on the part of students. By helping students to get a firm and articulable grasp on what moral principles they already held, via pertinent philosophical texts and case studies, I was able to help them see where their moral perspectives might have been flawed, in need of enrichment, or inconsistent with their everyday behavior. In the chapters to come, I will explain the coupling of ethical analysis and actual ethical problem-solving in much more depth. But let it be said at this point that merely "stimulating the moral imagination" of students in order to enlarge their moral perspectives even today seems both incomplete and a bit presumptuous, absent other necessary problem-solving elements.

PROMOTING ETHICAL ANALYSIS

Because I wanted to do more than merely cultivate a moral perspective in those first few years, at one point I attempted to transform my student professionals into analytical philosophers. I wanted them to become "ethical analysts," because this was what I thought some of the best moral philosophers of the day advocated (D. Callahan & Bok, 1979; Hudson, 1970). After all, I reasoned, to encourage students to identify ethical complexities, wrestle with opposing points of view, discover flaws in their own ethical biases, and reach thoughtful, informed, and logically defensible conclusions were exercises that any professor of philosophy would applaud. Cultivation of analytic skills, I believed, would keep my courses from deteriorating into platitudinous exhortation, arbitrary and doctrinaire imposition of opinions, and off-the-wall resolution of specific ethics cases.

At first, because I had no clearly thought-out goal or procedures for developing precise analytical skills, my teaching often elicited from students a variety of first-hand, experientially based opinions. For example, a physical therapist believed that lying about treatment outcomes was sometimes warranted because, in a few personal cases, he had possibly saved a patient from unnecessary psychological suffering. A teacher education student thought the threat of corporal punishment appropriate because, if she was able to quiet a troublesome child with it, why not? A social worker intern violated a promise of confidentiality because his agency supervisor said to "play it by ear" and use his own good "instincts." Although each of these actions could be analyzed and justified within a rigorous system of rules, principles, definitions, and ethical theories, students seemed to balk whenever I attempted to get them to scrutinize more carefully the leaps they were making from personal experience, to "gut" hunches, and, finally, to practical actions and decisions.

As I gained experience and confidence in the classroom, I gradually came to require more exacting documentation of all ethical disputation. I introduced increasingly subtle rule distinctions between deontological and utilitarian positions. I became a "metaethical hardliner": Each week the air fairly crackled with the analysis of the ethical language students were using; of the truth value of the claims they made in the name of right and wrong; and of the validity of cognitivist and noncognitivist epistemologies. A few students exulted in the rarefied intellectual experience; most failed to see the point of it all. I struggled during those early years to achieve an integration of normative and metaethical approaches in the teaching of analytical skills. But, disappointingly, I found the balancing act among metaethics, normative ethics, and professional application always delicate and exasperatingly tenuous, because it seemed so intangible to students.

While it is true that a "definitive" resolution to ethical problems can be established on morally defensible, objective grounds that are far more substantial than mere personal opinion, I know from experience that such a solution also contains the possibility of its own negation. I found myself haunted during those initial years of teaching by a nightmarish vision: A contingent of "ethical technocrats" would march out of my ethics classes, professionals who were technically skilled in analysis, but who were "scoundrels"—rational, defensible, rule-following scoundrels to be sure, but self-seeking scoundrels nonetheless. Derek Bok (1976) once observed that if ethics is taught exclusively as an analytic justification process, the chances are great that colleges will produce only "ethical logicians" who can clarify, sharpen, and analyze their moral presuppositions, but who still may not know how to do the right thing in morally ambiguous situations. Bok worried, as did I, that the temptation would be too great simply to fall back on a reasonable kind of "cost-benefit" formula: "If I do this, will I protect myself? Will the organization's policy be upheld? Will I get caught? What, when all is said and done, is in my own best interest?" In reaction to Bok's plausible fears, I wanted to develop in students something more: a sense of moral commitment and responsibility that would ground their rapidly developing analytical skills.

CULTIVATING A SENSE OF COMMITMENT
AND RESPONSIBILITY

Notwithstanding Bok's concern, I was sensible enough to know that, as in every other type of educational experience, there can never be a fool-proof, money-back guarantee that any single ethics course will make a student more ethical. When all is said and done, it is a matter of precious faith that an academic experience which enjoins students to think carefully and deeply about the complexity of ethical decision-making will make any existential difference at all. In the face of such realism, however, I still struggled to encourage students to make moral choices and to take responsibility for those choices. I was taken by Martin Eger's (1981) remark that too often ethical analysis is to ethical responsibility as soft porn is to Platonic Eros. Soft porn, you see, also talks of something it calls love. I agreed with Eger that unless ethical analysis leads to ethical behavior, then the study of ethics becomes merely a fig leaf for the shameless oppportunist and a cosmetic for the professional college that requires it.

In a way, for me to talk about fostering a sense of moral commitment and responsibility was easy. Many students had little patience for ethical instruction that merely pointed the way, through a disciplined process of defensible reasoning, to *their* ultimate responsibility to make a moral choice. Most resented what they perceived to be a type of professorial abandonment on my part at the exact point of making an ethical choice. To them, my efforts to avoid "imposing my views" smacked of a cowardly ethical relativism. As one educational administrator publicly charged me: "You are a moral voyeur who gets students all excited about ethical decision-making, but who then cops out when we ask for specific guidance in defining the content of what is morally good and evil."

On the other hand, few students wanted to be indoctrinated. Their instinctive ethical skepticism got activated very quickly whenever I consciously (or unconsciously) tried to smuggle into a case analysis an undefended personal moral preference. They wasted little time in pointing out my "shameless" efforts to propagandize in behalf of a favorite ethical stance. One could argue, of course, that to the extent students detected any ethical sleight-of-hand in my instruction, then I had done a good job in alerting them to sloppily disguised, ethical special pleading. But the issue still remained: For most students, a sense of moral obligation and personal responsibility, while highly important, was not enough. In addition, they wanted a clearly defined moral content by which to live their lives. I remember, to this day, a third-grade teacher challenging me in class: "Professor Nash, tell me what uncompromised, moral ideal you would die for at this very moment!" My flustered response, I am sure, was as unintelligible as it was unsatisfying. In those days, I wondered whether it was possible (or desirable) to furnish students with a prescriptive moral agenda. Was this what I was about as an ethics professor? Did I automatically become a privileged member of some "moral magisterium" simply because I was foolish enough to teach an ethics course to professionals?

In the early 1980s, I found two articles that shed some light on what I would call the analytic/normative dichotomy in my teaching. Peter Drucker (1981) and Mark T. Lilla (1981) raised the controversial issue of whether the study of ethics should ever be moral education. Drucker, a moral prescriptivist, argued for an "axiomatic ethics of interdependence" (p. 30), based on a Confucian moral model. He advocated measuring each ethical transgression against a universal ethic of "sincerity": Actions which are appropriate to the spirit of interdependence and, hence, promote harmony in specific relationships are "right behavior" and, therefore, ethical. And Lilla, a neo-Aristotelian, urged that applied ethics courses should teach people to do the right thing by teaching them the duties and virtues of "democratic moral behavior" (p. 5). For him, the correct virtues were "rather obvious": courage, tenacity, and prudence. Lilla would have ethics instructors be, first of all, good human beings who preach, witness, and exemplify what is moral.

Both articles stirred up considerable controversy among students. Some were ready to "send the philosophers home" and leave ethical training to the morally committed priest, parent, or social revolutionary. Others feared that such indoctrination would result in a theocracy or in some worse type of moral authoritarianism. In the early 1980s, the articles raised a host of moral issues that continue to surface in my courses even at the present time: How are ethics and moral education distinct and yet the same? What is the difference between "pure" and "applied" ethics? between absolute and relative morality? between skepticism and commitment? between "catching" and "studying" ethical principles? and between freedom and responsibility? I will explore these and similar questions in the chapters that follow within the context of developing a "real world" ethics.

PROMOTING TOLERANCE OF DIVERSE ETHICAL VIEWPOINTS

Notwithstanding the need to cultivate a sense of moral commitment and responsibility in students, my single greatest challenge in the early years was to help students deal with ethical ambiguity without becoming "absolute relativists" or pessimistic cynics. Because of the inevitable presence of a number of competing conceptions of morality in any class, eventually even the most intractable students learned that quick, easy answers to complex moral questions were impossible. Every moral choice inevitably raised new doubts, new issues, and new agendas. Gradually, students tended to catch on well to civil and rational modes of philosophical discourse. They learned to listen carefully, reason sharply, respond empathically, raise trenchant questions (all in a "nonjudgmental" way, of course), and, in short, deal comfortably with ethical complexity and ambiguity—at times, *too* comfortably, I worried.

Often, students came to confuse *understanding* another viewpoint with *accepting* it. Occasionally, some rushed to a premature and facile resolution of differences of moral opinion in order to relieve the tension of ethical combat. And more than a few students arrived at the conclusion that because disagreement and ambiguity were so common in ethical analysis, then there was nothing that could ever be unequivocally asserted about ethical behavior. Too many students thus became ethical cynics who sneered and mocked at the efforts of others to arrive at unassailable first principles for moral behavior. Attacks on religionists, who may have believed in objective moral norms, were especially harsh. Even more regrettable, some of these cynics were on the verge of becoming amoral opportunists who knew full well the "cash value" of an appropriate bibliographic reference or an adroit logical maneuver in ethics discussions, but who seemed to know almost nothing about making a personal moral commitment to anything beyond the advancement of a narrow, professional self-interest.

I have learned, through the years, that an effective antidote to the more toxic effects of an uncontrolled student skepticism is an up-front, "truth-in-packaging" set of announcements in my syllabus. I try to be as clear as possible that students can gain much from taking an ethics course. I declare that they will initially learn more than they thought possible, but less than they will probably be satisfied with by the end of the semester. It is in the first class that I and my students discuss their goals for the semester in light of my own. In general terms, we talk about the activity of ethical analysis, the need to stimulate our moral imaginations in order to develop a sense of commitment and responsibility, and the importance of learning how to respect diverse ethical viewpoints without compromising our own deeply held, carefully considered moral beliefs. We also explore, among other issues, the need to learn how to discern and challenge moral "error" in a mutually respectful way, the function of a sense of humor and perspective in weekly discussions, the question of whether a class on ethics should promote behavior change as its primary goal as opposed to simply achieving an "ethical literacy," and the folly of any quest for moral certainty

meant to secure unanimous agreement. Getting these issues out on the
floor early in the semester seems to fortify the class later against the appearance of corrosive cynicism.

CONCLUSION

What I will present in the chapters that follow are the fruits of much
that I have learned through the many years I have been teaching "real
world" ethics courses. I will probe more deeply many of the issues I raise
above. Although, as the aforementioned makes clear, my early failures were
(and still are) legion, I do not wish to suggest for one moment that classroom successes were rare in the early years or that I myself gained little by
way of moral and pedagogical insight. I offer the following personal reflections, as well as concrete, systematic recommendations for teaching (and,
by implication, for taking) ethics courses, with "cool passion," and with a
great humility leavened with a considerable pride. I offer them in the spirit
of someone who has not only "been there" for many years but also loves
what he does so much that he struggles valiantly to improve his craft every
single day of his professional life.

In Chapter 2, I discuss the difficulties of teaching ethics ethically. I
spend the better part of this chapter introducing a trichotomous "moral
languages" approach to teaching applied ethics, a method I have been developing for several years. I also argue that in an ethics course a syllabus
must be a type of fiduciary contract—a truth-in-packaging document
that spells out clearly the ethical obligations incumbent upon both instructor and students, as well as the content of the course. I offer my own syllabus
as a model and undertake an *explication de texte*, an elaboration of my syllabus's language, style, and content. Within the context of this *explication*, I
propose a series of aphorisms that operate as a code of ethics for "right
relationships" in my seminar.

In Chapter 3, I develop more fully what I call the First Moral Language—a language of Background Beliefs—which constitutes the "zero-
level" (those taken-for-granted, metaphysical assumptions) that forms the
metaphysical backdrop for students' ethical problem-solving. I present a
series of Background Belief "probes" designed to help students to identify
these zero-level suppositions.

In Chapter 4, I present what I call the Second Moral Language—a
Language of Moral Character—in order to help students discover and explore in a systematic fashion the personal and structural contexts for their
ethical decision-making. In this chapter, I discuss the strengths and weaknesses of a casuistic (case study) approach to applied ethical analysis, and I

methodically adapt the Second Moral Language to an actual case in order to show how a Moral Language approach works. I introduce a special typology for carrying out this analysis.

In Chapter 5, I present what I call the Third Moral Language—a rules and principles discourse—that students can use to logically defend their resolutions of ethical dilemmas. The Third Moral Language is the dominant ethical discourse in the professions today, and I systematically apply this language to another actual case. My Third Moral Language typology has been 20 years in the making, and I present it in detail here.

And in Chapter 6, I tie up the loose ends in the best spirit of what I call "moral bricolage": I attempt to integrate the various moral languages into a structured whole so that they form one usable ethical language. I argue that every ethics educator must become a "bricoleur" who engages continually in the "selective retrieval and eclectic reconfiguration" (Stout, 1988, p. 76) of various moral languages. Within this integrative Moral Language context, I critique three current ethics pedagogies that are gaining in popularity among ethics educators: what I call the self-help model, the political-analytical model, and the consultancy model. In this chapter, I also critically examine two newly developing moral languages—the languages of caring and of character education—and show how these two discourses contain both excess and promise for creating an integrative ethics pedagogy.

Finally, as I approach the imposing task of creating a "real world" ethics, I find it almost impossible to write in an impersonal or dispassionate manner about what has been the core of my professional life. I seek for the same type of salient balance in my writing that I have sought in my teaching: the achievement of a "cool passion." "[Hot] passions unguided," according to Hobbes (1651/1962), "are for the most part mere madness" (p. 65). "Cool passion," though, serves teachers and writers well, I believe, because it balances the forces of heart and mind, personal investment and critical detachment, private disclosure and professional distance. I have been at my best as a classroom teacher when I remain calm but cordial, dispassionate but responsive. I have been at my worst when my teaching has been so frenzied that it borders on the frantic or so imperturbable as to appear chilly. My intention, therefore, is to write with as much "cool passion" as I can muster, so that both impassive *and* impassioned readers might discover something worthwhile in its pages. In Chapter 2, I begin the journey by showing how my course syllabus tries to establish the appropriate ethical tone for an intense semester of study.

TEACHING ETHICS ETHICALLY

"Ethics and aesthetics are one and the same."
Ludwig Wittgenstein, *Philosophical Investigations*

It never fails. During preregistration week, the phone calls begin: "Professor Nash, I am planning to take your ethics course this semester. I have heard so much about it that I am a little anxious. Don't get me wrong. My friends [or colleagues] really liked the course when they took it, but I still don't know what to expect. I want to be sure I can do the work given my other responsibilities this term. Will there be a lot of reading? Do you, by any chance, have a syllabus I might look at so that I know what lies ahead for me?"

Such phone calls make me happy because not only am I feeling insecure that I will have sufficient enrollment to offer a course in ethics each term, but, believe it or not, I actually enjoy writing syllabuses! In fact, I look forward to writing a completely new syllabus each semester in order to clarify for myself, in a fresh way, just why I continue to teach ethics courses and what exactly I hope to achieve in any given semester. I have never been able to understand why some colleagues fail to put together a substantial syllabus. As a student confided bitterly to me: "Too often, course syllabuses tend to be one-page jokes for one-page courses."

As a parent, I have sometimes learned the hard way that the best way to teach morality to my children is to live my life morally. Similarly, over the years, I have learned that the best way to teach ethics is to teach ethically. Thus, in the true spirit of an ethics course, I believe my syllabus should be ethically exemplary. The above caller will soon learn that I consider the course syllabus to be a binding fiduciary contract I have with each student. It actually operates on two levels: It attempts to outline and summarize the major content to be covered in a course; and it strives to fulfill students' right to know exactly what is expected of them so that they can give their fully informed consent, not merely to formal course requirements, but also to my peculiar way of doing things as a teacher. Over the years, my syllabuses have grown thicker and thicker. Students jest that if they can get through my hefty syllabus in class on opening day, then they can easily complete any subsequent reading requirements during the semester. Because of its length, I believe my syllabus sets the appropriate tone of the course from the opening moments and spells out in considerable detail, with minimal jargon, just how seriously I take the work that faces us in the weeks to come. It also begins to build the trust that I believe is necessary for effective ethics teaching.

The one drawback of a substantial syllabus, unfortunately, is that a few students incorrectly experience it as a "weeder," calculated to eliminate the faint-of-heart, as well as the philosophical novice, from my class on the first day. This disturbs me. Because I have never seen myself as one who uses his syllabus to remove undesirable elements from a course, I make it a point to acknowledge at the outset that I consider a fairly comprehensive syllabus, written in an informative and entertaining manner, my way of showing how much I look forward to working with, and getting to know, my students. This disclaimer aside, though, the groans of some students, as they plunge into a reading of my beefy syllabus, are still painfully audible on opening day.

At this point, I will present a typical syllabus for one of my more generic applied ethics courses, as an example of what I mean when I speak of teaching ethics ethically. I will omit only specific logistical information (course requirements, reading lists, etc.) that the reader might not find relevant at this juncture. What comes next, then, is essentially what students receive on the first day of class. You will be reading what they read.

SYLLABUS:
ETHICS OF PROFESSIONAL RELATIONSHIPS

Greetings. As often as I have taught this course, I frequently hear the same questions from students about its purposes, content, expectations, and, yes, relevance. I will attempt to respond to many of these concerns in what follows, and I promise to be as clear and concise as I can. I will also introduce you to a basic moral framework and problem-solving approach to professional ethical dilemmas that I have been developing over a 27-year period. During the semester, I will do my best, with your assistance, to adapt my philosophical framework to your special professional issues, concerns, and dilemmas. I believe that our several readings, for example, will touch on many of your unique ethical dilemmas, whatever your profession.

Please know that, although I am a veteran teacher of sorts, I always begin a semester of ethics teaching with considerable trepidation. In my experience, students all too often harbor several unfortunate stereotypes and fears about ethics content and instruction. Permit me to try to dispel a few of these clichés and perhaps allay some personal anxieties for you.

In so doing, I will also be declaring my purposes in teaching this course and clarifying my expectations of you this semester as you strive to fulfill the course requirements.

"Ethics courses are too didactic."

Rest easily. I will not be teaching you what's categorically right and wrong about particular professional practices. This is the prerogative of someone far more insightful (and dogmatic) than I. I simply cannot give you surefire answers to complex moral dilemmas. I have no neat moral formulas. Although I do believe that objective ethical analysis is possible, even desirable, what I, an applied philosopher, intend to do this semester is to introduce you to a number of ethical languages as frameworks to think about ethical issues and resolve ethical dilemmas. During class time, I will frequently be a provocateur, a clarifier, an interpreter of texts, a dispenser of information, and a user of moral languages. If all works well, at the very least, you will be able to identify and understand the central ethical issues in your life and use the appropriate languages to frame the questions, analyze the issues, resolve the dilemmas, and defend the eventual decisions and judgments you will make.

"This stuff sounds pretty philosophical. What in the world can we do with philosophy?"

You are right. The course will be philosophical, but in a helpful way, I hope. The way I teach philosophy is active, applied, and conversational. I believe the most practical tool any professional can have is a good ethical theory. If you know what you stand for morally, and why, you can defend your ethical practices anywhere, anytime, to anybody. While I cannot guarantee that you can ever "do" anything with philosophy per se the way you might be able to "do" something with "hands-on" professional techniques, I can offer you an important opportunity to talk together in a systematic and thoughtful way about ethical ideas, ideals, policies, and practices.

Moreover, I will try to get you actively involved in what I hope are stimulating conversations about the "big" ethical issues, not only in your work but in society as well. I am talking about the importance of taking time in our busy lives to pause and to be reflective about what is morally significant in the work we do. One of my favorite political philosophers, Michael Oakeshott (1950), describes vividly what a university classroom experience should be. A university should "offer a moment in which to taste the mystery without the necessity of at once seeking a solution. The characteristic gift of a university is the gift of an interval" (p. 428).

It is only in this "interval," I believe, that we can step back from the daily fray and try to answer the most basic moral questions we will ever ask. While it is true that we will be learning how to resolve concrete ethical dilemmas during the semester, we will also be using the "interval" to respond to such "ultimate" moral questions as the following: Is all the effort I am making to help others (and myself) truly worth it? What is it that I believe deep down about the work I do, and why in the world, especially on my darkest, most despairing days, should I continue doing it? What exactly should I be doing to help people to be productive, self- and other-respecting, happy and responsible citizens? Do I have a vision of the good society and the good life that is both realistic and inspiring? And how can I persuasively defend that which is worth holding onto in my moral beliefs and practices, and how can I begin to dismantle that which must give way to the new?

It is important to note that a philosopher (*philo-sophia*, G.) is someone who loves the pursuit of wisdom so much that the process of discovering meaning and purpose in life is considered to be almost as important as the product. The reason why we do philosophy is simple: because we love the search for wisdom as much as the possession of it. Contrary to what you might think, a philosopher is not some calm and composed figure who attempts to cast everything in air-tight conceptual systems, or who spends inordinate amounts of time contemplating ethereal and unanswerable questions for their own sake. No, a philosopher's primary purpose is to inch ever closer to some fundamental moral truths about the human condition. This process is far from calm because fundamental truths, whether you know it or not, are the stuff we build our lives and careers on. Sadly, too many of us either take these fundamental moral truths for granted, or, worse, we dismiss them as impractical or inaccessible. We relegate them to the "metaphysical basement" and hope they never come up the stairs to the main living area to embarrass us. But these "background moral beliefs" always have a way of making an appearance and interfering with our professional practices and policies. It will be one of the pieces of business of this course to expose these "background moral beliefs" to the light of day in order to test, refine, and apply them. What, I ask you, could be more practical and valuable for professionals than this?

"Nobody's perfect. Who are you to think you can teach ethics?"

I'll be talking about who I am as a person and as a professional later when we introduce ourselves. At this point, though, let me say that *I* don't

pretend to be a perfect model of professional ethical deportment or philosophical articulation, although I certainly strive to become as morally sensitive and ethically articulate as I can. Neither do I expect *you* to be a paragon
of moral behavior and philosophical sophistication. One of the more embar-
rassing and painful advantages of teaching this course is that I become
keenly aware of my own ethical confusions, inconsistencies, and compromises. The daunting task of appearing before you as an ethics "expert" attempting to clarify and resolve moral issues keeps me honest and, yes, humble. Listen respectfully to what I espouse, please, but be forgiving when I fail
to live up to my own highest moral ideals. I will do the same for you. One
non-negotiable expectation I will have of you, however, is to take the course
seriously enough to work hard to master the ethical languages I will teach
you. At the very least, I hope you have the same expectation of me.

"Don't you think that some ethical decisions are more morally correct than others? Come on, admit it. You've got your moral biases."

I do have my moral biases, and I will identify them when I think the
timing is right, or when asked. But it does not follow that I will be foisting
them on you, or that I will expect you to adopt my ethical views. Not only
will I steadfastly refrain from issuing ethical imperatives (please call me
on it when I do), but I will never insist that certain moral decisions are more
politically, or philosophically, or religiously, or educationally "correct"
than others. I hope you will find very little intractable orthodoxy in the
various points of view I will enunciate throughout the course. If you do,
confront me. While it is true that I have strong moral beliefs, some of which
I hold tenaciously, I will try always to espouse my own ideals in a tentative, qualified way. I call this—teaching ethics with "tenuous tenacity."
But I do feel strongly, even uncompromisingly, about some things. I
have a conversational rule I apply in my courses: Find the truth in what
you oppose. Find the error in what you espouse. I will ask you to apply
this rule as well. The virtue of this rule is that, in practice, every ethical
pronouncement should be heard (and read) as containing some element
of truth. It is our responsibility to search relentlessly for this truth (no matter how tiny) before we proceed to refute it. Moreover, everything moral is
up for grabs in this seminar. All ethical propositions are arguable, including this one. In principle, no single ethical language is irrefutably the best
or the most complete. My major intention this semester is to help you cultivate the richest, fullest moral language possible so that you can achieve
some depth, balance, consistency, clarity, and precision in your ethical assertions and problem-solving.
Does this mean, therefore, that I will be promoting a kind of ethical

neutrality, or relativism, or situationalism? Although, when discussing cases, you will hear me frequently say "It all depends . . .", you will have to wait until the term ends, I'm afraid, to get what you might consider satisfactory answers to that extremely complicated philosophical question. (We will be discussing the question often, I hope.) I will say here, though, that I believe ethical decision-making for professionals cannot simply be a matter of subjective whim or arbitrary personal preference, if it is to be defensible. This course is about normative ethical behavior and, hence, defensible ethical actions, judgments, and decision-making. At this early juncture in the course, I note, minimally, that ethical understanding and defensibility are two of my highest pedagogical and moral ideals.

"Ethics instruction sounds too technical, too complicated. Why bother with ethical reasoning? Why can't we just consult a list of simple do's and don'ts that everybody agrees on? Why don't we just appeal to a code of ethics? Why give us all this terminological grief?"

Although I will frequently be using technical terminology and referring to certain philosophical writers and their ideas throughout the course, I will do this not to show off but to provide as serious and full a context for ethical understanding and decision-making as I can. Once you make the effort to see the everyday professional world through an ethical lens, and once you begin to understand and analyze problems from a series of systematic ethical frameworks, you will find yourself using the technical language more comfortably and referring to the particular authors more frequently and accurately. And you will learn all too quickly that no ethical dilemma is merely a matter of referring to a list of professional do's and don'ts. Ethical dilemmas are far more complicated than that. *Every resolution to an ethical dilemma, I maintain, must consider the act, the intention, the circumstance, the principles, the beliefs, the outcomes, the virtues, the narrative, the community, and the political structures.* In fact, we will be using codes of ethics mainly as broad (and suggestive) normative guidelines for behavior, not as definitive specifications for ethical decision-making.

"Why then should we bother taking a course in ethics? You're obviously not going to tell us what's right and wrong—either in our personal lives or in our jobs. This seems like an unnecessarily painful way to learn about ethics."

If I am not going to be giving you any specific solutions to ethical dilemmas, then you might be thinking, when all is said and done, that the best ethical decision-making is really subjective, intuitive, and impressionistic. After all, you might be wondering, don't we learn ethics by the "seat of our pants," or by trial-and-error, or by early socialization and indoctrination, or by imitation? Isn't it up to the family, the church, temple, or mosque, and the local community to create ethical people? Isn't the test of a good ethical decision if it works, or if it feels right, or if it convinces others, or if it keeps me out of court? Who knows with any degree of certainty what someone should do in particular ethical situations? Why should we read all these books, do all this writing, come to all these classes, engage in all this philosophical discussion, if everything is up for grabs? Why not settle for a little values clarification when we find ourselves stuck with an ethical dilemma, talk to a few respected professional peers, consult Kohlberg or Gilligan for the appropriate moral stage and developmental response, strive for at least a modicum of moral self-esteem, and, if necessary, flip a coin to make a decision? Down with all of this "ethics-babble"!

Although I cannot guarantee that you will be able to satisfactorily answer all of these questions for yourselves by the end of the course, I can tell you that the challenge of thinking broadly, deeply, and systematically about ethics for an intensive semester entails many professional and personal rewards. Among the "little" rewards are reading some good texts, engaging in some stimulating conversations, clarifying some core moral beliefs, thinking deeply about the moral life in general, learning to write with precision and clarity, and exchanging moral views with some very interesting people. Among the "big" rewards are rehearsing for major ethical decision-making in the actual professional world, learning to defend controversial and complicated ethical actions and judgments, understanding what makes you "tick" morally, finding the moral courage to stand up for what you believe even while respecting the views of those who think differently, and being able to translate your background moral beliefs and principles into defensible ethical problem-solving. The "little" rewards will make your life more intellectually stimulating. The "big" rewards could someday keep you from getting sued.

"You are beginning to convince me of the importance of an applied ethics course, all right, but you haven't said anything yet about the course content. What are these 'ethical languages' and 'systematic ethical frameworks' you keep talking about? What books are we going to read? It sounds to me like you are making a molehill out of a mountain. Won't there be any real content to the course?"

This is going to take a little time, so please be patient. I will try to be brief. After all, it will be the work of the entire course to respond adequately to these content questions. First of all, applied ethics is the implementation of general ethical theories, principles, rules, virtues, structures, moral ideals, and background beliefs to problems of professional practice, including professional–client relationships, delivery of services, and policy construction and enactment. During the term, it will be essential for us to examine a wide range of actual cases involving assumptions, practices, delivery, research, and policy. These cases will not only clarify and illustrate principles, virtues, background beliefs, and their conflicts; they will test and modify these elements as well. Without the applied dimension of ethical analysis, the entire exercise could prove to be arid and nugatory. Thus it will be necessary for you to know the meaning and implications of such ethical theories as deontology, utilitarianism, and virtue ethics, as well as such principles as autonomy, beneficence, nonmaleficence, and justice.

Also, you will learn to distinguish such ethical terms as moral relativism, universalizability, prima facie and actual moral duties, and rights and obligations. Other important terms will include narrative, role, character, power, structure, faith, caring, and community. Finally, you will be able to undertake an analysis and resolution of a professional ethical dilemma using three different kinds of moral languages: what I call the languages of *background belief, character,* and *principle* (Nash, 1991). When I use the term *language* I refer to a certain mode of moral discourse, one which features a particular type of vocabulary that both reflects and shapes a particular sociocultural context and professional organization and that prescribes and proscribes certain kinds of virtuous and vicious behaviors, as well as certain kinds of judgments and decisions.

Moreover, I will make the case that each of us lives our life in three overlapping moral worlds: a metaphysical life-space, a concrete moral world of small communities (Engelhardt, 1986), and a secular pluralist world of large organizations (Engelhardt, 1986). Each of these worlds features its own specialized language. The *metaphysical life-space* is the interiorized world of individual, philosophical consciousness. It is in this world that we attempt to formulate a comprehensive, coherent, and consistent account of morality grounded in a powerful set of "ultimate" background beliefs; these may be expressed in philosophical, theological, political, scientific, or other types of language. It is in this world that each of us understands and chooses to live out certain moral ideals, makes sense of the other two worlds we inhabit, and translates the messages of the other two worlds into conscious ethical practices. We often speak a very private moral *language of background beliefs* in this world.

The *concrete moral world of small communities* is the external, tangible world of moral origin and influence for most of us. Much of what we believe metaphysically and morally, and who we are as moral beings, has its roots in, and is mediated through, our various smaller, specific moral communities. We may claim membership in only a few, or in several, of these concrete moral communities. Some are permanent; others are transient. All are particular, however, and they send powerful moral messages. These intimate groupings may be ideological, religious, ethnic, racial, political, recreational, instrumental, or familial. In these concrete moral communities, we often speak a *language of character* grounded in communally sanctioned ideals, narratives, traditions, and virtues.

And the *secular pluralist world of large organizations* is the world of the workplace, the professions, the public arena. It is the setting where private individuals of diverse ideologies, values, and moral persuasions come together to make decisions of an ethical nature. The secular pluralist world requires an ethical *language of principle* rooted in mutual respect and a tolerance of moral differences. Secular pluralist language is, of necessity, an abstract language of general principles that diverse individuals and groups employ to reach mutual understanding, tolerance, and, possibly, agreement, regarding the resolution of ethical conflicts. It is the language of logic, reason, rules, and principles (Engelhardt, 1986).

I will make the case that ethical investigation must always operate in at least these three languages. The language of background beliefs is a "foundationally rich" discourse in the sense that it grounds the other two languages. It is the vocabulary of ultimate beliefs, truth, and metaphysics. It is well suited to helping us discover deeper meaning and purpose in our moral deliberations. The language of character is a "content-rich" discourse (a form of moral examination rooted in the concrete moral viewpoints of particular persons and communities), and it helps us gain a fuller personal understanding of our moral origins, intentions, and aspirations. It is well suited to explicating the influence of our concrete moral communities on our ethical activities. The language of moral principles is a "procedurally rich" discourse (a minimum form of moral discourse that is logically deductive without establishing the absolute "correctness" of any particular point of view). It is well suited to rational, defensible ethical decision-making in the secular pluralist society (Engelhardt, 1986).

All three moral languages overlap and are mutually interdependent. You will learn that your understanding and application of rules, principles, and theories are deeply influenced by your particular stories, traditions, and conception of the virtues. These in turn shape and are shaped by a number of structural realities that affect all ethical decision-making. Moreover, you will see that it is crucial to become aware of those background beliefs that underlie and drive the entire ethical decision-making process. My hope is that, even though these background beliefs are sometimes most difficult for students to retrieve, you will realize they exert perhaps the most powerful influence on all of your moral thinking.

Finally, I will assign a series of specific texts to exemplify and elucidate the various moral frameworks and languages. These texts are included in the annotated list of required readings at the end of the syllabus. I can assure you I have chosen each text very carefully after reviewing hundreds of titles over the years.

"Whew! You are going to have to go over all of the above much more slowly and carefully during the semester, if I am to understand and apply it intelligently. I will give you the benefit of the doubt, though, and assume you know what you are doing. It does sound intriguing. I must admit that I am very anxious. Do you really think you are going to get us to talk freely—using a technical language about difficult ethical issues—with virtual strangers? I'm no philosopher, you know. Moreover, why should I take the risk and disclose moral concerns I might have at my workplace or even in my personal life? Is this going to be a sensitivity group? If it is, count me out. I don't want anyone in this class to judge me, including you."

The last few years I have been developing an approach to ethics discussions I call the "moral conversation." The Latin root of the word "conversation," *conversari*, means to live with, to keep company with, to turn around, to oppose. Thus, for me, a conversation is literally a manner of living whereby people keep company with each other, and talk together, in good faith, in order to exchange sometimes agreeable, sometimes opposing, ideas. A conversation is not an argument, although it can get heated. A conversation is at its best when the participants are not impatient to conclude their business, but wish instead to spend their time together in order to deepen and enrich their understanding of an idea, or, in our case, the ideas in a text, or of a possible solution to a difficult ethical case.

A conversation that is moral, from the Latin *moralis* (custom), is one whose conventions emphasize the fundamental worth and dignity of each participant in the exchange, and this includes the authors of our texts as well. I believe the best way to get a person to talk publicly about ethical concerns is to treat that person with the utmost respect. I will always try to treat you with the highest regard in the sense that I believe all of you have a share of moral truth. No single one of us, though, has a corner on the market of ethical insight. No single one of us inhabits the moral high ground a priori. We are all moral *viators* (travelers with a purpose) on a journey to find meaning in the work we do, and because our journey is our own, it possesses intrinsic worth and is to be respected.

The primary purpose of engaging in a moral conversation this term is to test, expand, enrich, and deepen our moral languages through the disciplined examination of significant texts—and through the vehicle of pertinent ethical cases that you yourselves will construct, analyze, and re-solve—so that each of us can arrive at a fuller ethical language than we now speak. With the ideal of the moral conversation in mind, I hope we can be genuinely respectful of each other's efforts to work through diffi-cult readings, to find a common classroom language to express our indi-vidual interpretations of these readings, and to take conversational risks in constructing a more cogent moral discourse.

In brief, then, *good moral conversation starts with*

1. An honest effort to read and understand the assigned texts
2. An acute awareness that you have moral biases and blind spots
3. An open-mindedness about the possibility of learning something from both the author and your peers in the conversation
4. A willingness to improve your current moral language
5. A conscious effort to refrain from advancing your own current moral language as if it were the best one
6. An inclination to listen intently in order to grasp the meaning of other people's languages for expressing their moral truths
7. An agreement that clarifying, questioning, challenging, exemplifying, and applying ideas are activities to be done in a self- and other-respecting way
8. A realization that we will frequently get off course in our conversations because a spirit of charity, intellectual curiosity, and even playfulness will characterize many of our discussions, and because, as David Brom-wich (1992) says: "The good of conversation is not truth, or right, or anything else that may come out at the end of it, but the activity itself in its constant relation to life" (pp. 131–132).
9. An appreciation of the reality that it will take time for us to get to know each other, and a realization that eventually we will find ways to engage in robust, candid, and challenging conversation about ethics without being so "nice" we bore each other to death, or without being so hostile that we cripple each other emotionally and intellectually

Finally, I have devised several overlapping "ethical aphorisms" that have helped to foster moral conversation in past seminars. These apho-risms will constitute a code of ethics for our class discussions:

Do not force premature closure on the moral conversation. Genuine philosophical dis-course rarely speaks in clear and unambiguous messages. Rather it speaks in subtleties, sometimes in riddles, occasionally in circles and haltingly at that, and always in ambiguities, paradoxes, and unfinished business. Beware of the tyranny of quick-fix moral directives and impatient "final" calls to action.

Find the truth in what you oppose. Find the error in what you espouse. Then and only then declare the truth in what you espouse, and the error in what you oppose.

Read as you would be read (Booth, 1988). Listen as you would be listened to. Question as you would be questioned. Pontificate only if you would be pontificated to.

Speak with, not at or separate from, each other. T. S. Eliot once said that Hell is where nothing connects. Conversational Heaven must be where every comment is a link in an unbroken chain.

If you don't stand for something, you'll fall for anything. But know how to stand up for what you believe without standing over, or on, others.

Accept no text or opinion uncritically; it might be false. Reject no text or opinion uncritically; it might be true (Moran, 1989).

Find and express your own voice, but also find the right time to lower your own voice so that others might find theirs. The paradox is that we discover what we know as much by listening as by speaking.

But speak we must! Language is the primary tool we have to make meaning together. Without language, there is no meaning. It is a resource to be recycled frequently. There can be no conversation—moral or otherwise—unless people are willing to express their ideas, no matter how erroneous, outrageous, eccentric, enfeebled, or politically and morally unorthodox. Remember John Stuart Mill's (1859/1982) enduring insight: In a democratic society, all opinions must be heard because some of them may be true; and those that aren't true must be vigorously contested. In either case, free people only stand to gain.

Once you acknowledge your moral duty to speak up, even if your ideas are only half-formed or even half-baked, do not be afraid of appearing less than brilliant in your discourse. It will be our collective responsibility to discover if there is "brilliance" in those observations you consider merely ordinary.

Finally, remember what Ludwig Wittgenstein (1953/1968) once observed about ethics: Ethics and aesthetics are one and the same. Thus, at times we must stop to appreciate the beauty, as well as the truth, in our ethical utterances and conversations. Any moral belief that brings intense satisfaction to the mind or senses can be a beautiful thing, something to be admired by all.

"One last question, please. What is your teaching style going to be?"

The content of this course is, by its nature, very controversial. I fully intend to follow the rules of the moral conversation outlined above, but, being human, I am a flawed practitioner. Not by intention, I assure you, I am bound to step on everyone's moral toes at least once by course's end simply because I may have beliefs different from yours and because you may not like my pedagogical style. I will be both provocateur and explicator. At times, I will be a lecturer, a discussion leader, and an active seeker of truth in our moral dialogues. You will be amazed at how few irrefutable ethical answers I have to your most disturbing ethical dilemmas. But in spite of my paucity of final answers, I believe I do have considerable clarity on many pertinent ethical questions, themes, issues, and languages. I also have a problem-solving process many professionals have found helpful. I will not be laid back. Alas, I will be pushing you to reach beyond your pet ethical shibboleths, as I hope you will push me to reach beyond my own. I will be speculating and playing with moral ideas right along with you. If I unwittingly hurt your moral feelings, please let me know— in class if possible, outside of class if not. I can assure you I mean no comment personally, and I will take none of your comments personally either.

I like to think of our weekly forays into the various readings and professional dilemmas as helpful ethical conversations we will have. Because one of my own very strong background beliefs is that the best way to teach morality is to teach morally, I make a promise to each one of you that I will respect you as fully autonomous and responsible moral agents, and I will listen attentively to your own moral languages, even though, at times, they may be different from mine. I ask, in return, that you not be morally thin-skinned and that you give my ethical system a fair hearing.

SYLLABUS CODA

In the sections that follow, I intend to elaborate on key issues that I mention briefly in the syllabus.

Moral Languages and Moral Worlds

Generally, beginning students in my applied ethics classes belong to one of two axiological camps. One group believes that there are moral truths "out there" waiting to be discovered. These students are the "moral objectivists," and they come to class on the first day wanting to know with objective certainty what ethical principles have irrefutable truth value, what the source of their authority is, and precisely how these principles can be applied to the resolution of personal and professional ethical dilemmas. The other group believes that moral truths are created "in here." These students are the "moral constructivists," and their expectation for the course is to draw ethical understandings from diverse sources, in a tentative,

changing, and contingent way, in order to weave together a creatively useful, private "moral text"—one that seems well suited to their particular
personal and professional circumstances.

In order to avoid the endless, unresolvable battles that frequently
erupted between the two groups during my early years of teaching ethics
courses, I sought a more constructive third way to talk about morality. I
decided to approach the study of ethics as the study of moral language.
Thanks to such authors as Robert N. Bellah, Richard Madsen, William M.
Sullivan, Ann Swidler, and Steven M. Tipton (1985); R. M. Hare (1952);
Richard Rorty (1989); and Jeffrey Stout (1981, 1988), I eventually settled
on three modes of moral discourse, which I designate as First, Second, and
Third Moral Languages. In one sense, the three modes include the objectivist and constructivist perspectives, but they also transcend them. My designations also differ from those of Bellah and associates (1985) in the sense
that I do not use the terms narrowly or normatively to refer to "individualistic" or "biblical" or "republican" patterns of meaning, as they do. Rather,
my use of the Three Moral Languages is more pragmatic: to show students
that they can employ at least three distinct and cumulative vocabularies—
background beliefs, character, and principles—when discussing controversial ethical issues and dilemmas and that each vocabulary provides a
unique, and valuable, model for investigating, and resolving, ethical conflicts.

I am not interested in reconciling all the incompatibilities among the
three languages. Instead, I stress throughout the semester that there is considerable truth value in each moral vocabulary and, taken either separately
or together, they open up rich possibilities for ethical reflection and
problem-solving. At the very least, I make the argument that the three languages offer a plausible explanation of why some views on certain controversial moral issues remain so combative and intransigent in the larger society. Objectivists and constructivists, I contend, actually speak different
moral languages, and one interpretation of the "culture wars" currently
being waged in the United States is to realize that various groups are seeking to dominate the public conversation with their own moral languages
(Hunter, 1991, 1994). To the extent that one moral language can drown
out the others, then the dominant group gains ethical hegemony. I stress
continually to students that in my classroom no ethical language will become dominant. Instead, I want them to "try on" each of the languages in
order to appreciate the richness and complexity of moral discourse.

The weakness of a moral language approach to ethics teaching,
though, is that it can sometimes purchase linguistic insight and tolerance
at the cost of "objective" moral truth. Some students perceive me as per-
mitting the moral relativists to win the day by default. I am certainly aware

that a morality-as-language ethics pedagogy can go to the extreme of reducing all of ethical discourse to nothing more than the mastery of different
vocabulary systems that are presented as purely descriptive; and it can encourage students to choose a moral language mainly because it expresses a
personal ideological, intellectual, or aesthetic preference. "I know where
you're coming from," some could say, "but your morality isn't for me, because I don't like your use of Second Language. I prefer to use First Moral
Language, you see, because it's where I'm at." For these students, such an
ethical discourse can take the form of a "vulgar" moral subjectivism
whereby any ethical assertion and solution are as good as any other—as
long as they are relative to a personal preference for a particular lexicon.

Effectively countering such subjectivist thinking is not easy. I make it
a point often to remind students that I am not about the business of stipulat-
ing the once-and-for-all "correctness" of ethical objectivism or ethical constructivism. Rather, I remind them that because we are forced to live our
lives in at least three distinct and separate worlds—what I have called the
metaphysical life-space, the concrete moral world of small communities,
and the secular pluralist world of large organizations—it is necessary for
us to recognize and, at times, even to appreciate the functional utility of the
different languages that are spoken in each of the worlds. It is also important to know that one can be both an objectivist *and* a constructivist,
depending on the particular world one inhabits at any given time. In the
metaphysical world, someone may spend a great deal of time *discovering* ultimate beliefs; in the concrete moral world, someone may seek particular
communities in which to *express* those beliefs; and in the secular pluralist
world, we all need to *create* those minimal moral norms that bind us together
in spite of our moral differences.

I am in essential agreement with H. Tristram Engelhardt, Jr. (1986)
that because all of us live a major portion of our lives in common in the
secular pluralist world—where there will always be competing conceptions
of morality—we need to develop a common moral vocabulary that emphasizes the virtues of tolerance, liberality, civility, and fairness; this secular
vocabulary, I believe, will allow us to settle our moral differences peaceably.
But the common vocabulary notwithstanding, there will always exist an un-
eliminable moral chaos in a secular pluralist culture. And during the most
morally chaotic times, all we will have are our ethical vocabularies to discover and create moral meaning. What we will decide is right and wrong,
both at home and in the workplace, will depend largely on the moral languages available to us at any given time and on the moral purposes we want
these languages to serve. Thus the major challenges for me as a teacher of
ethics are to help my students to construct a fuller, richer ethical language
in order to express their moral truths to others and to avoid reifying the

three languages at the expense of trivializing or relativizing the moral realities the languages intend to describe and prescribe.

Teaching Style and Conversation

Students watch my teaching style very carefully on the first day of class. Inevitably, someone will ask me "Will you be lecturing this semester?" or "Will we be doing small-group work?" or "How will we be discussing the readings each class?" or "How will you grade us?" Behind these types of questions, I contend, there lurk several additional, more powerful, unasked questions:

- How is the manner in which you are expressing yourself indicative of how you feel about your discipline, your teaching, your students, and yourself?
- Is your pedagogical style graceful or elegant or provocative enough to keep me fully engaged for an entire semester?
- Will your teaching be all style and no substance, or all substance and no style, or do you even care?
- What is your dominant metaphor for how we learn? Is it the pump? or the funnel? Is it your style to "draw out" what we may already know about ethics? Or is it to "pour [ethics] into" empty containers?
- What modes of expression will you be rewarding and punishing this semester? Will you be partial to particular learning styles and deliveries? If so, which ones, and will any one of them be mine? Will you like me? Will I like you?

Because I am aware that I, like most teachers, raise many pedagogical questions for students, I adopt an easy, conversational style during the very first class. I do this in order to convey the fact that I predicate my teaching delivery on a fundamental commitment to the worth of conversation in a classroom. In Jane Roland Martin's (1985) words:

> A conversation is neither a fight nor a contest. Circular in form, cooperative in manner, and constructive in intent, it is an interchange of ideas by those who see themselves not as adversaries but as human beings come together to talk and listen and learn from one another. (p. 10)

I spend a good deal of time in the first few classes exemplifying, as well as elucidating, my belief that a good conversation is not a debate, nor an angry argument. Rather, an effective conversation amiably circles back on itself often, even as it pushes forward. The interchange continues at its best when the participants are not impatient to conclude their business but wish instead to spend their time together in order to deepen and enrich their understanding of an idea, or, in our case, the ideas in an ethics text. I try never to appear deliberately argumentative or arbitrarily stipulative.

My manner of engaging students is self-consciously dialectical. I think of the conversation in my ethics class as a kind of dialectical process whereby an assortment of ethics texts, languages, and perspectives—representing sometimes opposing and sometimes complementary points of view—are put in respectful confrontation with each other so that a fuller truth might emerge and our own meanings and vocabularies might be enlarged. The overarching purpose of my ethics dialectic is to get each of us to "improve" (deepen, enrich, crystallize) our own moral language and understanding first. We are not about the business of debunking particular ethical perspectives, or of converting each other to The Ethically Correct (EC) Way, or of discovering Categorical Ethical Truths that will eventuate in Moral Enlightenment for all.

I am not strictly Socratic in my use of the dialectic; I am not a priori critical of students' moral assumptions that I then try to "destroy," via an ironic style, so that students can eventually find their way to Ultimate Moral Truth. The truth is that I have never been good at Socratic irony. My "humility" always looks arrogant, and my "insight" always appears presumptuous. I have discovered over the years that when I use a strictly Socratic questioning approach, students find it to be supercilious and contentious. The result is that too frequently they become antagonistic, or they withdraw permanently from the conversation in order to avoid public embarrassment. Instead, the dialectical process I urge is primarily interested in enriching and enlarging the moral languages of each student in the conversation so that everyone, including myself, can leave the experience in the possession of a "better" moral truth than we had when we first arrived. I make no promise that students will ever possess the "best" moral truth, or that one even exists.

Neither am I Hegelian (Hegel, 1821/1953) in my practice of the dialectic; I do not have a formal conversational method that attempts to relate specific moral concepts to an absolute idea of the good by opposing one moral proposition to another contradictory one—with the purpose of reconciling all conflicting moral concepts and ideals. In my experience, most students are suspicious of preestablished metaphysical formulas; it does not take long for them to grow impatient with the imposition of simplistic dialectical models that mechanically attempt to reconcile contrasting ethical positions. Even though many students intensely dislike "either–or" moral positions, they will still resist facile efforts to rectify all opposing ethical judgments and decisions. The dialectic I employ carries with it no metaphysical guarantees that, in the end, reconciliation of contrasting moral views will occur, and that Ultimate Moral Synthesis will result.

And, finally, I am no Freireian (Freire, 1985) in my understanding of the dialectic. I do not frame the conversation exclusively in terms of moral forces that are either oppressive or liberating. I am not politically partisan in the sense that I see all texts, authors, and participants in the conversation as deliberately concealing self-aggrandizing arguments that are linked to special class, race, and gender interests. I have learned the hard way that whenever I get overtly political in my teaching, the entire tone and direction of my course shifts in unproductive ways. We start to read and discuss texts, as well as to analyze and resolve ethical dilemmas, mainly as political partisans. We tend to lump each other into groups based on our conventional political images. I end up getting stereotyped, and I lose the element of surprise in my teaching.

When I become patently ideological, students also get typecast, as they take on predictable roles in the conversation. After a while, some speak only as militant liberationists who see victimization and oppression everywhere. Others pigeonhole themselves as radical libertarians who perceive ubiquitous threats to individual freedoms and property in every moral dilemma. Others narrowly categorize themselves as radical egalitarians because they translate all ethical dilemmas into problems of social justice or equality. And still others straitjacket themselves into assorted theistic, or egoistic, or utilitarian, or distributionist, or meritarian categories. I stress that each participant in the conversation—instructor, student, and author—be recognized as having a prior nonpartisan integrity. This will require us to listen for the truth in other moral views and to challenge the taken-for-granted truth we always assume in our own moral views. This will also require us to "try on" a variety of ethical perspectives during the semester, if for no other reason than to become less transparent, and tiresome, to each other.

It is true that I am profoundly committed to the principle that good ethics conversation is a manner of living whereby a class keeps productive company with each other—by talking in good faith together about extremely important ethical issues—in order to arrive at a richer moral language than each of us now speaks. But I try never to be simply a "facilitator" or a "values clarifier" in the conversation. I have learned that I can never use these terms in a pedagogically neutral, or disinterested, way, as some educators urge, because, of necessity, all my classroom facilitation and clarification are grounded in particular moral standpoints and background beliefs that are very important to me. I can never truly be morally neutral, because I can never fully set aside my fundamental moral suppositions. Nor would I want to. On those occasions when I have tried to be merely an ethics facilitator, I have usually ended up "clarifying" other people's values with the unspoken intent of getting them to adopt the morally superior point of view—mine.

I also resist these labels because they connote a kind of pedagogical unassertiveness I find highly incompatible with my natural teaching style. I like to keep things stirred up so that, at times, the dialectic can become more animated and engrossing. At my best, I do more than merely facilitate a conversation; I often initiate, provoke, challenge, and complicate when the moment is appropriate. Likewise, I do more than merely clarify values; sometimes I criticize, challenge, espouse, and, when intellectually fitting, I deliberately leave discussions about morality in a muddle. Certainly, good conversations must be affirming and respectful; but if they are to work especially well, I believe they must also be stimulating and engaging. As conversational techniques, clarification and facilitation alone can lead to pedagogical boredom if they are not occasionally vivified by controversy and spiritedness.

On another note, I let my students know early on that I am *primus inter pares* (first among equals) in the conversation, because I have been officially authorized by the university to teach the course and because I am probably the only person in the classroom paid to be there. I inform them that I take their expectations of me to be a competent, understanding instructor as seriously as they take my expectations of them to perform as well as they can academically. Thus the message I deliver is clear: I believe I have a significant moral responsibility, as a fully qualified ethics professor, to be a vigorous and assertive classroom leader. I have found that, generally, students are grateful when I designate clearly both my preferred *modus vivendi* (a manner of living together) and my preferred *modus operandi* (a method of teaching procedure) as a classroom leader (Nash, in press).

CONCLUSION

Not long ago, a therapist said to me in class: "I appreciate the long syllabus, although I'm more than a little intimidated by your expectations. And I certainly love the idea of your moral conversation, because in the clinical professions we try to follow your principles. But is this all there is to morality, to ethics? Your syllabus makes it seem as if moral matters are simply contingent. Your approach sounds so postmodern, so liberal, so therapeutic. Where are the moral absolutes? Where is your concern for ethical truth? Why are you so humble about your expertise? Frankly, it sounds a little forced."

My response to her took this form: "For me to teach ethics ethically, I tend to think about truth in Parker Palmer's (1983) sense. Truth comes from the Germanic root *troth*, which has to do with faith and trust, betrothal and engagement. Thus I believe I am teaching ethics ethically when I enter into a faithful and trusting relationship with you, so that we might become an important part of each other's lives. For example, I have constructed my syllabus as a fiduciary contract, as something I hope secures your trust and initiates a relationship. While I am not exactly a postmodern, I do offer you this relational sense of truth, because I am convinced that only when we faithfully engage each other in mutually regardful dialogue can we talk honestly about our moral truths this semester. My greatest hope is that we will get to the point in our dialogue where we are willing to relinquish the dogmatic dimensions of our moral selves in order that together we might grow into some kind of binding (albeit tentative) ethical truth. For all of us, this will require considerable humility, I believe—a humility not forced, but natural."

Actually, the metaphysical question of whether there are absolute moral truths is one of the topics of the next chapter. And it is to First Moral Language that we now turn.

Chapter 3

First Moral Language: Grounding Ethics in the Language of Background Beliefs

> "Metaphysics is not something you can get rid of."
> Mary Midgley, *Can't We Make Moral Judgements?*

In the beginning of a course, I usually ask what many students believe is a preposterous question, "Why should we bother about being ethical professionals anyway?" Without hesitation, students tend to respond in the following, often indignant ways:

"You mean we have a choice? Tell that to my supervisor or my clients."
"Professionals are expected to be ethical persons. That's why we have a Code of Ethics. Right?"
"Ethical behavior protects us against law suits."
"My conscience would bother me if I did something immoral. Wouldn't it bother you?"
"It's important that my clients perceive me to be an ethical person."
"People have a right to be treated fairly and compassionately."
"My parents brought me up to be an ethical human being. I don't intend to stop being ethical when I become a professional."
"I have a set of ethical ideals I strive to live up to in all areas of my life, but especially in my profession."
"I consider myself a Christian, and I practice the Golden Rule. Isn't this what ethics is all about? What more is there?"
"Why do you think I am in this course? Obviously I want to become the most ethical person I can be. I hope this won't be the kind of question you'll be asking throughout the term. If it is, I'm afraid I will be looking for another course to take."

After composing myself, I then ask a series of far more difficult questions: "Remember what you have just said. Now, tell me, if you can, upon

35

what conception of moral authority do you ground your ethical views? Do
you have any moral ultimates that might be the source of your ethical beliefs? What are the important background beliefs that support your understanding of moral truth and your conceptions of ethical behavior?"

The silence is unnerving. For a very long time, students look at each
other in embarrassment, and at me in panic, and finally at their watches.
Most are not ready for these types of inquiries during the first few meetings
of the course. Eventually, a few brave souls fumble for such replies as:

> "I believe in the Bible (or the Torah). Doesn't the ultimate truth lie
>   there?"
> "Why do I need a 'moral authority' to explain my ethic? Can't I be
>   my own 'moral authority'?"
> "I don't understand what you mean by 'background beliefs.'"
> "Why do I have to 'ground' my ethic? This sounds very abstract. How
>   will this be useful to me in my work?"
> "Could you give us an example of 'moral ultimates'?"
> "I don't understand the issues. It's been a long day. Why are we both-
>   ering with these kinds of questions anyway?"

WHY BOTHER WITH BACKGROUND BELIEFS?

Indeed, why *are* we bothering with these kinds of difficult questions? I
propose to my students that whenever they speak of responsibility, the law,
conscience, rights, ideals, and religious obligations, they are actually predi-
cating their assertions on a set of Background Beliefs, many of which reside
in what Polanyi (1966) called the "tacit dimension." In a detailed and intentionally didactic presentation at the beginning of my unit on First Moral
Language, I attempt to explain what I mean by the "tacit dimension" in
the following words:

I believe there is a compelling reason why we should bother with Background Beliefs: You probably have not had the opportunity to think
deeply enough about the questions I raise above, because you lack a language—what I call First Moral Language—to discuss them in any depth.
First Moral Language is foundational language. This is one of the reasons
why I hope you will find this course useful. When I talk about "moral authority," I mean the most fundamental assumptions that guide our percep-
tions about the nature of reality and what we experience as good or bad,
right or wrong, important or unimportant. I believe that these assumptions—what I refer to as Background Beliefs—are the "ultimate" bases

by which we make our ethical decisions. If we were to compare Background Beliefs with mathematical systems, they would be like axioms, the most basic elements of ethics (McGrath, 1994).

In fact, one contemporary writer, James Hunter (1991), goes so far as to say,

> The point needs to be made that all individuals ground their views of the world within some conception of moral authority. Not only those who are religious in a traditional sense, but also those who claim to have no religious faith at all base their views of the world in unprovable assumptions about being and knowledge. To imagine otherwise would be philosophically naive. (p. 119)

I believe Hunter is right; therefore, one of the primary purposes of the course is to help you to understand your ultimate, "unprovable" sources of moral authority, even if these sources are not "religious" in the conventional sense.

It is at this point that I would like to explain the notions of the metaphysical life-space each of us inhabits and the First Moral Language of Background Beliefs that I believe each of us speaks, but which few of us can articulate with any kind of clarity or cogency without careful reflection and much practice. In existential terminology, I submit that each of us lives in what can be called a metaphysical life-space where we experience ethical dilemmas from the vantage point of our own unique "horizon of meanings" (Barnes, H. E., 1971, p. 65). This life-space is our moral vantage point, our ethical center of reference, our primary moral subtext.

To be sure, I am aware that ethical dilemmas are objectively present to us—outside us—in the sense that they always involve others. But I believe ethical conflicts are also subjective—inside us—in that we each bring a unique center of reference to these objects. This center of reference maintains its irreducible areas of privacy. It is the location of our most fundamental beliefs about the world, the self, others, knowledge, and morality. Sometimes we are able to bring these background beliefs into the foreground through a conscious act of retrieval. Sometimes these background beliefs remain inaccessible to us. So powerful are these beliefs, however, that even though we all look at the same ethical dilemmas, we do not always see the same dilemmas. To some extent, we each remain trapped in our own metaphysical life-space, our own "tacit dimension."

But I do not believe we are doomed to stay enclosed there forever. Even though we speak a private language in this world—a language of

ultimate meaning that contains elements of faith, reason, and imagination—I know that it is possible, even desirable, to go public with this language. The philosopher John Rawls (1971) argues that every moral action
must meet the "test of publicity" (p. 175): It must be capable of public
statement and defense. I agree with Rawls. For my part, I hope to make
it possible for you to develop an even richer, fuller background language
than the one you now have by raising the right questions, assigning the
appropriate texts, and engaging you in probing conversation with each
other, in order to prepare you to meet the test of publicity successfully.

And I hope to make the case that a full understanding of this language of background beliefs is desirable because without it you will remain seriously handicapped as ethical analysts and problem-solvers.
Worse, you will remain unable to articulate a coherent moral life plan for
yourselves, because you will not understand the impact your deepest,
most taken-for-granted moral beliefs have on your entire life. Nor will you
be able to explain and justify your moral choices with depth or conviction. If you are to evaluate and defend your ethical actions in another
world we inhabit—the secular pluralist world—I contend, with Rawls,
that you must speak compellingly and persuasively to others about those
moral reference points that are of utmost significance to you, and by implication, to others as well. This, in a nutshell, is why I believe we should
bother about background beliefs.

CLOSET METAPHYSICIANS

I have yet to meet a student who is not, in some sense, a metaphysician.
I believe that all people, including my students, cling to "unprovable
sources" of moral authority. Moreover, all ask the sorts of ultimate questions
about meaning, purpose, and being that cannot finally be resolved on rational grounds, because they are fundamentally undemonstrable. To be a
metaphysician is to seek the deepest truths to the most existentially central
human dilemmas. This is not to say, of course, that all students are at the
same levels of interest, readiness, background, or intellectual ability to do
classical metaphysics. Very few want to become engaged in an Aristotelian
study of being itself; or to embark on a Socratic examination of unchanging
first principles or Forms; or to undertake a theological investigation of a
transcendent realm of Being; or to plunge directly into Immanuel Kant's
The Metaphysics of Morals (1797/1991) or into St. Thomas Aquinas's essays
on the existence of a God in the *Summa Theologica* (1256/1948).

I have found, however, that most students are deeply curious about
metaphysical inquiry in two less specialized senses than these. First, they

are intrigued by the opportunity to identify some important systems of morality and their accompanying claims about what is right and good. They also appreciate the chance to examine critically the underlying assumptions employed by these systems. Second, they like the chance to develop a comprehensive, coherent, and consistent account of their own moral convictions. It is truly important to them, as professionals, to be able to articulate, and defend, the most fundamental sources (the Background Beliefs) of their working ethic to others. To the extent that I can entice students to come out of the metaphysical closet early in the course, then all of our subsequent ethical study becomes more challenging and percipient.

When it works well, the language of Background Beliefs helps students to emerge from the metaphysical closet. This language provides access to a world most know only dimly. In my experience, it takes awhile for students to get accustomed to the language of Background Beliefs because it is foundational language. I ask them to think of this moral language as "basement language," because it is that part of their ethical edifice that is mostly below surface level. It is the most fundamental part of their ethical philosophy because it serves as the foundation for the two subsequent languages they will learn and because it grounds their ethical thinking and behavior in something more than moral whim. My primary pedagogical intention in teaching this language is not one of immediate utility, however. I do not ask students to apply it to the analysis and resolution of a particular ethical dilemma, although I firmly believe that the language of Background Beliefs is an essential basis for the other two problem-solving languages.

Instead, my purpose is to help students to develop a more conscious, and articulable, understanding of what Charles Taylor (1992) calls each person's "background of intelligibility," those "moral horizons against which things take on significance for us" (p. 37). To this end, I require each student to construct a First Moral Language Manifesto of 15 to 20 pages about a third of the way into the course. The Manifesto is a written philosophical declaration of those background moral beliefs that prop up a student's ethical system. When I first announce the assignment, most students are terrified, not just because this assignment is the first paper of the course, but because it deals with metaphysical, epistemological, and axiological material that at this point is alien to most of them. At first, the language seems unnecessarily theoretical and overly technical.

Furthermore, students become even more alarmed when I caution them to resist the habitual behavior of running to the library in order to pad a lengthy paper with the insights of "experts." I tell them to go easy on any outside references unless these authors have truly made an intellectual difference in their lives. These are the authors I want to hear about because, if they have precipitated "aha!" moral insights that students have retained, then they are truly the authors worth writing about in a personal Manifesto. I urge them to construct their *own* original ethics papers by drawing from their personal reflections on our class conversations, from their interpretations of the course readings we have completed up to that point, and from those defining moral texts that have touched their lives in some prominent way outside the course. I promise them that my Background Beliefs Framework—a series of questions that act as "metaphysical probes"—will help them to develop an appropriate language for writing their Manifesto.

THE BACKGROUND BELIEFS FRAMEWORK

As we begin the unit on Background Beliefs, I introduce a series of general metaphysical, axiological, and epistemological questions calculated to help students think in First Language terms about their sources of moral authority. I use these "probes" to initiate what I hope will be a penetrating investigation of foundational moral assumptions. *I stress continually that the purpose of First Language is not to solve concrete problems.* That will come later. The major purpose is for students to go as deeply as possible into the "metaphysical basement" (the zero-level of beliefs) in order to understand their unique, "inescapable" horizons of meanings, their ethical centers of reference. The questions introduce students—many for the first time—to some of the perennial issues in moral philosophy. Students also begin to develop a facility with some of the technical vocabulary in First Language, especially when I am able to keep the conversation free-flowing and unintimidating. This is not always easy to accomplish.

I try to keep the questions open-ended, thoughtful, and even a bit playful, in an effort not just to relax my students, but to get them in a mood to asseverate freely about their fundamental moral beliefs. I stress that there are no right or wrong answers to any of the questions. After all, I remind them, their metaphysical beliefs are grounded in "unprovable sources." The purpose of First Language is not to "prove" or to "justify" anything; it is to "locate" ethical judgments, decisions, and actions in a Background Language that deepens, explains, and reveals. This language helps students to understand what is truly important to them, and I have found that when they work well, the questions surface what has hitherto been mainly tacit, half-formed thinking about morality. The all-inclusive First Language question I am really concerned about is this one: *What underlying beliefs help you to make sense of the world?* The following starter questions (the "probes") are meant to help students to formulate some thoughtful responses to this master question. I will also include my commentary on each of the questions, based on students' responses to them through the years.

1. What does it mean to be moral? Immoral? Who says so?

Without formal ethical training, students generally tend to resort to simple formulas when discussing the content of their morality. Many will cite the Golden Rule as their ultimate authority for moral behavior. Some will talk of the "do-no-harm" principle—the moral obligation to refrain from unnecessarily hurting innocent people. A few will mention in passing what they consider to be the cardinal helping virtues: service, caring, compassion, empathy, and nonjudgmentalism. Still fewer will point to some "canonical" text—e.g., the Bible, *The Fountainhead,* the Hippocratic oath, *A Theory of Justice,* the Florence Nightingale Nursing Code of Ethics— as being the authoritative source for what they believe to be right and wrong. And, occasionally, a moral cynic in my class will refer to some proof-text in Nietzsche to demonstrate that morality is nothing more than a social invention of the ruling class meant to keep the "herd" in its proper place.

Notwithstanding the tendency for students to spout conventional moral formulas, however, I find this to be a good starter question because it forces students, many for the first time, to consider publicly the actual content of what they believe to be moral and immoral. In my experience, the majority of students, regardless of moral conviction, developmental level, age, and level of education, come at this question as "mild relativists" and constructivists. For many, the very question itself conceals the ominous threat of moral indoctrination or imposition, which they see as inegalitarian, authoritarian, arbitrary, and "judgmental." While students do, indeed, hold certain convictions about what, for them, is moral and immoral behavior, they are always very careful to acknowledge that their conceptions are subjectively constructed and peculiar to their own personal contexts.

In fact, I find that, today, students are increasingly unwilling to specify publicly what they consider to be moral or immoral, because, for them, any declaration on morality seems "judgmental," and, after all, they assert, "Who is anyone to judge?" I actually relish those times when the topic of "nonjudgmentalism" comes up in class, because I believe it to be one of those unexamined orthodoxies in students' lives that cries out to be disputed. The chief influence that fuels the runaway engine of nonjudgmentalism in the culture is popular culture, I believe. High school and college educators, like the rest of the general population, are not immune to the blandishments of the media. On nearly every television talk show, for instance, the visiting expert—a therapist—is trotted out to proclaim the gospel of moral neutrality, which often takes this form: "I am here not to judge you, but to help you to heal. Let's leave morality out of it." Morality thus becomes the culprit in a public, therapeutic ritual. "Value-free" professional technique is presented as the only cure. This therapeutic ethos is so widespread throughout the culture—talk shows, advice columns, 12-step recovery programs, self-esteem workshops, sex education, parenting workshops, AIDS awareness groups, textbooks—that it has infiltrated virtually every high school and professional training program in the American university.

In class, we frequently end up talking a great deal about the impossibility, even the undesirability, of avoiding judgments when discussing morality. In fact, it is a commonplace that every professional must continually make informed moral judgments about which professional and client behaviors are acceptable and which are not. Students come around eventually to the realization that making ethical judgments about client behavior may even be professionally obligatory if "healing" is to occur. And as we discuss the reasons why we do, indeed, find some actions more or less morally tolerable than others—in spite of our "value-free" protestations—we start to make sharper terminological distinctions. We begin to understand, for example, that "judgment" and "imposition" do not have to be synonyms. All action begins with a judgment, which may or may not lead to an imposition. Along the way, there exists a continuum of different ethical responses that include approval, disapproval, suggestion, exemplification, persuasion, habituation, formation, indoctrination, and coercion or imposition. Sorting out the most effective ethical responses in any given situation is the work of discerning professionals who, in some ways, must always function as moral educators.

On the matter of nonjudgmentalism, I have recently begun to assign Mary Midgley's *Can't We Make Moral Judgements?* (1991). Her text always stirs up considerable controversy among my students, because she challenges the epistemological assumption extant in so many of the helping professions today that nobody can ever be in a position to question the morality of others, because nothing at all can ever be known with any degree of certainty about morality. Midgley's view is that such a position is itself an absolute judgment about morality in that it has become a type of "dogmatic skepticism" required of all who would work with people in the human services. She also attributes a "false universality" to the pronouncement that morality is ultimately unknowable and, therefore, unprescribable, because "the characters who talk like this are in general quite as ready as other people to live most of their lives by existing standards, to pass judgments about others, and to invoke morality where it happens to be on their side" (Midgley, 1991, p. 8).

2. Is there a spiritual as well as a physical, intellectual, and emotional realm of existence? To what realm do you attribute primary importance? Why? Can you be moral and not believe in a God?

I believe that religion and spirituality are an integral part of ethical investigation. This kind of question is an important one for me to ask because it encourages students to talk on a deeper level about what gives "ultimate" meaning to their lives. While few have remained faithful to the mainline churches of their youth, many students have explored religious and spiritual themes in Eastern mysticism, New Age movements, Goddess worship, 12-step recovery groups, Native American spirituality, and environmentalism, to name but a few. I agree essentially with Andrew M. Greeley (1990) that religious "pictures" are the foundations upon which all moral worldviews rest. Without an understanding of what they consider to be of spiritual significance, I do not think that students will ever be able to dig deeply enough into the metaphysical world in order to discover what gives ultimate moral meaning and purpose to their lives. Thus I try to be a very empathic listener whenever students discuss their spiritual "pictures" during class, because I want to make sure I hear what is "sacred" to them.

I admit, though, that it is difficult to get some students to conceive of separate "realms" of existence wherein they think of one as more important than the other. Many conceive of existence as a seamless web of being, a "holistic" experience whereby the physical, intellectual, emotional, and spiritual realms are inextricably interrelated, and of equal importance. In fact, at one time, from the late 1970s to the late 1980s, it was almost impossible for me to get students even to acknowledge a spiritual component to their lives. Spirituality was not in vogue in those days; materialism and commercialism were. Today, it seems that students are more than eager to trumpet the significance of a "spiritual" dimension in their day-to-day existence. For many, spirituality summons up oceanic images of incorporeality, the sacred, the breath of life, the animating principle that bestows life in a person, the environment, otherworldliness, health, happiness, "feeling good about oneself," and what the theologian Matthew Fox (1990) calls "heart-knowledge." Wade Clark Roof (1993), a sociologist, actually talked to hundreds of "baby boomers" in the early 1990s about their "spiritual journeys," and his findings confirm my observation that student spirituality is experiencing a major renaissance today. It is important to note, however, that many students refuse to equate the "spiritual" with the "religious" realm, because, for them, the latter connotes a kind of sectarian dogmatism that they almost always associate with negative childhood church experiences.

I have had much success in getting students to consider the function of a spiritual component in their lives by using three very stimulating, First Language texts, each of which is radically heterodox in its conceptions of spirituality and religion. Peter L. Berger's *A Rumor of Angels: Modern Society and the Rediscovery of the Supernatural* (1970) is a text written by a "heretical Christian," who argues that in his view "all phenomena point toward that which transcends them" (p. 94). He advocates a rediscovery of the supernatural as a way to understand the "true proportions" of human existence. When we become sensitive to the "signals of transcendence" (p. 94) all around us, Berger believes that we will be better able morally to confront the anomalies of the age we live in, because we will be living in a perspective that transcends the age. We will be more likely to live with a moral courage to do what must be done in any given moment, because such a perspective entails that no given moment is ever the "be-all and end-all" of our existence. Thus we are likely to regain the capacity to laugh and to play. Students delight in identifying those "signals of transcendence" all around them—especially "signals" like nature, pets, loving relationships, friendships, parenthood, sexual orgasm, aesthetic pleasure, satisfying work—although most disagree with Berger that a belief in "transcendence" is necessary for morally courageous living.

Russell Pregeant's *Mystery Without Magic* (1988) speaks to those students who have long since abandoned any interest in the supernatural or spiritual realm of existence. He argues that spiritual awareness necessitates a paradox: Life appears to point inexorably to some mystery that encompasses it, and yet to acknowledge and affirm this mystery is to make a leap to a realm we can never fully know or understand. Pregeant contends that without this leap to a "faith-commitment," there is simply no foundation for moral beliefs. Secular consciousness alone provides no real basis for moral judgments and actions. For him, the "religious quest" is a quest for a foundation for morality, "the search for some final court of appeal in the case of conflicting values" (p. 11). He reasons that if there is no way that the moral beliefs we assert are grounded outside our subjective wills and judgments, then we can have no basis whatsoever for maintaining the superiority of one kind of moral behavior over another. Everything ends up in moral arbitrariness. Students appreciate the elements of mystery, quest, and faith commitment in Pregeant's analysis of religion. They are deeply touched by the existential quality of his writing. Many, however, reject his view that we need a "foundation" or a "final court of appeal" in order to resolve "conflicting values."

Those students who are more anthropological in their religious interests find Ninian Smart's *Worldviews: Crosscultural Explorations of Human Beliefs* (1983) very challenging. For Smart, religion is a "system of beliefs which, through symbols and actions, mobilize the feelings and wills of human be-ings" (p. 1). His approach is to study religion through an analysis and com-parison of such worldviews (religious and secular ideologies) as Christianity and Buddhism, Islam and Marxism, and Platonism and Confucianism. Smart believes that we are all religious beings, not necessarily in any con-ventional sense, but in the sense that each one of us has a worldview that forms a "background" to the lives we lead.

He further maintains that our worldviews always contain six dimen-sions:

Doctrinal (fundamental principles)
Mythic (stories with special or sacred meaning)
Ethical (prescribed rules and precepts)
Ritual (ceremonial rites, laws, customs)
Experiential (expression of strong, ego-transcending feelings)
Social (particular organizations and groups)

Smart offers students a secular, quasi-scientific way to think about religion. They take very quickly to his nonsectarian, worldview approach to the study of religion, because his definition of the term resembles their notion of spirituality. And they can readily identify the six dimensions in their own worldviews.

Does this flirtation with different types of spirituality, coupled with an antipathy toward institutional religion, mean, therefore, that students tend more toward pantheism, agnosticism, or even atheism, than theism? It is true that during the late 1960s and early 1970s, many students were more likely to consider all "God-talk" to be muddled or wishful thinking. They thought that theism was prescientific—an anthropocentric myth. They were inclined to agree with Nietzsche that God is dead, and with Marx that human beings must now take control of their own social destiny. At the present time, however, I have many more agnostics in my classes than atheists. The agnostics, for the most part, are not willing to foreclose on the possibility of theism. They believe that atheism is too harsh; it appears to be the denial of the existence of anything even remotely corresponding to theism, including even a personal spirituality defined in the broadest of senses. Today, few students are willing to go as far as Nietzsche and Marx. These students tend to assume an agnostic view, because, even though they have seen no decisive data (scientific or otherwise) that a God in fact exists, they are willing to consider any future evidence. The existence of a God remains for them an open, coherent possibility (Gaskin, 1984).

Where, then, do students stand on the relationship of morality and a belief in God? I would say that most hold that people can believe in, and follow, the rules of moral conduct without the need for any authoritative grounding in religious belief. These students would prefer to omit religious justifications for morality in the classroom, on the job, and in the "naked public square." The minority, however, are aware that a major part of all religious teachings is concerned with morality. For example, the Ten Commandments, the Old and New Testaments, the Koran, even the pagan religions of the pre-Socratics and the ancient Greeks and Romans establish almost a de facto inseparability between religion and morality. While these students can hardly be classified as strident religionists (some may not even be believers), they are concerned, nevertheless, that without a religious warrant, morality is, at best, a very fragile matter in a pluralistic society. They are likely to agree, at least in principle, with John Gaskin (1984) that

> the loss of . . . a metaphysical good and evil under atheism is serious. . . . Only when set against the powers of an eternal or divine good or of a Satanic evil can the things we are now capable of be adequately experienced in moral terms . . . the genetic mutilation of all living things, the poisoning of the earth, the burning of most of the cities of the northern hemisphere. (pp. 163–164)

In practice, students are not radically disjunctive in their thinking on the issue of morality and religion. Most are willing to accept the peaceful coexistence of two kinds of morality in a pluralist society: secular and religious. For most practical purposes in students' work and personal lives, the demands of secular and religious morality coincide. Where students get very nervous, though, is when the demands of religious morality vie for preeminence over the demands of secular morality in the public square— as in current disputes over abortion, physician-assisted suicide, capital punishment, and even alternative sexual lifestyles. Students are rightfully skeptical whenever religious moralists appeal to a type of theological voluntarism, or Divine Command theory: the belief that the standard of right and wrong for society must be the will or law of God (Gaskin, 1984). They ask, as did Socrates in the *Euthyphro:* "How can we know with any certainty what God commands or forbids?" Or as one student cynically noted: "Why is it that God talks to the televangelists, to Jimmy Carter, to Ronald Reagan, even to my mother, but never to me?"

In my classroom, our most intense conversations concern those ethical dilemmas with major social policy implications. However, in spite of the cogency of arguments mounted by each side of the abortion, capital punishment, and euthansia controversies, for example, very few students of either persuasion are willing to accede to the imperatives of religious moralists solely on the grounds that religious morality transcends the demands of secular morality. In fact, when we read David Hume (1748/1930), both my religious *and* secular moralists are likely to agree with him that the "secular moral sentiments" are often sufficient enough to see us through even the thorniest ethical dilemmas. For Hume, "some particle of the dove is kneaded into our frame together with the elements of the wolf and the serpent" (p. 109). It is in our human nature, he contends, to be benevolent and to observe a moral code toward others in the hope that others will reciprocate. We also seek to be highly regarded by others so that we will avoid estrangement and attain an "inward peace of mind." Hume believed that even if these sentiments fail, most of us will be responsive to the threat of social ostracism or other types of civil punishment (Gaskin, 1984).

3. Would you characterize your moral philosophy as being predominantly rationalist? intuitionist? emotivist? naturalist? sensualist? theist? secularist? humanistic? communitarian? individualistic? egoist? Explain.

I believe it is important for students to know how to discourse about morality in these technical terms for two main reasons: First, each term provides a richer, more systematic way for students to structure how they *think* about morality; and, second, the terms give us all a common language with which to *talk* about morality. Initially, however, many students find these technical terms to be too theoretical, constraining, and even tendentious. After we read Hunter Lewis's *A Question of Values: Six Ways We Make the Personal Choices That Shape Our Lives* (1990), however, most change their minds. Lewis greatly simplifies the above terms by putting them into non-philosophical language. He starts with two simple questions: "Why do I believe what I do?" and "How do I know it?" He argues that there are basically six modes of moral reasoning that describe how we think about the world, and how we develop and choose morality. They are authority, deductive logic, sense experience, emotion, intuition, and science. Some of us, according to Lewis, are likely to rely on authority (teacher, Bible, politics, science), or on observation (direct sense experience), or on logic, or on intuition, for example, in order to answer the questions he raises.

Moreover, for Lewis, human beings cannot separate the way they arrive at morality from the morality itself. Whenever we adopt a particular framework of moral reasoning, and emphasize that one over the others, we tend to turn it into our dominant personal system of morality. It becomes our moral good. For example, if my dominant mode of moral reasoning is authority, then authority itself is likely to become my good. Or someone might insist on the moral superiority of logical reasoning, or intuition, as the way to think about, and resolve, ethical dilemmas. It is not a difficult task for students to identify their own dominant epistemological modes; not only do they enjoy this activity, but they (especially the sense experiencers and the scientists) quickly see its usefulness. They can also readily identify the dominant modes in their families, friends, and colleagues. A few are more than ready to point out what they think is my principal epistemological bent as well. Despite students' lingering skepticism regarding Lewis's claim that there are only six ways of knowing, they do appreciate his invitation to organize and categorize what is otherwise a chaotic maelstrom of personal beliefs. I like Lewis's work because he makes it easier for me to introduce more technical, and diverse, philosophical terms, some of which are equivalent to his own.

Another way I confront students' concerns head-on is to choose persuasive classical and contemporary texts that argue for a particular moral position grounded in one or another of the above perspectives. I then place these texts in dialectical opposition to each other. For example, we have recently contrasted the moral philosophy elucidated in *Forbidden Fruit: The Ethics of Humanism*, by the humanist Paul Kurtz (1988), to the one in *Making Choices: Practical Wisdom for Everyday Moral Decisions*, by the theist Peter Kreeft (1990). We have also read *After Virtue: A Study in Moral Theory*, by the communitarian Alasdair MacIntyre (1984), in tandem with *On the Genealogy of Morals*, by the individualist Friedrich Nietzsche (1887/1967). Each of these authors, and dozens of others I have chosen over the years, is a powerful, convincing voice in behalf of a particular moral point of view. When students have to refute the views of authors like these, the terms, and the positions they signify, suddenly become less abstruse, less stereotypical, and more useful.

And when we begin to talk about the pervasiveness of each of the points of view in contemporary politics, religion, and the helping professions, the terms get grounded in reality very quickly. Students come to appreciate the utility of such vocabulary, because they discover that technical terms can be parsimonious; they can succinctly encapsulate significant, and revealing, philosophical tendencies in people's thinking, and they can effectively explain, and predict, people's ethical behavior. For example, after reading the egoists J. L. Mackie (*Ethics: Inventing Right and Wrong* [1977]) and Joseph Butler (*Five Sermons* [1949]), students sometimes change their initial negative impressions about egoism. They begin to realize that, at least for Mackie and Butler, there need be no unresolvable moral tension between ethical behavior and the rationality of self-interest. In fact, a few students become so intrigued with egoism as a defensible ethical position that they begin to resurrect the works of a popular 1960s egoist, Ayn Rand (1961).

4.   Is an objective morality possible? or desirable? If yes, what is the object of your morality, and how do you avoid the excesses of dogmatism and absolutism? Or is all morality subjective? If yes, how can you ever expect others to be moral, and how do you avoid the excesses of moral relativism and nihilism?

These are important questions for me to ask because they reveal major prejudices and blind spots in students' moral thinking. These questions flush out the objectivists and the constructivists in my classes early on, in spite of students' angry protestations against being pigeonholed. *Objectivists* are Cartesian foundationalists who believe that knowledge, to be secure, must rest on indubitable premises that take on the character of bedrock certainties. These objective certainties might be natural law, God, or a universal moral law. Objectivists maintain that moral truths exist prior to and apart from observation and thought, and it is the project of all human beings to discover these mind-independent realities. Unfortunately, unchecked objectivism leads all too easily to absolutism and dogmatism, as well as to a general devaluation of the active role of human consciousness in constructing its own realities. Two objectivist texts that have evoked a strong reaction from students in recent years are Brian Hebblethwaite's *The Ocean of Truth: A Defence of Objective Theism* (1988) and Hadley Arkes's *First Things: An Inquiry into the First Principles of Morals and Justice* (1986).

Constructivists are neo-Kantians who believe that the human mind, through the imposition or projection of its own concepts on experience, "constructs" its own world. Some moral constructivists go so far as to declare that there is no way we can ever get outside of our basic linguistic categories, and so, with Wittgenstein (1953/1968), they take a "linguistic turn" when thinking about ethics. Unchecked constructivism, though, leads all too easily to relativism and extreme subjectivism. Its toxic influence can be seen in the more nihilistic wings of such postmodernistic twentieth-century movements as existentialism, poststructuralism, and deconstructionism. Two constructivist texts that students have found especially compelling are Hazel Barnes's *An Existentialist Ethics* (1971) and Barbara Herrnstein Smith's, *Contingencies of Value: Alternative Perspectives for Critical Theory* (1988).

In my experience, no two categories more aptly sum up the dominant moral perspectives of the vast number of students who find their way to my ethics courses than do objectivism and constructivism. No two categories have better predictive or explanatory value for me as a teacher. The constructivists are easily the majoritarian party in my classes, and, with notable exceptions, I find them to be well represented among the ranks of psychotherapists, younger clergy, elementary and middle school teachers, school and university counselors, and clinical social workers. The objectivists are the minority group in my classes, and, with several special cases, I am more likely to find them among older clergy, physicians, lawyers, high school subject-matter teachers, allied health workers, high school and college administrators, and law enforcement officers.

Pedagogically, I appreciate the sharp dichotomy between objectivist and constructivist perspectives on the topic of morality, because I am free to navigate a middle course between the contrasting viewpoints. Sometimes, I am even able to find a common ground in students' basic moral beliefs. At their worst, though, I find objectivists and constructivists to be equally dogmatic and fundamentalist. Both are certain that their perspective is the "right" and exclusive way to think about morality. Both tend to resort to ad hominem attacks when cornered. Libertarian constructivists and born-again Christian objectivists, for example, can be equally vituperative and close-minded when ethical debate grows heated in my courses. My task as a teacher is to point out rhetorical excess and hyperbole, as well as contradiction and inconsistency, in each of the views. I must confess, though, that I find extremists in both camps to be equally objectionable at times. Fundamentalists come in all stripes, and they can become serious obstructionists in the moral conversation.

5. Do you believe that any moral actions, or standards, should be universalizable? If yes, which ones, and why? If not, why not?

I contend that what we are willing to universalize by way of "right" moral belief and action is what is truly important to us as moral individuals. And what we are not willing to universalize is less central to us. How students stand on this question says a great deal about what is of utmost moral significance to them, and, for this reason, the question is invaluable in getting students to probe the deeper layers of their Background Beliefs. Actually, the problem of universals can be traced back 2,500 years to the debate between the Platonists and the Sophists: Socrates argued that a universal good did exist in the world of Ideas, while Protagoras contended that "man is the measure of all things" and, thus, goodness exists, not in the universal, but only in the particular. (See, for example, Plato's *Protagoras* and *Theaetetus* [1961].)

In applied ethics, universalizability is the principle that if one judges a particular action or decision to be the ethically right or good one, then one is ipso facto committed to the judgment that anything like that action or decision in relevant respects is equally right or good (Frankena, 1973). Obviously, the principle that if a moral judgment applies to a particular case, then it must equally apply to any exactly relevant case, has affinities to the Golden Rule, utilitarianism, and Kantian ethics. Nevertheless, this principle poses huge problems for most of my students, because they think it conceals an obligatory, prescriptive subtext. Even when they agree on the moral validity of such maxims as the Golden Rule, for them, the principle appears to command consistency at all costs; furthermore, it seems to insist on the imposition of moral consistency on others whenever they must act in similar situations.

The constructivists and subjectivists in my courses are reluctant to universalize anything in the realm of morality. They tend toward the belief that no moral judgments can ever be objectively certain, and no two situations are ever exactly morally similar. Thus they argue that moral agents have a right, indeed a responsibility, to change their minds in all subsequent ethical decisions and actions, depending on their intention and circumstance. As situationalists, they believe that they should never be bound to prior ethical judgments, because these cases may ignore highly specific details in other similar cases.

The objectivists and theists in my classes are somewhat more willing—but not much—to universalize their moral beliefs and standards, but only if these can be grounded in a consensus that there exists some irrefutable natural law, revealed religious truth, constitutional authority, or cross-cultural universal. As certain as some of these students are about their beliefs, however, I still find that most are extremely unwilling to generalize them to other people in other settings, for fear of being accused of moral imposition or absolutism.

When we read R. M. Hare's *Freedom and Reason* (1963), though, students begin to understand the extent to which they, in practice, actually assume a certain day-to-day universalizability in their ethical reasoning and problem-solving. When we really talk with each other about ethical issues in our local communities and organizations, we find ourselves using moral language that we expect others to understand and even to accept. Also, students agree essentially with Hare's larger argument that global morality itself depends on a universalizable language; in order to adjudicate national and international differences regarding solutions to pressing geopolitical ethical dilemmas, we need a prescriptive and proscriptive language that is binding on all nations, in spite of grave international differences. Closer to home, however, as our organizations grow increasingly diverse, and as some individuals' competing conceptions of morality threaten to erupt into irreconcilable conflict, students realize the necessity of a genuinely universalizable moral language. They know that constructive ethical discourse with each other is impossible without this language.

Students learn how to check the excesses of the universalizability principle, however, when we read J. L. Mackie's *Ethics: Inventing Right and Wrong* (1977). Mackie, who believes in both the logical and functional necessity of the universalizability principle, nevertheless issues three cautions: First, be aware that your universalizable moral judgments may be largely a matter of personal taste, predicated on a set of distinctive preferences, values, and ideals. (Bernard Shaw once said about the Golden Rule: Do not do unto others as you would have them do unto you. Their tastes may be different.) Second, refrain from universalizing some moral maxim or behavior until you put yourself in the place of the other person. Ask whether you can accept the maxim as a directive guiding the behavior of others toward you. Third, take account of the different tastes and rival ideals of others. How do your own tastes differ from, and intersect with, the tastes of others. Is there room for compromise?

The chief virtue of Mackie's caveats for students is the reminder that although there may be basic moral standards that are indeed universalizable, morality still has its subjective elements. And it is out of these radically divergent personal preferences and values that the more obstinate ethical disagreements are likely to arise. Thus, it behooves each of us to lower our moral sights a bit in order to look for those moral principles that represent an acceptable compromise. Mackie reassures us that we can be both universal *and* particular in our ethical decisions, if we are willing to be realistic and modest about our moral maxims.

6. Do women and men approach moral dilemmas differently? If yes, how? If no, how do you know? Do you agree that women are more likely to subscribe to a caring ethic and men to a principled ethic? Or is there a natural, gender-neutral impulse to be ethical?

This is a quintessential First Language question, because it challenges the dominance of taken-for-granted perspectives on morality. It strikes at the very foundation of the argument that there can truly be a natural, "impartial," context- or gender-independent moral perspective. For example, no less a moral luminary than David Hume (1751/1952) indicated that a "disinterested," "sympathetic" moral point of view was indeed possible, even desirable. He spoke of the need for moral agents to be free, impartial, and informed. Kurt Baier (1965) held that one took the moral point of view only if one was detached, unbiased, altruistic, principled, universalistic, and even-handed. Now it is quite true that many students are at least subliminally aware of the self-interested, subjective, and socially constructed components of ethical decision-making. And it is also true that most believe ethical behavior to be more a matter of education than heredity. I find, however, that few have thought seriously or deeply about the above questions, because, at least at the outset of a course, both male and female students (even the most political) reject the possibility that a moral point of view might be genderized in some way. Some even get quite vehement in their negation, because they consider such a claim to be sexist.

For example, when I first assigned Carol Gilligan's *In a Different Voice: Psychological Theory and Women's Development* (1982) in the early 1980s, and Nel Noddings's *Caring: A Feminine Approach to Ethics and Moral Education* (1984) later, both male and female students did not know what to make of their work in regard to actual ethical decision-making. How, they wondered, is it possible to resolve ethical dilemmas without recourse to moral principles? Students found the authors' use of moral language too "personal," their sources too "literary," and their attack on males too "extreme." Both authors rejected outright a "masculine" language of principle in favor of a more "emotional, personal" language. They preferred a "feminine" language that, for many students, relied too heavily on such "soft" words as *caring, feeling, response,* and *relationships.* Moreover, the authors appeared to students to be "angry" feminists, who, in their attacks on the male monopoly in ethics, seemed to throw the "baby out with the bathwater." Gilligan, in particular, was perceived to be a "turncoat," because she was "unloyal" to her mentor, Lawrence Kohlberg. She was thought to have pronounced him guilty of introducing an exclusive male bias into his research on moral stage theory, and then, to make matters worse, she proceeded to issue a "death sentence" to his research by spending much of her early career attacking his work.

Over the years, however, Gilligan and Noddings have become virtual icons for some in the ethics field, and now, whenever we read them, students genuinely respect them for their important, early critique of male-dominated ethical language. They are rarely in awe of them, however. (To this day, several students of both sexes get almost apoplectic over the color pink in the cover of Noddings's paperback edition of *Caring.* For them, pink connotes stereotypes of women who are "soft," "feminine," and "touchy-feely"—which they find particularly abhorrent.) While most students are willing to acknowledge the existence of two moral languages—the masculine and the feminine—they are unwilling to grant hegemony to the latter, as some advocates for a caring ethic do. In fact, those women in my classes who are in male-dominated professions such as medicine, business, and law, and who wish to establish themselves as "tough-minded" colleagues, equally capable as men of making emotion-free decisions, tend to be especially vociferous in their criticisms of the caring ethic.

Actually, I sense a growing aversion among professionals of both sexes to sweeping indictments, and ultimate dismissal, of what these writers call the "masculine" moral language. Noddings, in particular, seems to have become increasingly shrill in her repudiation of what she labels the "language of the father" (1989). In fact, the majority of my professional students still find the "masculine" language of rights, principles, moral dilemmas, discursive reasoning, and lexical ordering of alternatives to possess considerable validity. While they like the particularity and concreteness of the Gilligan–Noddings perspective, and while they endorse, in principle, a moral philosophy that stresses networks of relationships, connection, cooperation, caring, and communication, they nevertheless turn eagerly to the masculine language of logical reasoning and moral principles for real-world ethical analysis and problem-solving. For them, this functional ethical language ought to belong to everyone, not just to men.

In order for me to move the analysis of the two moral languages to a deeper level, and to restore some balance to the class conversations, I assign two texts that postulate a naturalistic, nongendered basis to morality. William Damon's *The Moral Child: Nurturing Children's Natural Moral Growth* (1988) argues that morality emerges naturally in the context of children's everyday social life from the very earliest years. It is through common activities such as sharing and helping, as well as through "universal," "natural" emotions such as empathy, shame, and guilt, that children acquire their deep-seated moral standards. And James Q. Wilson's *The Moral Sense* (1993) argues that we are born with a "moral sense," an intuitive, directly felt belief about how we ought to act. He gives four examples of such a moral sense—sympathy, fairness, self-control, and duty—and, in his account of the sources of these "moral sentiments," he examines the influence of human nature, family experiences, gender, and culture in the development of these sentiments. It is striking that neither author ever speaks of a masculine or feminine moral language. I intend to say more about an ethic of caring in my final chapter.

COMING OUT OF THE METAPHYSICAL CLOSET

At the end of every unit on First Moral Language, for feedback, I ask students to do an anonymous, brief, in-class "free-write" account of what they honestly think about the Language of Background Beliefs. I then tell them they may choose to keep or to give me their free-writes with the stipulation that I may use them any way I wish. Through the years, only a few students have refused to hand over their written remarks. What follows are some recent, uncensored responses:

My First Moral Language is a foundation from which I begin acting as a moral being. It is important to be in touch with our First Moral Language in order to fully understand from where our values and morals arise. They are our vital reference points, our subterranean beliefs.

The First Moral Language is the heart of what I believe and the rock on which I stand. It is the truth in my life that underlies all that I value. I must admit I am a devout Orthodox Jew, and so my religious beliefs are my ethical bedrock. I think about them all the time. In fact, you could say that I am ethical because I am a Jew.

Background Beliefs are so much a part of us that it takes a terrific amount of work to identify what they are. They are difficult to convey because most of the time these beliefs exist at a taken-for-granted level in our thinking. The hardest thing I have ever done is to put these beliefs into words.

These beliefs help me to determine what is right and wrong. In some sense, the First Moral Language exists outside of me in that it is objective and fundamental. This language puts me in touch with my philosophical roots. It is prior to my experiences, feelings, and even my intuitions. As a philosophy major, I have always liked reading metaphysicians. Hegel is my favorite ontologist, and Kant is my favorite moral philosopher. But the comic strip, "Calvin and Hobbes," is my favorite metaphysical text.

First Moral Language is a personal search for underlying truth, knowledge, and morality. The search is excruciatingly painful for me today, because I have had very little practice in learning and speaking this language in my life—except maybe in church when I was a child. Where do I go today to learn to become fluent in this vocabulary? I hate to say it, but I am an illiterate in this language, and I am deeply embarrassed whenever someone asks me what it is I believe about right and wrong and why. I usually find myself uttering platitudes or quoting the television shows *Seinfeld* or *Friends*.

I find this language incoherent and misplaced. It was almost impossible for me to write your first assigment, the Ethics Manifesto. For me, morality has no foundation whatsoever. I agree totally with the author of one of our texts this semester, Richard Rorty (1989), that only metaphysicians and clergy look for rock-bottom certainties and absolutes when they discuss morals and ethics. My morality is con-

stantly changing. It doesn't need any grounding or certitude. It is an
evolving, random product of my past experiences, my present relationships, and my always-changing interpretive perspectives. Besides,
I don't know how you can separate this language from the other two
languages you teach. I guess you could call me a scientific realist, because I find so much of the metaphysical rationale for morality ab-
surd and meaningless. I did find the reading interesting, though,
even if it was biased toward a metaphysical point of view.

This language completely escapes me. I am a realist, a high school
principal, who must set aside the luxury of philosophizing in the
work I do. Besides, if it's all unprovable anyway, why bother? I resolve ethical dilemmas according to my feelings and intuitions, and
on the basis of 20 years of experience. Not one author we've read
this term could even understand, let alone do, my work.

I am struck by something Mary Midgley (1991) said in one of our
readings: "Metaphysics is not something you can get rid of . . . metaphysical [beliefs] about human nature and human destiny are the
most general presuppositions of our thought, without which it would
remain a hopelessly shapeless collection of scraps" (p. 169). One
thing I realized during our study of First Moral Language is that
much of my moral thinking seems "shapeless" only because I haven't
taken the trouble to define what is truly important to me. When you
first asked us to react to your probes, I thought you were crazy. They
seemed so abstract. But because you kept pushing these questions at
us, I was forced to consider what is really deep down important to
me. I do have a metaphysic, and it has been with me for a long time.
Native American spirituality and an environmental ethic form my
"moral picture," as you say, and whenever I think about ethical issues
I find myself falling back on these "presuppositions." Thank you for
helping me to retrieve them.

CONCLUSION: HERMENEUTICS AND
BACKGROUND BELIEFS

I have long been a student of hermeneutics in the tradition of Hans-
Georg Gadamer (1976). Hermeneutics derives from the Greek *hermeneuein*,
to interpret into one's own idiom, to give expression to, to attribute meaning to. One of my First Language beliefs is that the world of ethics is an
endlessly interpretable world, and rarely is there a final or definitive re-

sponse to an ethical dilemma. In this sense, I am an unrepentant ethical constructivist, perhaps even a moral postmodernist. For me, the goal of a hermeneutical approach to ethics is to determine what morality means to each of us in the present, to interpret and translate this understanding in our own idiom, and to give concrete expression to this interpretation by our daily ethical actions (Bernstein, 1992).

I frequently remind students that ethical interpretation begins with our Background Beliefs, our moral reference points. Without this standpoint, I argue, a coherent moral dialogue between ourselves and the world cannot take place; neither is it likely we will ever achieve the deepest ethical self-understanding that leads to fully informed (and defensible) ethical action. While it is true that most students in my classes accept and embrace the importance of Background Beliefs in developing an interpretive perspective on ethical reality, some remain unconvinced, as a few of the above free-writes make clear. These students simply want to get on with actual problem-solving—without the metaphysics. Regardless of their position on First Moral Language, though, most students eagerly await the time we will move to the more concrete Second Moral Language, the subject of the next chapter.

Chapter 4

SECOND LANGUAGE: THE LANGUAGE OF MORAL CHARACTER

Non in dialectica complacuit Deo salvum facere populum suum. God does not save the world by logic.

St. Anselm

While students often struggle with the complexities, and the abstractness, of First Language, most can barely conceal their enthusiasm when we get to Second Language. This is the language of "thick description," and it allows a fuller, much more colorful moral response to ethical dilemmas than either the First or Third Language. Earlier in my career, when I taught only the First and Third Languages, some students would complain that the study of ethics seemed too cerebral and "bloodless." I vividly remember a physical therapist once asking me in class: "Why do you abstract out of our lives all the truly important stuff when you teach us how to resolve ethical dilemmas? It is like you are teaching us to write by giving us only nouns but no adverbs, adjectives, or verbs!" As I recall, the gist of her reasoning went something like this:

> It is true, as you say, that I draw from a personal philosophy whenever I enter a moral situation, but I also draw upon so much more. I know I bring to my ethical problems something greater than an assortment of Background Beliefs and rules. I cannot philosophize about ethics in an intellectual vacuum. I am the daughter of two strict Italian parents, both of whom are still living, and they taught me most of my morality—old-world Catholicism mixed with a lot of common sense—when I was young. I don't think either of them could write one defensible sentence about their morals, and yet they are the most thoroughly decent people I have ever known.
>
> There was a time when I thought I'd rejected most of their teachings as "uncool," but, as I get older, I find I'm teaching the same stuff to my own children. I grew up in a very special, loving Italian family, attended a Catholic church every Sunday and a parochial

school for 12 years, belonged to several influential groups throughout my early and middle life, held a bunch of jobs, and now I am in the midst of a messy divorce trying to retain custody of my two children. My feelings seem to be affecting my morality in some pretty intense ways these days. I didn't suddenly arrive at an ethic, you know. I've been growing into one all my life, and I'm almost ashamed to say, the whole process has been mostly unconscious. In fact, you might say my life's vocation up to this point has been to learn the difference between right and wrong, and then to have the courage to live my life the right way. Unfortunately, most of the time I'm not sure what's right or wrong, and, I don't mean to offend you, but philosophy doesn't always help me to know. Don't I actually draw from my whole life's experience when I think about ethical dilemmas? Isn't my entire life my philosophy? I'm sorry; I know this sounds anti-intellectual, but I'm glad I said it.

MORAL CHARACTER

In her own way, the physical therapist was calling my attention to the reality of another world each of us inhabits: the concrete moral world. In addition to living in a metaphysical life-space, where we speak a more private, foundational, and philosophical language, we also live in a number of small, tangible communities, where we speak a "thick" language of feeling, memory, intuition, and imagination, a language that St. Anselm (in the quotation that introduces this chapter) believed God speaks. It is in these communities, I contend, that we first begin to think about, and develop a perspective toward, those "metaphysical" questions I discuss in the previous chapter. The physical therapist was reminding me that a large part of who we are as moral beings "living out our vocation to know what is right and wrong" has its roots in our various face-to-face communities. These are the settings for the institutions and people that exert such a formative influence on our moral development that without them, I submit, we have little moral identity. These concrete moral communities provide us with a framework for thinking about right and wrong, because they are our primary context of morally significant people, ideals, and language (Sichel, 1988). They comprise the inescapable basis for our personal moral narratives, our language, our virtues, and our ideals.

Concerning the centrality of concrete moral communities in our lives, Aristotle (1976) taught in *The Nicomachean Ethics* that people do not become virtuous by nature or through spontaneity. He believed that excellence of character occurs, if at all, only as a consequence of a systematic and de-

voted community effort wherein everyone is a moral "teacher" to the
young, wherein everyone embodies and implants the important moral dispositions. Children learn to be moral by imitating adult exemplars. A contemporary Aristotelian Christian, Stanley Hauerwas (1981), has even gone
so far as to assert that without a moral account rooted in the traditions and
practices of closely knit sectarian communities and exemplified by devotees
of a special way of life, most behavior ultimately becomes lonely, selfish,
desperate, and destructive. Those young people today who join gangs,
commit random acts of deadly violence, and indulge in careless and irresponsible sexual and drug behaviors are living proof of the timelessness of
Aristotle's teachings. In the last few years, a growing number of students in
my classes are of one mind with Aristotle and Hauerwas. They concur that
"selfish and desperate" youth are prone to turn toward gangs, violence, and
self-destructive activities precisely because they are without the strong
moral exemplars and the morally vibrant, supportive concrete communities necessary for responsible character formation.

I found the physical therapist's comments jarring and, in their own
way, quite insightful. She was able to put into words what I and my students
were only vaguely sensing: Something fundamental appeared to be missing
in our readings and conversations about ethics. Robert Coles (1989), a
writer my physical therapist found to be a sympathetic soulmate, made a
parallel observation:

> I remember my father talking at the dinner table about character, telling my
> brother and me, when we were young, that "character is how you behave
> when no one is looking." . . . Are we ever in a situation when "no one is look-
> ing"? . . . For those of us who try to be conscientious, someone is always "look-
> ing," even if we are as solitary as Thoreau at Walden. (p. 198)

Earlier in the same text, Coles says,

> We all accumulate stories in our lives . . . no one's stories are quite like anyone
> else's . . . and . . . we become our own appreciative and comprehending critics
> by learning to pull together the various incidents in our lives in such a way
> that they do, in fact, become an old-fashioned story. (p. 11)

Coles is saying, as is the physical therapist, that my moral character
has as much to do with *who* I am as with *what* I can put into discursive
language. And who I am is the embodiment of my entire life lived in a
variety of small communities, shaped by pivotal experiences in a number
of institutions, and touched by influential others (real and fictional) who
come into my life at various points and who stay with me in lingering moral

memories throughout my lifespan. These communities, events, and people are "always looking" at me when I make moral choices. Moreover, when I think about my life as a continuing moral narrative, I become a self-critical author; I create unique and illuminating stories that give purpose and meaning to the life I lead. Coles would offer one wide-ranging definition of moral character, therefore, as the way I behave in response to all of the events and people, seen and unseen, that constitute my lifelong story. The physical therapist, likewise, was challenging me to consider the profound impact of all of these elements of moral character on her ethical decision-making.

Consequently, during the last decade, I have amplified my own understanding of character considerably. I now think of moral character in five ways: First, it refers to an overall aggregate of moral characteristics that distinguish one person from another. Second, it includes the practice of certain virtues and the avoidance of certain vices, in the pursuit of a moral life. Third, it is a complex amalgam of intention, thought, action, disposition, intuition, and feeling. Feelings and intuitions especially are focal to the formation of moral character, and their positive and negative influence on intention, thought, and action must never be overlooked. Fourth, it is always formed in communities, which provide the defining personal, historical, political, cultural, and professional settings and structures, as well as the exemplars, necessary for the development of moral strength. And fifth, it originates in, and is nourished and transformed by, the appropriation of normative stories with their unique moral vocabularies.

In my estimation, one of the major limitations of First and Third Moral Languages is that they do not offer an adequate explanation for growth in moral strength and integrity. Their language is "thin." They presume that personal integrity depends mainly on a set of Background Beliefs, and on a single principle and theory, to determine every ethical action. Hence, they posit the character of a moral self as developing as a result of discrete ethical decisions and actions that are grounded in a metaphysic and that are justified by appealing to specific principles and theories. This, I believe, is valid, as far as it goes, but, like the physical therapist and Robert Coles, I do not think it goes far enough. Neither, evidently, did many students in the early days of my course. Thus over the years I have worked to construct a Second Language of Moral Character that incorporates such elements as virtue, narrative, community, feeling, structures, and ideals. This is a language of "thick description," and I teach this as an actual framework for ethical decision-making, which I will spell out later in this chapter.

Today, I teach that moral integrity, in large part, is the lifelong outcome of actions and people that shape particular kinds of character. It is mainly through a continuing narrative of actual choices that individuals learn to acquire a moral character. I agree, to some extent, with Aristotle that to be moral requires constant training. (It also requires continual confirmation, reflection, action, and critique, of course.) And the character that develops is like the narrative of a good novel: It gives a coherence to all of our ethical decisions and forces individuals to claim their actions as their own. This is essentially the claim that many character educators in the public schools are making at this time: They advocate systematic classroom instruction to form a specific kind of moral character, one that is respectful, diligent, responsible, and self-disciplined (Kilpatrick, 1992; Lickona, 1991; Wynne & Ryan, 1993).

With such instruction, the character educators hope to offset what they perceive to be a runaway moral nihilism in the larger culture, and they believe this nihilism is reflected in the permissiveness of many sex- and drug-education programs in the schools. While I intend to say more about the weaknesses of character education in the final chapter, at this point I will simply note that contemporary character educators go awry because they ignore the roles of First and Third Moral Languages in constructing their programs. They choose instead to concentrate overzealously on only one aspect of Second Moral Language—virtue training—and they focus exclusively on the school as the site of such training. If Aristotle is right, moral education must begin early, and it must pervade the whole of a person's life. This is the classical Greek notion of *paideia*, the understanding that only through lifelong practice and precept could a person be initiated into the ways of the community. The ancients would be very skeptical of the idea that the schools alone could do much to correct the moral deficiencies of the larger culture. Aristophanes (448 B.C.–388 B.C.), for one, declared in *The Clouds* that moral virtue is not acquired in schools, but rather within the family, neighborhood, and circle of friends. Moreover, he felt that virtues and vices are probably fixed by the age of 7.

In the work I do, however, the advantage of a moral-character component to ethical decision-making is that generally students learn a very important lesson. They realize that when they make a moral decision they do not simply *do* something; they actually shape their own moral character in new ways, even while they express those moral dispositions and ideals that they have been developing throughout a lifetime. This is frequently a major insight for students. They have suspected all along that moral choice is always something more than a Third Language exercise in a type of case law, or a First Language exercise in metaphysical system-building; now they understand that every moral choice must take account of the moral agent's character as well. Each ethical choice is always a choice about what kind of character to become, about what choice will best preserve their moral integrity in such a way that their actions will fit their best moral images of themselves. The paradigmatic Second Language question to ask is not only, "Is this the right thing to do?" but "*Which decision has the most integrity in terms of the kind of person I either perceive myself to be or am striving to become?*" This type of question has proven to be invaluable to students in sorting through their complex ethical dilemmas. It is the single language they write to me about years after they have taken the course.

THE MORAL CHARACTER FRAMEWORK FOR ETHICAL DECISION-MAKING

The Second Moral Language provides a useful framework for understanding actual ethical dilemmas. Throughout the remainder of the chapter, I am going to explain this framework in greater depth by applying it to a real-life case. Moreover, I intend to reflect on the strengths of the framework as an instrument for resolving ethical conflicts, based on my many years of teaching it. The truth is that I myself came late to this framework, in spite of my students' continual prodding, because I was least comfortable with this way of thinking about ethical decision-making. My own philosophical training was largely discursive, and it seemed to reinforce my bias that reason alone was the superior source of moral knowledge. I will discuss this more in the sections that follow, but now I want to talk about case studies and their utility for an applied ethics course.

The Case Study

Because I insist that all students write their own cases, I urge them to think of a *case* as a brief narrative of an ethical dilemma and as a problem to be solved. The narrative tells a little story in four or five compelling paragraphs and includes all of the morally relevant actors and events, as well as significant times and places. A case can be retrospective (a reexamination of a past experience), ongoing (an examination of a current experience), or prospective (a rehearsal for a case that could happen in the future). I also accept fictional cases from students as long as they meet my criteria for an ethics case. (Whatever type of case students choose to construct, I always promise them complete confidentiality; I also urge students to change names and pertinent events in a true case in order to protect the identity of those involved.) An ethical dilemma is a situation in which two or more courses of action (moral choices) are in conflict, and each action can be plausibly defended as the "good" one to take. The primary moral agent is the student, the one who must make the ultimate ethical decision, either individually or as a member of a group. I insist that each student write the case in the first person.

I have found over the years that the best provenance for cases is in my students' own work lives. Initially, I might use a series of ready-made cases from the professional literature to give them a sense of what an ethics case looks like and to provide a common pool of experience for us to examine. A good case can be a provocative, almost indispensable tool for teaching the relevant moral concepts, and there are several professional ethics texts at the present time that present engaging cases (e.g., Beauchamp & Childress, 1979; Glaser, 1994; Strike & Soltis, 1992). The difficulty I have with some textbook cases, however, is that they are oftentimes so overly dramatic they make no claim to verisimilitude. While they can be occasionally absorbing, and even entertaining, many cases do not ring true for some students. Thus they do not take them seriously as facsimiles for their own work.

Moreover, in certain professions cases tend to focus on repetitive themes. For example, in the counseling/social work professions, the cases have to do mostly with rights-to-autonomy, confidentiality, and privacy issues. In the allied health field, the cases are concerned mainly with themes of scarce-resource distribution, professional competence, and conflicts with physicians and other superordinates. And in the teaching field, the cases deal predominantly with other peoples' encroachments on teacher autonomy, discipline, fairness, and conflicting loyalties to different constituencies. While I readily acknowledge that these issues are of utmost importance to professionals today, the reiteration of the same topics and dilemmas sometimes serves as a soporific; many students tune out because they have heard the same issues over and over again. Or, worse, students narrow their ethical scope to these few, familiar themes, and thus they miss a variety of additional ethical issues that may actually be more true to life for them.

I have become much more insistent that students construct cases that report on their own experiences in the workplace. At the outset, some students will complain that they have no ethical dilemmas to discuss. "My life isn't nearly as complicated or as dramatic as a physician's or a lawyer's," some will reply. Or "How can I top what we've just read about?" Usually, I will get this response from undergraduates and from educators in the public schools and in universities. My reaction is always to be patient, because I know that education is above all a moral profession with a profusion of ethical choices that professionals confront on an almost hourly basis. I believe what all students (both pre- and practicing professionals) require is training in moral discernment. They need practice in the ability to distinguish between what is morally relevant and what is not. They need help to see what is not evident to the ethically untrained mind. They need to learn to speak the technical ethical languages in order to identify the moral factors in the work they do. In this respect, moral language can be empowering, because without it the ability to discriminate is lost. Once my students develop some skills in speaking the three languages, though, their confidence soars; and both the quantity *and* quality of their cases improve dramatically.

A *case study* is the primary moral agent's systematic examination of the case narrative; this entails applying the relevant framework in some depth to the analysis and disposition of the case. The purpose of a Second Moral Language analysis is not to defend or to justify a particular ethical decision, although it can be used in this way. This is the major function of Third Moral Language. *Instead, its central function is to provide important contextual information for the decision-maker for whom it can be an instrument of rich self-revelation.* Its data are mainly personal and include much psychological, sociological, political, and professional content. A Second Moral Language analysis differs from a First Moral Language analysis in that the former is more psychological and the latter is more philosophical; the former is an exploration of personal motives, intentions, origins, and contexts, while the latter is an examination of first principles, truth, metaphysics, and ultimate meaning. Third Moral Language analysis, in contrast to the other two, is a minimum form of moral discourse that is logically deductive, and it is well suited for rational, defensible, quasi-legal, ethical decision-making in the secular pluralist society. It is a justification language. I will be examining this framework more extensively in the next chapter.

Every application of a moral language must begin with a case. Therefore, in order to illustrate how this Second Language Framework functions, I will work with a fictional case I constructed featuring a high school guidance counselor, Jonathan. I will then spend the major portion of this chapter applying the Moral Character Framework to this case as Jonathan might have.

"KEEPING A FRIEND'S SECRET"

I [Jonathan] am a guidance counselor at the local high school. My friendship with a colleague, Sam, a history teacher, goes back 20 years to the time we were roommates at the state university. I have lately been worried about Sam's behavior, because reports from students and the central office have been alarming. Sam's classes have grown unruly and disrespectful, and one day he even dozed in full view of the students. Sam has become a social recluse, pulling back from all involvement with his colleagues and friends. He has become the talk of the school. On a recent weekend, I was drinking coffee alone at the local mall in a doughnut shop, when, after an awkward entrance, Sam sat down beside me. Following a few minutes of social chatter, he began to get very serious. It did not take long for Sam to reveal to me how "messed up" his life had become.

His wife, Martha, had walked out on him several months ago in order to live with her newly divorced boss, with whom she had been having an affair for over a year. The affair completely stunned Sam, who declared that he still loved his wife very much and would take her back in a moment. Sam had become increasingly lonely and despondent over the last few months and had sought psychiatric help. He had also begun self-medicating diazepam, an antianxiety drug, taking more than three times the amount his therapist had recommended. Sam told me that he would be mortified if any of these disclosures were to get out at school. He would work things out in his own best way. He only needed a little more time. Besides, "things weren't really that bad at school, right?" The reason he shared all of this with me, he said, was that he needed to "unload" to the "only friend in the world I can trust." He had little confidence in his therapist and had been thinking, for some time, about finding another one.

Now, I think, Sam's behavior at school makes some sense. But what should I do with this information? I am Sam's closest friend, and I am profoundly grateful for Sam's allegiance and support through many of my own crises over the years. How can I violate Sam's privacy? I have been under considerable pressure from Sam's colleagues, and from the school administration, to find out exactly what has been troubling him.

Several ethical questions arise for me. Does the disclosure in a coffee shop at a mall require an implied promise of confidentiality, as such a disclosure almost certainly would if it had occurred in my office at school? Why does betrayal of a dear friend's secret seem so much more upsetting than betrayal of a colleague's or client's secret? Can I keep the two roles separate? Do I have an obligation to report what I know to the principal, who is a kindly woman and who would certainly be understanding of Sam's problems? And what about the harm to Sam's students, who are learning nothing this term? His seniors in particular are complaining about not being properly prepared for the Advanced Placement exam in history. Is keeping his secret in Sam's best interest? Will Sam's drug overdosing cause him serious psychological and physical damage? Should I at least inform

Sam's therapist about the drug abuse? Just who are my clients anyway, and to whom do I have the greatest obligations? And should I even get involved? Why can't I draw the line between my private and public life? Everybody else does.

Second Language Moral Brief

The major task in analyzing the above case is to construct a Moral Brief. This Moral Brief is the framework for a 15- to 20-page paper that I require of my students when we have finished the unit on Second Language, about two-thirds of the way through the course. In the mid-1970s, a lawyer in one of my classes recommended that an effective way to do a structured analysis of a difficult ethical case might be to do what the legal profession does: Make a legal brief—a concise outline of the major themes and contentions in an argument. Through the years, almost without exception, my students have expressed appreciation for the systematic and practical assistance that a Moral Brief offers in working through an ethical dilemma. At its best, it gives them a concise, formal method for gaining access to important personal data in ethical decision-making. The Second Language Moral Brief asks the following questions:

1. What are your immediate moral intuitions and stirrings about this case?
2. Are you experiencing any conflicting moral feelings as you think about this case?
3. What would happen if you were to make a decision both *in* character and *out of* character in this case?
4. What do you think are some of your profession's expectations regarding your decision in this case?
5. What is your decision?

In what follows, I will explain the ethical meaning and pedagogical significance of each question. I will also respond to each of these questions as Jonathan might, but in the third person. If Jonathan were a real moral agent, he would address each of the questions in the first-person singular, as someone who is actively working through an ethical dilemma in the present. Jonathan is actually a composite of several counselors and therapists who have taken my ethics courses over the years; I believe I have accurately captured their professional personas and concerns. In constructing the actual case and in developing Jonathan's moral character and story, I have consulted at length with a school counselor in order to achieve a more realistic case portrayal and analysis.

1.   What are your immediate moral intuitions and stirrings about this case?

Sidney Callahan's *In Good Conscience: Reason and Emotion in Moral Decision Making* (1991) has been an excellent guide for my students in understanding the influence of intuition and feelings on ethical decision-making. For her, moral intuitions are "thoughts and ideas that come spontaneously to mind" (p. 63). Callahan is a firm believer in rational problem-solving methods, but she also understands that much rational thinking is "nonconscious, that is, the processes are unavailable to, or unnoticed or unappreciated by, our conscious phenomenological awareness" (p. 75). Callahan urges us to consult, and trust, our hunches, our immediate apprehensions, our intuitive stirrings, when contemplating ethical decision-making. She recommends that we turn inward to listen to our "inner stream of [moral] consciousness" as we reflect on the courses of action we might take in resolving ethical dilemmas such as the above. For her, this is a kind of "covert [moral] self-talk" (p. 76) that flows through our minds.

I think of myself as a very intuitive person. My scores on intuition tests are always extraordinarily high. Over the years, I have come to trust the insights of my nonconscious rational mind. I enthusiastically agree with Callahan that often we can get an immediate sense of the "right" thing to do when we let the solution to a dilemma just come to our minds, without the initial deployment of First and Second Languages. Because I have always been more of an intuitive thinker than a rational skeptic, I tend to rely heavily on my intuitive sense when I initially confront a problem in ethics. I think of the human mind as a tripartite container that includes a conscious rational part, a feeling part, and a nonconscious rational part. The nonconscious rational part of my mind, the intuition, can be a powerful aid to ethical problem-solving, and it sometimes delivers its "solutions" to me in a flash.

Moreover, because most of these hunches and flashes of insight actually coincide with my reason and common sense, I believe they can generally be trusted to produce both rational insight *and* moral discernment. And so, I propose to students that when our Background Beliefs and moral principles give no immediate guidance on what course of action we should take, we must find ways to tap into our intuitive resources. I say this even as I stress that the best solutions to ethical problems will always be a synthesis of First, Second, and Third Moral Languages, a composite of philosophy, nonconscious reason, and conscious rational problem-solving. Nevertheless, in the Second Language Moral Brief, I still reserve an important place for consulting the intuition.

Jonathan's immediate, primary intuition is to keep Sam's disclosures secret. He senses that neither Sam's nor the school's best interests would be properly served if he were to reveal what Sam has told him at the mall. He also suspects that Sam has sought him out as a good listener and friend, not as a professional colleague or school administrator. Perhaps, then, his duty to Sam at this particular time is defined more by his friendship than by his professional relationship. Maybe, in this one instance, he should keep his private and professional roles separate, and marshal whatever resources he can to help Sam get through this period of crisis. He recalls out of nowhere something his mother used to say about friendship: "Nothing, not even the truth, is worth the loss of a friend."

He also keeps hearing the words "primary loyalty" as he thinks about the meeting with Sam at the coffee shop. When he was a teenager, his father once gave him advice that a person's primary loyalty must always be to loved ones and friends; thus, whenever he had to make a choice between conflicting loyalties, his father instructed him that the primary loyalty should always take precedence. If his father's loyalty principle is true, then Jonathan believes he certainly owes his allegiance to Sam in this instance. Finally, Jonathan wonders what would be gained by "dumping" Sam's problems in the principal's lap. This action seems counterintuitive, because he knows this is not likely to get Sam to stop overmedicating or to return to his therapist, and it most certainly will not bring about a reconciliation between Sam and his wife. It will probably raise Sam's anxiety level even higher. Although Jonathan's intuitive stirrings to keep Sam's secret are strong, he is still not fully convinced on a conscious rational level that such an action would be the most judicious one.

2. Are you experiencing any conflicting moral feelings as you think about this case?

H. Tristram Engelhardt, Jr. (1986) sums up the usual response of philosophers regarding the role of feelings in ethical decision-making: They are always "irrational and surd" (p. 10). He worries, as do most ethicists who speak exclusively in First or Third Moral Languages, that feelings are too subjective, arbitrary, and distracting to be of much help in problem-solving. He opts for a rigorous impartiality and objectivity in constructing rational moral arguments. I must acknowledge that for years I shared Engelhardt's critical assessment of feelings in ethical analysis. I was tone-deaf to my moral feelings. I considered feelings sentimental, messy, and far too volatile to be a dependable ethical resource. While I was able to see the wisdom in my moral intuitions—which I was convinced were simply reasonings not made fully conscious—I could not understand the value of my feelings. And so I treated them as an intoxicant that could only produce stupefied ethical analysis. I came very close to agreeing with Kant's observation that feelings are "probably always an illness of mind because both emotion and passion exclude the sovereignty of reason" (S. Callahan, 1991, p. 98).

I have my wife to thank for the insight that I am at my best as a parent (and husband) whenever I recognize, and acknowledge, the worth of family members' feelings in trying to make sense of their experiences. Her training as a counselor has alerted her to the "feeling tone" of all discourse, including the moral. Even though I still tend to challenge her insights on occasion, she has helped me to understand that an absolutely detached moral reasoner, like Mr. Spock in the original "Star Trek" series, is, at best, the ersatz creation of science-fiction writers. Neither she nor I have ever met a Spock in the classroom, in church, at the supermarket, or even in the science lab. So, too, I am at my best as a teacher, I believe, whenever I remember that students often consult their feelings when working through an ethical dilemma. Like me, they frequently think, judge, evaluate, even believe, through their emotions. The kind of moral knowledge that is truly worth defending, perhaps even dying for, is what people feel most deeply about. Our most authoritative First Language beliefs around religion and politics, for example, are often accompanied by the strongest feelings; and our most abstract beliefs become real when they are expressed in the language of joy or love or excitement.

In Sidney Callahan's captivating phrase, feelings are "hot cognitions" (p. 100) because they motivate. Our feelings get "hotter" the more we are subjectively invested in our ethical decision-making. In some cases, moral problem-solving can actually activate the limbic system and other brain pathways. It can arouse biochemical, muscular, and related physiological mechanisms. There have been times in class when students have become so emotionally involved in a case analysis that tempers have flared and tears have been shed. I remember a nurse who lost his composure one evening in class while trying to defend his decision to ignore a dying patient's advance directive to forgo the use of a feeding tube. This professional became so distressed as he recounted his reasons for forcing a tube down a reluctant patient's throat that he actually had to flee the room in order to regain his poise. Upon returning, he apologized profusely to the rest of us because he had acted so "unprofessionally" in front of us. What disturbed me was not the "unprofessional" outburst. Rather, I wondered whether he had experienced those same feelings at the time he made the decision to use the feeding tube; and, if so, had he discounted the "cognitive" worth of those very strong sensations in coming to a prudential ethical decision regarding forced feeding?

The challenge for me is to encourage students to treat their feelings as a potentially rich source of insight in thinking about ethical dilemmas. Because our feelings are complex combinations of sentiments, biological responses, and thinking patterns, they can signal possible directions to take in sorting through the moral complexities in a case. In fact, I believe it is our emotional systems that make empathy and understanding possible in the first place. I would argue that such primary feelings as excitement, joy, anguish, anger, disappointment, remorse, and guilt, for example, can motivate us to think more deeply, and caringly, about all of the morally relevant issues and people represented in an ethical dilemma. It is equally true, of course, that relying on feelings alone to find answers to ethical problems can be seriously distorting. For this reason, the best approach to ethical decision-making will always be one that fully integrates feelings, reason, and intuition.

Jonathan recalls that when he first saw Sam approaching him in the coffee shop, his immediate feeling was one of anger. Why, he wondered, was this person, who had so obviously been avoiding him for months, now violating his privacy, and in a coffee shop on the weekend? How brazen of Sam to think that he could disturb Jonathan during a moment of relaxation in a neutral, anonymous space—on Sam's terms, and not Jonathan's. But this feeling of anger also competed with a sense of elation that perhaps Jonathan's old friend was feeling better and was now ready to continue their relationship. He had always enjoyed Sam's company, especially over dinner, or at the theater, or at ballgames in the city. Jonathan's wife also appreciated her friendship with Sam and his wife, Martha. Finally, Jonathan remembers that as he was listening to Sam discuss his problems, he felt both disappointment and sadness: disappointment because Sam seemed so totally oblivious, even a bit insensitive, to the damage he was causing at school; and sadness because Sam was so obviously hurting and helpless, and Jonathan did not know how to make him feel better.

As he mulls over the case at the present time, Jonathan senses in his gut (a part of the anatomy he has always trusted) an enormous relief that for the first time he understands the reasons for Sam's erratic, unprofessional behavior. He also feels relieved that he has something concrete he can finally tell his colleagues when they question him about Sam's aberrant conduct. But this course of action just does not feel right because it has the flavor of betrayal. And it seems in direct conflict with Jonathan's overall feeling of deep apprehension about the deteriorating physical and mental health of a truly precious friend. He feels a genuine sense of solicitude in Sam's behalf, and he knows it would be very difficult to do anything that would further injure his dearest friend and colleague, including possibly violating his confidence in order to help him. The task for Jonathan now, though, is to determine the right course of action that would be most consistent with his strongest feelings about the case.

3. What would happen if you were to make a decision both *in* character and *out of* character in this case?

My character is the sum total of all those moral characteristics that make me a unique person, different in important respects from all other persons. In addition to my intuitions and feelings, these unique moral characteristics include my very special defining *communities*, my continuing *story*, and my formative *virtues*. Thus, to act in character is, first, to understand the decisive impact of my primary and secondary communities on who I am and on who I hope to become; these communities are the important contexts of places, people, events, ideals, and language that are the sine qua non for my virtues, my vocabulary, and my narrative.

Second, to act in character is to act with a critical awareness that with every moral choice I make I am continually "writing" new chapters in my personal moral text, a story that includes a beginning already constructed, a middle in process, and an end that may or may not be far off. It is to act with the full realization that with every decision I make, I bear full responsibility for creating a moral self. As I construct my moral narrative I link the disparate places, events, ideals, and people in my life into a coherent, ongoing autobiography, and, along the way, I fashion an authentic and unique moral identity.

And, third, to act in character is to act in a way that fulfills particular virtues that are important to me. To act in character is to act consistent with my very best motives, intentions, and dispositions. For me to act out of character is to betray all that is precious to me for the sake of moral compromise, expedience, or utility. Even though I may be able to justify my moral turnabout from my own best self, I know that I am living a lie in the sense that I have abandoned my "true" ethical self. I have turned my back on those communities, stories, and virtues that have nourished and transformed me throughout my life. I am a character in moral exile because I have lost my rightful ethical identity.

Community. In determining whether he is acting in or out of character, Jonathan must consider the possible impact of his key moral communities in his decision-making. This is less difficult for Jonathan, a second- and third-generation Greek-American, than for many of my less ethnically conscious students, because so few of them think of themselves as belonging to a bona fide, moral community. In Andrew Oldenquist's

(1986) words, a moral community is one that "depends on its members' awareness of having a core of deeply and confidently held moral values together with people, customs and ceremonies which bear witness to them" (p. 62). While I agree with my students that there is a paucity of monolithic moral communities in our pluralistic society, I believe we are still, by nature, tribal creatures, even as we are autonomous individuals pursuing our particular conceptions of the good in our own best ways.

We each exist in unique assemblages of nested and overlapping groups from our earliest years, and these groups—what I prefer to call our concrete moral communities (Engelhardt, 1986)—are the training grounds for our ethical development. These concrete moral communities consist of our families, churches, schools, political organizations, unions, clubs, recreational groups, professional associations, and so forth. And one of their essential functions—sometimes overtly, sometimes covertly—is to shape us as moral beings through precept, example, exhortation, encouragement, and reward. It is largely in these communities (small or large, transient or permanent, sectarian or secular), I contend, that we write our personal moral narratives and cultivate our virtues.

Michael J. Sandel's *Liberalism and the Limits of Justice* (1982) has been a very useful resource for students because of his fine elucidation of three conceptions of community. He has helped them to understand that because a secular, pluralist society seeks not to impose a single conception of the good on us, but rather to leave us as free as possible to choose our own ends, we often seek membership in groups. We do this, he maintains, in order to define, and pursue, our private and public moral purposes, including the meaning of such principles as justice and autonomy. At first, many students reject the surmise that community belongingness is necessary for the construal of moral purposes. Most are unwilling to locate themselves in formative moral communities because they honestly believe they belong to none, or else they regard themselves as authentic individualists who have freely chosen their own moral principles and thus have no need for communal involvement. But whenever we read Sandel, students not only become more aware of the three types of groups he believes exist in a liberal society; they are also more willing to acknowledge the *moral* impact such groups might have in their own lives.

According to Sandel, one type of community is "instrumental" in the sense that it is where individuals freely choose to come together out of mutual self-interest in order to pursue their own private ends. For my students, these groups are their predominant ones, and they usually involve their associations at work and play. As a student once put it, and she was not being cynical: "Instrumental groups are those where members give their full consent to mutual exploitation." Another type is "sentimental" in that members are emotionally involved in the community, and they may share final ends and moral ideals. Members might even be willing, in some instances, to make sacrifices in behalf of others' welfare because they are linked by powerful ties of affection and sentiment. Some students do acknowledge belonging to such groups, usually of a familial, political, or educational nature, but talk of sacrifice, and the possible loss of autonomy, is bothersome to them, because moral pluralism is still their chief preference.

And a third type of group is "constitutive" because members are connected not simply by self-interest, feelings, and shared aims and values, but also by the fact that their very identities are defined by the community of which they are a part. Jonathan, as we shall see, is a product of a constitutive community, but such communities are rapidly disappearing for most Americans. Certain familial, ethnic, racial, and religious groups, however, still manage to serve a constitutive function for some. In fact, one way to understand the tendencies of some racial and ethnic groups to segregate themselves in the American university, and of gangs to form in the urban environment, is to see them as attempts to give atomistic, disenfranchised individuals a sense of group solidarity and purpose. The need for some fragmented souls to identify with a movement larger than the self can be as seductive on a college campus as it is in an inner city. According to Sandel, whether a person's group fits any one of his three categories depends, to a large extent, on the interests, needs, and expectations of its members. Most students in my classes can readily identify their instrumental, and their sentimental, associations. Few, however, have ever experienced the moral puissance of constitutive communities in their own lives.

When we first begin discussing the role of community in the formation of their moral character, most students think of their instrumental and sentimental communities mainly in lifestyle terms: They see their involvement in groups as being chiefly private, recreational, and consumption-oriented in nature. And, for many, these groups are voluntary, secular, sometimes even ad hoc and transient. They wonder how such groups can ever be morally determinative, or even why they should. The more we talk, however, it soon becomes apparent that for many the lifestyle group is a fragile and shallow substitute for genuine community. I sense students' increasing anxiety and uncertainty each semester about ever achieving more important and enduring relationships than are possible in their lifestyle groups. The therapists and pastoral counselors in class often call our attention to these fears, and many of them talk about encouraging their clients to get involved with more stable, morally grounded, groups.

As we continue to talk, it is clear that many students have sought to join "churches" (albeit nondogmatic ones), support groups, recovery groups, or political action groups in order to "reconnect" with others. Their reasons for doing so are palpably moral. It becomes more and more apparent to me that it is the moral content of community that fulfills their needs for standards of right and wrong and for a common commitment to the good. In spite of a religious community's inherent authoritarianisms, for example, such a community does have one advantage: It is able to provide common understandings so that a rough moral consensus is possible. Not everything ethical is up in the air all the time. Traditional needs to relate in certain ways—familial, religious, civic, ethnic, racial—persist stubbornly in a pluralistic and mobile United States, I suspect, because they provide an answer to the search for common moral understandings. And, as we continue our discussion of community in class, it is evident that at least, at some level, several students agree with me.

Jonathan is one of those students, and he finds his reflections on community to be helpful in understanding some of the ambivalence he is feeling about his dilemma. The strong pressures he feels to be faithful to both Sam *and* his school have their origins, he thinks, in the constitutive community of his childhood. Jonathan realizes how pivotal his Greek heritage has been in defining who he is. Jonathan was raised by a first-generation Greek father and a second-generation Greek mother to be proud of his Greek-American background. Jonathan also belongs to a number of instrumental and sentimental communities, and their moral messages regarding this case can be confusing. Sometimes they validate, and sometimes they contravene, the moral lessons of his youth.

He has heard since early childhood, from his parents, relatives, and friends, how important it is for a Greek to be a good worker. A Greek not only "works" for an organization; he "becomes that organization," as a way of showing respect both for the people who hired him and for the people he serves. While he was growing up, many of the influential adults in Jonathan's particular ethnic community were workaholics who were "married" to the job. He recalls as a boy hearing his grandfather giving advice to his father. To this day, the words remain with him: "Ted, all you've got in life are your family, your church, your friends, and your job. But without your job, you could lose everything else. This is why we came to this country. Be thankful. Nothing else matters. The job is right up there with the family, and both should always come first. Forget your own selfish interests." He realizes that his family's high estimation of a person's work is a major factor in his intense discomfort regarding Sam's irresponsibility at school.

The particular quandary for Jonathan, though, is that the work messages he received from his community sometimes conflicted with the compassion messages he received from the same community. A friend is ipso facto considered to be a member of a Greek family. Sam has been Jonathan's friend for more than 20 years. Many times he invited Sam to dinner at his parents' house. On several occasions, his relatives commented on how much they liked Sam. Jonathan suspects that if his mother were alive today, she would probably give him this advice regarding Sam's troubles: "Jonathan, be understanding. Have Sam over for a meal so we can talk with him. The poor man is obviously devastated that his family is falling apart. Let's get him to talk to the priest. If he needs money, we'll lend him some. We're like his family, so we have to be there for him. And reassure him that good Greeks keep family secrets secret." Jonathan knows that the priest at the Greek Orthodox cathedral would echo his mother's words exactly. In fact, compassion and love were frequently key words in Father Stavrotokos's Sunday sermons.

Jonathan realizes that Sam has been an integral part of his adult community life. Both of them belong to many of the same lifestyle groups: a book discussion club, a poker group, a baseball-card collectors' association, a wine-tasters' party, and an exotic-meal-of-the-month circle. They have also been very active and faithful members of their college alumni association, a sentimental association if ever there was one. Curiously, though, Sam seems never to be as involved with his colleagues at the high school as Jonathan. Sam always manages to avoid out-of-school contacts with other teachers and students, because he wants "to protect his privacy."

In contrast, for Jonathan, the school represents a kind of "second family," a "home away from home." He has made many lasting friendships there, and he often socializes with his colleagues outside of the workplace. He feels strong obligations to his principal, a woman he respects and likes. She has been both a mentor and confidant to him. He is very close to his department head, a former graduate school classmate who went through the counseling program with him at the local college. His friendships with some students who have long since graduated are a continual source of satisfaction and pleasure. And his activities with certain professional groups at school have resulted in a number of warm and devoted relationships with colleagues.

How can Jonathan even begin to weigh his love for his friend against his love for his school? And how can he harmonize what seem to be the opposing moral messages he has received from those who matter most to him in his constitutive community? He wants to be compassionate, but he also wants to be responsible. He wants to help Sam, particularly with his drug problem, but he also wants to prevent harm to his colleagues and students at the high school. He understands the trauma Sam must be experiencing over the dissolution of his marriage, but he also knows how easily an irresponsible teacher can tear apart the fabric of a school community. He wants to keep his friend's confidence, but he also wants to keep faith with all of those people at school who trust and respect him, and who look to him for some answers regarding Sam's mysteriously destructive behavior.

Story. "A story is a narrative account that binds events and agents together in an intelligible pattern" (Hauerwas, 1977, p. 76). I hold that personal stories are indispensable if moral agents are truly to know themselves. Those elements that make up the story of a person's life—birthplace, parents, ideals, communities, friendships, education, vocation, religion—create a powerful sense of identity for moral actors. They focus a moral understanding of the self over time in a way that is both dramatic and penetrating. Just as a religious story can be invoked to give answers to the anomalies of human existence, and a profession's dominant story can give meaning to a person's work, so, too, personal stories can be retrieved to help individuals understand what their moral commitments are about. In this way, personal stories answer moral questions. Thus I maintain that at least part of the "truth" of an ethical decision is that it be consistent with a person's ongoing moral story and that it add further depth and richness to the moral story that the person is living. I believe a person's story is a moral necessity because it provides the ethical skills to form a life truthfully, committedly, and courageously.

Ethical decisions like Jonathan's are always made from within a personal narrative that all moral agents inherit. When I restricted ethical decision-making to rational deliberation and analysis only during the early years, I was sending out the false message that students' stories were irrelevant to ethical problem-solving. Today I teach that it is the personal story that provides the context necessary to pose the terms of an ethical decision—and even to determine whether a decision should be made at all. For someone like Jonathan to understand that he has inherited (and is in the continuing process of re-creating) a moral story underscores how his moral intentions and motives originate in, and are formed by, significant people, ideals, and events in his life. His personal moral story links the disparate elements of his life into an integral and coherent narrative. Thus the question I want him to ask in Second Moral Language is not "Is this the right thing to do?" but "Which decision will best fit the story I am attempting to live by way of my highest ideals?"

It is important to note here, before we look at Jonathan's particular story, that our personal stories include our ideals, and our stories can help us to decide whether our contemplated ethical actions fit the ideals we want to emulate. Frequently, students have a tendency to confuse ideals with principles. Strictly speaking, a moral ideal is not a moral principle. A moral principle is a primary rule of conduct that becomes a general guide to action. Thus a moral principle is a way of *doing* something. I will be discussing moral principles in the next chapter. In contrast, a moral ideal is a way of *being* something (Frankena, 1973). When one has a moral ideal, one wants to be a certain sort of moral person, with certain traits of moral character. One wants to live life in a special way. In the Platonic sense, a moral ideal can be some overarching Good that we try to execute in our everyday lives. Or in the Aristotelian sense, it can provide us with an account of the virtues we need in order to live our lives more ethically. In this last sense, a moral ideal is less a search for an unattainable perfection than it is a realistic goal we can hope to achieve.

How important are moral ideals to the language of moral character? I often say to my students: "Tell me your moral ideals, and I will tell you who you are. Tell me what readings have moved you morally, and why, and I will tell you what 'narratives' have been 'canonical' in shaping the moral premises that have stayed with you throughout your life. Tell me what people, living or dead, have had the greatest influence in shaping your highest moral standards, and I will tell you what kind of a person you wish to become." Most students are eager to explore their moral character by responding to these sorts of requests, because they like to think of their lives as continuing epic adventures complete with powerful, formative characters, watershed events, conquerable obstacles, and heroic aspirations. Students are grateful for the opportunity to tell their moral stories, and the above solicitations frequently open up the narrative floodgates. Their "stories" usually include the following plot elements: the necessity of setting attainable career goals in order to be successful, the hurdles they have overcome, the importance of establishing an overall life-plan, and the mentors who have served as examples and started them on the "right track."

One recurring subtext that emerges in my students' narratives is a teleological (*telos*, G., end or purpose) theme. A narrative structure, by its very nature, endows a person's life with meaning and purpose and therefore is teleological. To think of one's life as a continuing and connected series of defining events and people is to design one's life in such a way as to find order and content there. Thus I have met very few students, no matter how hard-nosed, who weren't, in some sense, teleologists. A teleologist is someone who believes that life is better when it is shaped by certain purposes and directed toward certain ends. I use the term in an active, rather than a passive, sense: One needn't be a theist, a determinist, or a fatalist to be teleological. I believe that a true teleologist is one who is an active agent in designing and implementing a life-course. The sine qua non of contemporary teleology is the principle that an unordered, purposeless life is not worth living; that there is more merit in having a purposeful, ordered life-plan, complete with realizable goals and ideals, than there is in any imaginable alternative.

The reason I always elicit an enthusiastic response in my classes to questions about moral mentors is because moral mentors tend to be exemplary teleologists; they appeal to students because they live lives of high resolve, direction, and agency. This is why moral exemplars like Socrates, Jesus, Abraham Lincoln, Mother Teresa, Eleanor Roosevelt, Dorothy Day, Simone Weil, and Martin Luther King, Jr., for example, have played an important role in generations of moral education. Each is a supererogatory character, because each is a praiseworthy moral hero who has gone far beyond the normal call of duty; each has led a life of exemplary conduct. These people, and others like them, have become our moral mentors over time. Whenever our moral exemplars "slip," however, and give in to the lure of their baser selves, we are crushed. The biographical disclosures that both Martin Luther King, Jr., and John F. Kennedy were adulterers and plagiarists shatter our illusions that these men were moral nonpareils. We struggle to put the flaws in their moral characters into some kind of comprehensible perspective. When we fail to separate their private vices from their public virtues, we become moral cynics. When we succeed, we are able to continue venerating our fallen heroes, albeit far more realistically.

William Damon (1988) has established several criteria to identify "moral exemplars": They are committed to high ideals; they act in accordance with these ideals; they take risks in behalf of these ideals; they are inspiring; and they are humble, dedicated, and responsive to the needs of others. My students take great pleasure in identifying their moral exemplars. Frequently, they name their parents, siblings, mates, and influential teachers. Occasionally, they refer to a character in a favorite novel, a historical figure, a writer or artist, a sports figure, or a religious figure. Only rarely do they mention a colleague, however. What all of these individuals have in common is that they instantiate those standards of moral excellence my students want to exemplify in their own lives.

Jonathan's moral exemplars include his deceased parents, hardworking, compassionate, dedicated family people who always managed to find time to assist those relatives and friends in the community less fortunate than they. He admires the determination of his wife, who was the first person in her family to graduate from college and who subsequently earned four graduate degrees and went on to teach at the local university. Her intelligence and dedication to her work have always inspired him in his own profession. Jonathan has enormous respect for his principal, a visionary professional who is deeply concerned about the professional *and* personal needs of her staff and pupils. He has learned a great deal from her about how to win important political battles without compromising personal integrity in the process. He admires her courage, tenacity, and equanimity under stress, and her willingness to make the unpopular—but right—professional decisions, even when they are certain to alienate influential people in the community. And, ironically, Jonathan also counts Sam as one of his mentors, because through the years, Sam has been one of the most gifted teachers in the school and one of the most generous with his time. Sam seemed always to be there for students, and for Jonathan as well, especially during the early years when Jonathan was frequently overwhelmed by the demands of hundreds of troubled adolescents and needy staff.

Jonathan is a teleologist in the sense that he tries to live a purposeful, ordered existence. What gives his own story integrity, he believes, is that the events of his life fit together in a predictable, sensible pattern. His wife often says: "There are no surprises with Jonathan. What you see is what you get. He is a kind and decent man who rarely deviates from the script. He is the epitome of rock-solid stability." He is proud that his life has a coherence and a wholeness to it, although at times he fears he may be a little dull. One of the reasons he became a counselor is because he appreciated the dominant story of the counseling profession, with its Rogerian elements of caring, concern, and compassion. This was the story of his family, and he deliberately chose a profession whose story matched the normative power of his constitutive community's controlling story. In fact, he has always found himself at odds with his profession when he has been tempted to act in a brusque, bureaucratic way with colleagues, parents, and students, either because of the pressures of time or scheduling or because of conflicting loyalties and obligations.

Jonathan wonders what particular course of action regarding Sam would be most true to the moral story he is attempting to live. Stanley Hauerwas (1981) says that what we require in our professions is not simply a story but a *true* story, one that "enables us to know and face the truth of our existence" (p. 149). The "truth of our existence," according to Hauerwas, is that "we acquire a narrative that gives us the skill to fit what we do and do not do into a coherent account sufficient to claim our life as our own" (p. 151). Jonathan knows that his motives and actions must never be fully separable from the story that has encouraged his moral growth through the years, one that has allowed him to claim his life as his own. He also knows that he is continually writing his story with every action he takes. Would betraying Sam's confidence, for whatever good and defensible reasons, and however obliquely or directly, be in keeping with his own best image of himself? Would keeping Sam's secret be consonant with the story that has given Jonathan's personal and professional life meaning? What will either decision mean to his story in terms of who Jonathan is striving to become as a moral person?

Jonathan actually thinks of his overall life-story as a series of tragicomic events with generally good outcomes. Because his own life has been a complex blending of tragic and comic elements, he has been attracted to fiction, such as Pat Conroy's *The Prince of Tides*, that spans decades and provides a generally happy ending to potentially devastating interpersonal events. He loves the comic strip "The Far Side," with its black humor and keen sense of the absurdity of the human condition. He is drawn to domestic romances and comedies in film and theater that mingle serious and light moods and that feature personal relationships that seem doomed but, through inexplicable reversals of fortune, grace, love, and perseverance, are saved.

Jonathan's own life imitates his choice of fiction in that the crises that have occurred in his life around career choices, the early, tragic deaths of his parents, and the serious illness of one of his two children have always seemed to produce much good following the pain. For this reason, he is an optimist who is usually full of hope regarding life's events. He is also grateful for his droll sense of humor, inherited from his dad, for giving him some perspective on life's more ravaging incidents. He is confident that not only will Sam someday resolve his problems successfully, but that the two of them will be able to share a few laughs and postmortems together over a sumptuous Greek meal.

Virtue. "An ethics without virtue is an illusion," I will sometimes assert at the beginning of a unit on virtue. Few students know how to react to such a declaration, and immediately some will go on the attack. "That sounds pretty old-fashioned. What's virtue got to do with me or my job?" Or "Whose virtues? Yours? Mine? My parents'? The church's?" Or "The last time I heard that word my mother was telling me to protect my virginity, and she referred to it as my 'virtue.'" Or "One person's virtue is another person's vice, so who's to say?" Or "You mean values, don't you?" At that point, I ask students to think of one adjective they might use to describe the quality of the relationships they strive to have with their clients. The steady drumroll of terms fills the classroom: *caring, compassionate, competent, helpful, involved, committed, fair, thoughtful, honest, trusting, sensitive, sincere, understanding.*

Next, I challenge them to make a decision about their particular ethical dilemmas with one ground rule: They must bracket any concern with such dispositions. Few students are able, or willing, to play this foolish game, because they cannot separate their own best images of themselves as moral people from the ethical judgments and decisions they must make as professionals. Finally, I ask what they will do if a conflict arises between their professional obligations to act in certain ways and their personal aspirations to be certain kinds of moral human beings. Almost before we know it, our conversation about virtue has intensified, and its ethical relevance for the professionals in my classroom becomes luminously clear.

One of the reasons students struggle with virtue talk, I believe, is that we moderns frequently ask the sorts of ethical questions that promote a concern with rights, duties, and utility, rather than with the cultivation, or strengthening, of desirable personal habits, qualities, dispositions, and skills. "What is the ethical thing to do in this situation?" is a different kind of question from "What kind of person should I be in this situation?" Kant's (1797/1991) answer to the former question is that one must follow universal laws that constitute one's duty. John Stuart Mill's (1861/1957) answer is that one must maximize utility. Contemporary secular pluralists respond that one must arrive at a decision which is fair, tolerant, and open-ended. And some values clarifiers (Raths et al., 1966), perhaps embarrassed by the word *virtue*, answer that one must strive for sincerity, integrity, and authenticity in ethical decision-making. They see anything more than this as "prescriptive," "judgmental," and inflexible. The classical thinkers, in contrast, thought of ethical behavior as dovetailing with virtue, which for them was any trait or capacity that enabled individuals to discharge their social role selflessly and to move toward the achievement of a natural or supernatural telos.

Virtue came to signify for the Hebrews, Greeks, and Romans the qualities of a full humanity—strength, courage, capacity, and moral excellence. And eventually, for them, virtue meant moral goodness as well—the practice of moral duties, uprightness, and rectitude. For Plato, the four chief virtues were justice, prudence, temperance, and fortitude. For St. Paul, they were faith, hope, and charity. For the Romans, the cardinal virtue was a capacity for public leadership in statecraft and in war. Other virtues associated with the *mores maiorum* (the ancient Roman manners) were reverence, seriousness, equitableness, firmness of purpose, tenacity, steadiness, frugality, and self-restraint. Aristotle taught that virtue was of two kinds, moral and intellectual; moral virtue grew out of habit and was learned informally in the family and neighborhood, while intellectual virtue was developed through systematic instruction in philosophy, literature, history, and other related humanities (Kirk, 1987). What all the ancients had in common was the belief that it was the quality of a person's life that was of ultimate moral significance. There were objectively desirable states of character that every rational being had reason to acquire. And only the virtuous person, the person who possessed these states of character, could be truly happy.

Today, in almost any view, a common theme emerges from these different formulations of virtue: Virtuous persons are those who strive to achieve a balance between noble intention and just action; they aspire to act habitually in a good way because they are committed to being morally decent human beings who pursue excellence in personal, professional, and community life, even when, in Robert Coles's words, "no one else is looking." No profession or community, I contend, could survive for long without individuals who are committed to living their lives in this way. Santayana's words in *Dominations and Powers* still ring true: "Human society owes all its warmth and vitality to the intrinsic virtue in its members," and these virtues "hover silently" over every system of ethics (quoted in Kirk, 1987, p. 3). Notwithstanding the important philosophical problems entailed by a virtue ethic—whether there is a unity or nonunity of the virtues, whether they are teachable, their relationship to First- and Third-Language conceptions of ethics, their functional relevance to professional practice, the lack of a virtue consensus in a secular pluralist society—it appears counterintuitive to suppose that a society or profession could endure only on an ethical foundation of rights and duties, or intuitions and feelings.

Jonathan was raised in a constitutive community that taught him an essential truth: His virtues are rarely independent of the good of his community. As with the ancients, Jonathan understands that there is simply no way of pursuing a good that is not shared by others and that does not advance the welfare of others. Aristotle presents his conception of friendship, for example, as the ideal form of human relationship, and it is always drawn in terms of shared virtues. Jonathan finds it very difficult to conceive of human happiness in any kind of community where the intimate connection between individual autonomy and communal solidarity is sundered. Jonathan, unlike Sam, seeks a unified moral life, one where his central communities—home, church, school, and other associations—are able to agree on fundamental goods and on the virtues necessary to achieve those goods. He wonders how his friend, Sam, with whom he shares so many virtues, has been able to fragment his own pursuit of the good, relegating his professional good to the school and his personal good to the privacy of his interior self. Perhaps this split explains Sam's apparent lack of concern about the harm he is doing to the school community.

For himself, Jonathan knows that to counsel virtuously requires certain fundamental clinical dispositions, including compassion, caring, concern, empathy, meticulous respect for autonomy, understanding, and open-mindedness. But he knows that virtuous clinical practice requires other dispositions as well. He has been greatly impressed with Gilbert C. Meilaender's (1984) definitions of the core "human" virtues, because they strike a responsive chord in his own professional life. For Meilaender, prudence is a "fundamental openness to the truth of things" (p. 26). Love is "always essentially the affirmation that it is good you exist" (p. 30). Courage is "a willingness to accept insecurity" (p. 34). Caritas is the "love of God which makes possible a sharing in God's affirmation of all of his creation. Creatures are made for God" (p. 35). Justice "looks toward the needs and claims of fellow human beings" (p. 20). And hope is the "expectation that something good will happen to us, but only as God's gift." Jonathan realizes that while Meilaender's virtues are necessary to secure a virtuous professional practice, they also exist independently of counseling. In fact, for Jonathan, they are central to the practice of a good life in general.

But Jonathan is troubled, because, in this dilemma with Sam, his professional and personal virtues are at odds in some crucial respects. Concerning his professional virtues, Jonathan knows that he cannot simply be open-minded and nonjudgmental with Sam. Jonathan perceives his professional strength to be his ability to make difficult clinical decisions, and this is a time when hard judgments must be made. His sense of himself as a highly competent professional is at stake. He wants to be compassionate, caring, and empathic, but he has more than one "client" in this case, and he worries that the needs of his school constituency loom larger than Sam's personal exigencies. And while he certainly respects Sam's autonomy, his respect cannot be absolute because so many autonomies are in virtual collision in this case.

Concerning his personal virtues, prudence is an important disposition for him, to be sure, but he finds he is becoming more and more close-minded regarding Sam's professional misconduct. Where, he ponders, is the truth in Sam's blatant disregard for the welfare of the school and community? He sees himself as a loving person, but it is not clear that Sam's continued existence at school is beneficial to others, or even to Sam himself. He thinks of himself as a courageous person, but the insecurity created by Sam's daily crises is beginning to keep him up at night. He knows that he cannot "stonewall" the students, principal, school board, and parents indefinitely. He wants to be a just person, but how can he reconcile the needs and claims of his students and colleagues with Sam's? And, as he agonizes over his choices, he is becoming less hopeful that good things will happen, even though, as noted, he is basically an optimist who often recalls his father's maxim: "Like a painful kidney stone, this, too, shall pass."

4. What do you think are some of your profession's expectations regarding your decision in this case?

Profession and moral character are closely related, I believe. Students are generally surprised when they consult the dictionary definitions of the term *profession*. The *Oxford English Dictionary* (*OED;* 1993) lists as its first meaning: "The declaration or vow made by a person entering a religious order." Other definitions include: "Any solemn declaration or vow." "A vocation, a calling." "The action or an act of declaring, affirming, or avowing an opinion, belief, or custom, as opposed to putting it into practice." A *professional*, according to the *OED*, "professes publicly one's faith in, or allegiance to, a religion, principle, or belief." By extension, then, a professional is someone who is engaged in a profession, who possesses not only advanced knowledge, training, and competent practice, but also a willingness to declare or avow a belief in something. I am continually reminding students that professionals actually express their moral character in every public declaration of belief they make, because if professionals do anything at all, they are always professing, always declaring openly, by their words and actions, what is morally important to them. The religious origins of the term serve to underscore for my students the moral content of all the professions, by reminding each of them that their professional roles are extensions of their moral characters.

But while it is true that a profession is a moral calling, it also "requires advanced knowledge or training in some branch of learning or science" (*OED*, 1993). Thus no profession can ever be without its significant formal and informal educational structures to teach the relevant knowledge and skills. These structures usually include classroom learning, workplace training, exposure to appropriate codes of ethics, the demands of work-related role specifications, and the influence of overt and covert reward systems and workplace norms. Jonathan is a high school counselor who, in some very important respects, has been shaped by his formal and informal educational structures to be a certain kind of professional. Any ethical decision he makes regarding his dilemma with Sam, therefore, will be guided in part by his profession's expectations. In Jonathan's case, these expectations have been formed during a 20-year exposure to some powerful formal and informal educational structures. In some respects, these structures have been apposite to the moral character he has been becoming; in other respects they have been antithetical to it.

Donald Light's *Becoming Psychiatrists: The Professional Transformation of Self* (1980) has been a useful text in pointing out to students the influence of formal and informal training structures on their professional and ethical development. And Karen Lebacqz's *Professional Ethics: Power and Paradox* (1985) is the one text I can count on to demonstrate the political power that the professions in general, and that individual practitioners in particular, wield in the everyday world. I find these texts to be generalizable to a number of helping professions. Students initially find disconcerting the idea that there may be several external professional factors to consider in making ethical decisions and that they may not be able to depend exclusively on the internal dynamics of moral character.

Few are willing to agree with Lebacqz, for example, that there may be critical structural differences between the roles they inhabit in their concrete moral communities and the roles they occupy in their professional practices. Students like to think of themselves as living authentic and continuous lives whereby their professional roles are coextensive with their personal ones. But this is not always the case. Jonathan's relationship to Sam is a dual one—friend and colleague—and each role carries with it different responsibilities and expectations. For Lebacqz, the former role has less to do with overt displays of influence and control than the latter. At first, many students are intimidated by Lebacqz's premise that power is a central and defining characteristic of the professions and that, consequently, the question of the distribution and use of power must become a pivotal consideration in making ethical decisions.

But eventually students come around. They begin to take seriously the impact of various external structures on their professional ethics. Before Jonathan can make a fully informed ethical decision about Sam and the school, for example, he needs to examine both the subtle and obvious pressures exerted by his formal training, his workplace, his professional role, and the profession's reward system. He will have to consult his profession's code of ethics for possible guidance. He will need to explore potential discontinuities between what his profession would have him do in this case and who he is striving to become as a particular kind of moral person. He will have to reflect on how he can more effectively link the counseling profession's central virtues of caring, concern, and compassion to what it is he actually does in the workplace. And he will have to identify and expose any maldistributions of power that might exist in his workplace and that might seriously diminish the autonomy of his various constituencies, including Sam, the principal, his students, and himself.

Formal Training. One of the major purposes of formal professional education is to reproduce a set of structured technical responses in its practitioners—to imbue a fledgling generation with the techniques and knowledge that set professionals apart from clients. Jonathan's technical training as a counselor was rich in theoretical understandings and practical internships. He was taught, both in the classroom and in his practicum experiences, to be a disciplined but responsive therapist, one who could be detached but always present to his clients. Two rules predominated in his graduate program: (1) Know where to draw the line with clients between empathy and sympathy, between objective understanding and subjective overidentification, between clarification and advice-giving, and especially between nonjudgmentalism and judgmentalism; (2) protect client confidentiality at all times. Jonathan worked hard to master these rules throughout his graduate training.

As a result, clients flocked to him at the college counseling center and at the local high school—two sites where he did internships—because of his growing reputation. He was perceived as having the remarkable capacity to drop whatever he was doing and give full attention and support to a needy human being. And he always seemed to do this with a great deal of empathy, supportiveness, and professional self-restraint. He remembers one of his college clients saying to him: "I like your balance. You don't wear a bionic detachment mask, but neither do you get so overinvolved with my issues that you are useless. You know where *you* end and *I* begin. And I know that what I say to you stays with you. I feel I will never be betrayed."

Likewise, his high school clients especially appreciated his refusal to sermonize or to sit in superior judgment of their personal issues. In fact, Jonathan consciously tried to model himself after a very popular prac-titioner at the college counseling center who was so open-minded and un-critical that students considered her the "neatest" adult at the college. Her daily schedule was always jammed. Today, Jonathan is less admiring of this woman's absolute reluctance to make overt moral judgments, because he believes that, when done sensitively, a professional's expression of a moral conviction can be an excellent counseling tool and precisely what some stu-dents may need. On the whole, though, Jonathan is certainly grateful for the fine technical training he received in graduate school, especially in the skills of clarification, diagnosis, empathy-building, and active listening. He wishes, however, that his earlier classroom training had included more con-frontational practice and ethical decision-making skills. He has only lately attempted to correct these gaps in his formal training.

On that day in the mall, Jonathan instinctively listened to Sam with sensitivity and compassion—virtues that were his forte as a graduate stu-dent. Without trying very hard, he was able to listen actively and to be present to Sam. But Jonathan found it nearly impossible, at least at the beginning, to listen to Sam objectively. He had forgotten where *he* ended and Sam began. Jonathan was so consumed with conflicting feelings of alienation and anger, compassion and relief, that, at one point, he remem-bers stifling an almost unbearable urge to tell Sam to "get lost." Graduate school had not prepared him to "counsel" a person who was simultaneously colleague, turncoat, friend, and ad hoc client.

Neither had he learned in any formal classroom how to balance his clinical responsibilities with his ethical obligations. Why, for example, did he find it so difficult to confront Sam morally on his excessive self-absorption and diazepam overdosing, and their harmful consequences to students, colleagues, and the entire school community? And what had he learned at the local college about resolving issues of conflicting loyalties, especially, as in this case, when they required ethical discernment? Finally, although he tends to agree with the thrust of the message in his graduate training that confidentiality is a sacrosanct counseling principle, he never-theless feels ill prepared in Sam's case to know what defensible exceptions would allow for its violation.

Workplace Norms. Renee Fox (1957) has described well the doubts most students feel about their professional education. First, they are overwhelmed by all that they have to learn, and they constantly wonder if they will ever be able to master the necessary knowledge and skills it takes to become an effective professional. Second, they become painfully aware of the "indeterminacy" of their professional knowledge. They do not know which knowledge they have been taught is real or useful or merely conjectural. They come slowly to realize, for example, that law, medicine, counseling, and education are not "true" sciences; for the most part, these disciplines lack irrefutable theories, laws, or, in some cases, even systematic observations to support their practices. And, third, they find themselves increasingly unable to distinguish between their own imperfect mastery of the knowledge they have been taught and imperfections in the knowledge itself.

It is my sense that these epistemological uncertainties get largely resolved when students become practicing professionals and enter the workplace. Then the questions become less epistemological and more mimetic: Whose example should I imitate? Who knows what I should be doing? What does the situation call for? What schools of professional thought and practice are dominant? Which ones should I adopt? Who appears to be doing the right things? Where does my responsibility lie? How can I gain increased professional autonomy and authority? Who is in charge, and to whom must I defer? For what will I get rewarded or punished? What must be changed in the work setting so that my needs, and my clients' needs, can best be met? And how can I make those changes? I believe that professionals learn to look to the workplace norms—those implicit and explicit standards of action that serve to guide, control, or regulate acceptable behavior—in order to allay the philosophical uncertainties in their formal education. In fact, if Eliot Freidson (1973) is correct, the workplace norms are such highly important determinants of professional behavior that they become as structurally important as formal education in the shaping of professionals.

Certainly, the impact of workplace socialization has been well documented, although I for one do not accept the claims of some sociologists that new professionals are absolutely passive vessels when they enter their work structures. Donald Light (1980), for example, speaks of professional socialization as the process by which nonprofessional selves are transformed into professional ones. For Light, becoming a professional is a profoundly metamorphic process, and, at the very least, it entails internalizing a whole new set of values and attitudes. In most cases, says Light, this necessitates a radical transformation of the professional's moral character. It seems to me that Light seriously underestimates the internal complexity of character development, as well as the huge impact that a number of other institutions and communities have on the formation of moral character. While I remain skeptical of such extravagant and oversimplified claims in behalf of the workplace impact on moral character, I do accept Howard Becker's (1970) much more moderate assertion: "Values learned in school persist only when the immediate [workplace] situation makes their use appropriate" (p. 93). I think it is safe to say that the workplace shapes the practice of professionals through the values, skills, rewards, and folkways it transmits, as well as through its structural links with formal training programs, the larger profession, related social institutions, personal communities, and key self-understandings based on story and virtue.

In Jonathan's workplace, there is minimal overlap between some of the key values he learned in graduate school and those he has developed in the high school setting where he works. One of the "values that persists" in the two settings, however, has been the importance of a counselor's establishing personal relationships with teachers and staff as a way to promote their professional development, a critical job responsibility of Jonathan's. The principal and counseling department head have made it clear that Jonathan "must make connections" to teachers, administrators, and support staff. The upshot of this has been that presently Jonathan feels as close to some of them as he does to Sam. But what does he do when one of them inquires about Sam? How should he respond when someone complains about the personal harm Sam has done to one of them? Regardless of his final decision in the case, Jonathan knows he will end up hurting someone. Why is it, he wonders, that nobody at graduate school told him what to do when one person's professional development happens at the expense of another's?

Another norm at the high school that is identical with his graduate training is the need for the counselor to get into the classroom occasionally. Jonathan prides himself as much on spending some time in classes as he does on doing one-on-one counseling and college advising in the office. Consequently, he has come to know first-hand how frustrated teachers and students have become with Sam, because stories about Sam's latest bizarre behavior make the rounds when he visits classes. Not only is he embarrassed when he hears these tales, because his close friendship with Sam is a matter of public record, but against his better judgment he is beginning to show visible signs of irritation in class whenever somebody recounts one of Sam's most recent antics. More than once he has been ready to "kill the messenger." To make matters even worse, Jonathan is becoming so paranoid each time Sam's name comes up that he actually dreads making a classroom appearance.

Moreover, there are few explicit or implicit norms at school to help Jonathan sort through the more troubling *ethical* complexities of his dilemma. In his graduate program, Jonathan learned continually about the importance of professional autonomy for counselors. In the high school, Jonathan actually has very little autonomy; he is always responding to ad hoc student, teacher, and staff crises throughout the day. His time is rarely his own. The unwritten norm at school seems to be that the quest for professional autonomy is selfish and isolating. Jonathan knows, though, that while he may have negligible professional autonomy and prestige, he does have variety, dialogue, and close relationships with people at the school. The price of autonomy in the workplace can be loneliness; the price of communal responsibility and close personal relationships can be a failure to gain critical distance and authority. Jonathan wonders whom he can turn to for dispassionate advice in his case. He seems to be so excessively dependent on the personal and professional support of his colleagues, especially the principal's and his chairman's, that he frequently doubts the worth of his own independent judgment.

Two additional norms in direct collision at school are confidentiality and collegiality. The written and unwritten law at graduate school was: Keep secrets, no matter what. The unwritten law at the high school is: Keep secrets, but remember how important it is to gossip. In graduate school, one was not expected to criticize a colleague publicly. In the high school, it seems that one must criticize someone publicly in order to "belong to the club." Teachers-room gossip is perhaps the most powerful folkway at the high school, and whenever Jonathan tries to withdraw from the latest round of cruel backbiting, something he has always detested, he becomes the object of teasing. One of the English teachers has started calling him "Saint Jonathan" because of his "pious" refusal to be "one of the guys." His words, "Saint Jonathan is too good for us," are stinging. Jonathan understands only too well the overwhelming implicit pressure in his workplace for the norm of collegiality to prevail over the norm of confidentiality. Not only would some of his colleagues relish the idea of learning something scandalous about Sam in a gossip session, but they would probably counsel Jonathan to report Sam to the principal. A few would gratuitously add: "But do it gently. We know you two are friends."

Finally, the official and unofficial reward norms at the school are confusing to Jonathan. At the official level, as a counselor, he tries to maintain a visibly supportive presence at all times for all parties. When necessary, he is called upon to be teacher, administrator, therapist, and advocate. To the extent that he can be available as a helping person to anyone at the school—from janitor to teacher to student—whenever he is needed, then Jonathan receives many tangible compliments from administrators, colleagues, parents, students, and, not least, school board members. Thus what gets Jonathan publicly recognized are those official, role-defined functions he performs so well: Counsel troubled and troublesome students who are self- or teacher-referred; advise college-bound students, and do the endless paperwork required by these students; visit classrooms; counsel beleaguered staff and faculty when necessary; offer a series of extracurricular, counseling-oriented workshops to the community; and be available for meetings, staffings, and policy-setting sessions both before and after school. Everyone knows that Jonathan truly enjoys his work at the official level. Not for him is the rule that "what gets rewarded gets done," because he genuinely derives both extrinsic and intrinsic gratification from his official job responsibilities, and he would continue to do the work even in the absence of public recognition.

But the unwritten reward norms at the school are powerful as well, and, as a counselor, Jonathan finds many of them in conflict with the official reward system. Some of these informal reward norms are: Avoid close liaisons with faculty "renegades." Support administrative policy initiatives no matter how unpopular with teachers and parents. Be loyal to teachers when their interests are opposed to students' and parents' interests. Do not engage in activities that might cause scandal in the community, but "be yourself" and "get a life" outside of work. Keep students' secrets, but when pushed by teachers release information about students that will "make their jobs easier." Keep colleagues' secrets, but when relaxing with them during a break or after school hours do not be so close-mouthed about their peers' private lives as to appear "standoffish" and morally superior. It is the unofficial reward norms that pose special problems for Jonathan's ethical decision-making in this case.

Jonathan senses that the extrinsic rewards would be greater for him if he were to share what he knows about Sam's personal life with his department head and principal. Both would be deeply grateful to find out "what Sam's problem is." Though an excellent teacher, Sam has always been perceived as a kind of school renegade. They would assure Jonathan, of course, that this disclosure would be in everyone's best interests and that they would never reveal the source of the information to Sam. And, certainly, they would see to it that Sam would benefit the most, because, after all, "Our community is a caring community, one that you yourself have done so much to nurture, Jonathan. Why you're practically an administrator here." Jonathan would be seen as an administrative ally, a "friend," who can be trusted to do what is best for the whole community, as someone who put his concern for the school over a questionable promise to keep some very dangerous information confidential. Jonathan knows that as an ally he would be invited to be more directly involved in administrative decision-making, an activity he has always appreciated.

Moreover, Jonathan has felt a bit marginalized in recent months be-

cause of his principled refusal to join the teachers' union, a decision that
upset quite a few of his colleagues at the school. He realizes he needs to
"hang out" with his peers a little more than usual. Jonathan feels that if he
were to drop a few lightly veiled comments about Sam's personal issues in
the teachers room during the day or maybe over drinks at the town's Fireplace Lounge on Friday afternoon after school, he might reestablish his
position as "one of the gang." He could do this, of course, with much solicitude for Sam, and he could carefully monitor the content of his revelations
by simply "whetting their appetites." But this feels deceitful to Jonathan,
and not in keeping with his desire to be a person of integrity and honor,
someone who is a trustworthy and caring professional. At this point, Jonathan is fairly clear that whatever decision he makes regarding Sam will be
based on what he genuinely believes is the right thing to do, not on what is
calculated to get him the most rewards in the workplace.

Role Expectations. A role is a capacity that indicates how professionals ought to act in a structured situation. Thus a role always entails
a normative content. Ethical choices are, in large part, a function of expectations that arise according to the roles that professionals inhabit. For
school counselors such as Jonathan, a commitment to advance the welfare
of students and colleagues is not simply one prima facie duty among others;
it has a central normative position. It is a formidable role expectation. The
promise to keep secrets is another. The obligation to be trustworthy is another. But this expectation of absolute commitment to the emotional well-
being of students and colleagues does not thereby solve all the problems of
ethical decision-making. As a school counselor, Jonathan must know what
is in the best interests of all the people he serves. He must also know how
to balance the claims of his diverse constituencies when these are in conflict. And he needs to understand that because the enhancement of student
autonomy is such a dominant duty for school counselors, other duties—
fairness, nonmaleficence, beneficence—could be overridden or ignored,
thus setting up a number of future dilemmas for the school. Jonathan must
ponder his role responsibilities before making an ethical decision.

At the outset, many younger students reject associations of role with
professional practice. For them, the distinction between *occupying* a role and
playing a role is untenable. Both seem inauthentic. The *OED* (1993) points
out some critical differences, however. On the one hand, role is "the characteristic or expected function of a person or thing, especially in a particular
setting or environment." Thus to occupy a role is to perform in a predictable and expected way. Professionals behave in a way that is consistent with
their status in a particular profession. This predictability is essential if the
professional and the public are to know exactly what work must be done

and if the public is to have any protections from the possible abuses of professional power. Once we know, for example, that Ms. Smith is a university professor, or that Mr. Jones is a physician, we, and they, are able to have certain warranted expectations about their behavior in professional settings. And when they deviate from our expectations, we have grounds to challenge them or, at the very least, to be wary. School counselors, such as Jonathan, exhibit an authorized capacity to perform the work of caring, concern, and compassion. If, however, school counselors practice beyond or beneath their competence and inappropriately try to be psychoanalysts, social workers, politicians, or preachers in their work with clients, then students, and others, are justified in demanding role accountability.

Another concern is that some professionals become so identified with the role that they "become" the role. Their "characteristic function" in a "particular setting" gets generalized to atypical environments, and role confusion occurs. They lose the ability to step back and challenge the abuses of the role. They are unable to discern the ethical obligations incumbent on every professional role. A familiar figure in some school districts is the school counselor who is always "on," whether at parties, ballgames, or shopping at the mall. His behavior gets stereotyped, and he often becomes the target of parody. One of Jonathan's problems is that with Sam he has "become" the role of friend, colleague, and confidant, and this peculiar admixture of roles has turned combustible. Jonathan must sort out the complications attendant to each role and decide "who" he will be in this particular ethical dilemma. He does not want to become a counseling caricature.

On the other hand, role-playing is "the acting out or performance of a particular role, either consciously, as a technique in psychotherapy, or unconsciously, in accordance with the perceived expectations of society as regards a person's behavior in a particular position" (*OED*, 1993). This "acting out" or "performing" as a professional is what some of my younger students renounce as counterfeit. For them, an authentic person *is* the role. No role-playing is necessary. Role-playing professionals are likely to be perceived by younger students as insincere, incompetent, or self-aggrandizing. They are seen as "actors," characters who simply play roles or take parts and who lack "commitment" and "integrity." They are "bad" professionals who use their roles to exempt themselves from responsibility; they no longer take their professional and social obligations seriously. They have broken faith with clients and have pledged primary allegiance to their own narrow interests.

Jonathan is a professional who "occupies" a special role. This role—school counselor—is defined in his job description. Jonathan is viewed by his peers as the consummate counselor. For example, his willingness through the years to be available to anyone in need takes the form of receiving phone calls at home, late at night, even on weekends. His availability to help is of near-mythic proportions in the community. He is the last person in the school someone would accuse of merely "playing" a role. He is fully committed to his position, and he would never consciously do anything to undermine the integrity of his profession.

The difficulty Jonathan faces in his particular role as school counselor, however, is to know where his primary responsibilities lie in his dilemma. According to his job description, his obligation to students at the school appears to precede his obligations to staff and parents. His principal is always saying: "We have a caring community here. The students come first." If this is true, then Jonathan has sufficient reason to break Sam's confidence in order to benefit his students. But Jonathan also has a major responsibility to his friend and colleague for whom he cares greatly. And he has an obligation to his profession as well. In this respect, perhaps the most central role-activated obligation for school counselors is to honor confidentiality. He knows that Sam wants his disclosures to be held in strictest confidence and that keeping secrets is one of the most important duties of counselors. There is a hallowed aura surrounding the norm of confidentiality for Jonathan, and he wants to be very sure that violating the norm is in the best interests of everyone who is involved in Sam's case.

Furthermore, Jonathan is still considering the ethical impact of where the encounter with Sam took place. Was he in his professional role as a counselor during an ad hoc meeting with a disturbed friend in a public coffee shop? Also, because Jonathan made no explicit promise to keep Sam's confidence, is his duty to keep a secret less stringent than if he had? Unfortunately, his job description offers no tangible answers to these questions. Finally, Jonathan wants to be true to himself. Because his professional role is intimately related to moral images of who he wants to be, Jonathan needs to examine who he is becoming as a professional and the extent to which an ultimate decision in this case is consistent with these moral images. It is at this point that Jonathan considers turning to his professional code of ethics for clarification and guidance.

Code of Ethics. Whenever I ask how many students have consulted their profession's code of ethics in the past year, I rarely see more than a few hands in the air. Some look at me incredulously, wondering if I am serious. Snickers and sarcastic asides usually greet my query. An alarming number of my students tends to think of codes of ethics as "window-dressing" statements so vague and idealistic as to be virtually useless. Some students are scathing in their attacks, declaring that codes are "guild-protective," or preoccupied mainly with "remuneration and etiquette," or filled with "pieties and deportment," or "elitist." When the angry outbursts subside, however, the truth surfaces: Few have actually read their codes. I have never had as a student a single public school teacher who has even heard of the National Education Association's code, let alone read it. Educational administrators are likely to have seen their local school district's statement of policy and practices—if there is one—and they construe this as a code of ethics. Few remember anything noteworthy in it, though. Occasionally, a special educator will respond to my question affirmatively, even a bit self-righteously, because her code "safeguards the interests of special-needs students." But she will recall little by way of specifics.

Allied health professionals—especially nurses and physical therapists—are the most likely to know their codes well. But even they are confounded as to how the codes apply to their actual practice. I have found few social workers who regularly consult their codes, however. I have yet to meet a physician in my consultancies who has read the American Medical Association's code from beginning to end. Most have heard of it, but none have ever studied it. Few lawyers I have seen at my workshops have read the Code of Professional Responsibility of the American Bar Association. College personnel professionals are totally unaware of the existence of a professional code, because until recently the National Association of Student Personnel Administrators did not even have one. I remember only one college teacher's ever having read the American Association of University Professors' code. I myself had never even owned a copy until I started teaching applied ethics courses.

What are we to make of this almost universal disparagement of professional codes of ethics? What does the nearly total disregard of professional codes mean? For years, I thought it was something in my delivery that evoked such strong, antagonistic responses. For example, whenever I ask students to bring their codes to class, few know where to locate them, and most get utterly surly when I make such a request. I understand now, however, that they do not want to be bothered with what they consider a trivial, irrelevant assignment, because they simply do not see a correlation between learning how to make ethical decisions and appealing to a code of ethics.

Karen Lebacqz (1985) says many wise things about professional codes, but the most insightful observation she makes is that we tend to view them in the wrong way because we "expect them to do things they cannot" (p. 67). For example, in respect to the medical profession, Beauchamp and Childress (1979) claim that a professional code of ethics should always "specify normative standards for situations likely to arise in the practice of medicine, in health care, and in research" (p. 9). I have come to understand that codes are not meant to be precise ethical action guides, and they should rarely be applied in the way Beauchamp and Childress recommend.

Codified principles and practices can never cover every situation, because circumstances vary and discretionary professional judgment is always necessary. Universal "normative standards" for particular practices are very difficult to apply and to enforce.

Rather, for Lebacqz (1985), a code might best be understood as embodying "statements about the image of the profession and the character of the professional" (p. 68). While codes will typically indicate something about a particular profession's ethical dilemmas, loyalties, tasks, conflicts, role expectations, remuneration issues, and so forth, they are most useful, according to Lebacqz, when read as "guideposts to understand where stresses and tensions have been felt within the profession, and what image of the good professional is held up" (p. 68). Carr-Saunders and Wilson (1933) found in their archetypal study on the professions that most professional codes of ethics include a service orientation, a demand for competence, and a commitment to the virtues of trust, confidentiality, colleagueship, respect for the client, fairness, honesty, fidelity, and goodwill. They are in essential agreement with Lebacqz that professional codes should aim at establishing expectations for moral character. For them, the most effective codes are those that make assertions about the kinds of virtues necessary to be a good professional.

A code of ethics embodies the highest moral ideals of the profession. I believe that if a code does nothing else, it should be concerned, at the very least, with presenting an ideal image of the moral character of both the profession and the professional. In addition to designating a number of prima facie duties—and I would argue that this is still an important function of codes—a code must help us to act with the right attitude. One of the fundamental premises of my Language of Moral Character is that being the right kind of person is basic to doing the right action. As Jonathan peruses the Ethical Standards of the American Association for Counseling and Development (AACD; 1988), he hopes it might shed some light both on what he might do concerning his dilemma and on how he might be true to the highest ideals he holds as a person and as a professional. Whatever decision he makes, he wants to make it with integrity, self-respect, and honor. Surprisingly, Jonathan finds much that is valuable in the Ethical Standards, especially when he reads the code as an ethics of character. He also discovers much that is problematic, particularly when he turns to the code for concrete assistance in decision-making.

Jonathan is struck with the code's painstaking protection of the client in the counseling relationship. The counselor is depicted as a trustee for both the general public and the individual client—as someone entrusted to function as a public defender and client benefactor. The code makes it clear throughout that protection of a client's autonomy is the counselor's highest moral obligation. The major intent of the AACD statement seems to be to encourage counselors to be thoroughly professional, truthful, just, "guardians of individual rights and personal dignity," vigilant about maintaining the "norm of confidentiality," and scrupulous about not practicing beyond trained competence. What is most impressive to Jonathan, however, is the prevailing underlying intention of the code to deal with what might be called the "problematics of professional power." A professional's formal education, workplace norms, reward systems, and role definitions often combine in complex ways to create gross imbalances of power. The code appears to be highly sensitive to the de facto power gap that exists between counselor and client, and consequently it tries to check the abuses of a counselor's authority whenever possible.

Jonathan appreciates that the AACD code is responsive to the need for client protection. He has always felt that the counselor's task is more than simply helping the client. The counselor must also try to check the excesses of professional power by sharing it with clients whenever appropriate. The code expressly forbids any activities that "meet the counselor's personal needs at the expense of the client's"; sexual harassment; "racial and sexual stereotyping and discrimination"; and "any type of sexual intimacies with clients." The major restraint on professional power, Jonathan notes, is the code's rigorous insistence on full informed consent at all times and the demand that a counselor must always "respect the integrity and promote the welfare of the client." He realizes that whatever course of action he takes concerning his ethical dilemma, he must consider protecting Sam's right to privacy. He must also think about securing Sam's full consent.

Lebacqz (1985) argues that perhaps the professional's greatest prerogative is the "power of definition"—the right to define reality. Counselors construct reality for clients by using a specialized psychological language to describe their issues and problems. According to Lebacqz, this authorization to construct reality automatically creates a maldistribution of power whereby some professionals wield virtually unlimited control over clients. Jonathan is less interested in control than he is in cooperation; thus he consciously tries to avoid using overly technical language with his clients. He does not want to increase the power divide between him and them by using arcane counseling jargon. The particular problem he has with Sam, though, is to find the appropriate helping language. Should he be speaking the language of a friend? a colleague? a counselor? or a judge? Moreover, he has been careful not to "psychologize" Sam's moral problems. Sam is both "victim" and "perpetrator," and while he has a right to be treated compassionately, he must also accept moral responsibility for his damaging actions at school.

Jonathan certainly likes the overall image of professionalism drawn in the AACD code, and he hopes to spend the rest of his life becoming a living embodiment of its noble ideals. It is in the code's details, however, that Jonathan discovers some potentially conflicting advice regarding his dilemma with Sam. In Section A, Number 3, the AACD code stipulates that "when information is possessed that raises doubt as to the ethical behavior of professional colleagues, the member must take action to attempt to rectify such a condition." But while the stipulation to blow the whistle on unethical counseling colleagues is clear, nothing is said about taking action against noncounseling colleagues such as Sam. In Section B, Number 2, the code advises that "the counseling relationship and information resulting therefrom must be kept confidential." But in Number 4, the code states that "when the client's condition indicates that there is clear and imminent danger to the client or others, the member must take reasonable personal action or inform responsible authorities." Jonathan believes that Sam has placed both himself and students in "clear and imminent danger." But in what sense can it be said that Sam is a "client"? And the danger to students does not appear to be physical in nature. Does this make a difference?

In Section B, Number 11, the code recommends that "the member may choose to consult with any other professionally competent person about a client. In choosing a consultant, the member must avoid placing the consultant in a conflict of interest." Does this mean that Jonathan can consult with the principal or his department head about Sam, or do these individuals represent conflict of interest to Jonathan's "efforts to help the client"? In Number 13, the code stresses that "When the member has other relationships . . . with an individual seeking counseling services, the member must not serve as counselor but should refer the individual to another professional. Dual relationships with clients that might impair the member's objectivity and professional judgment must be avoided." It is not clear to Jonathan that Sam has "sought [Jonathan for] counseling services," and if Sam has not, then any attempt to refer him to another professional would be futile, although Jonathan has tried.

Finally, in Number 18, the code urges that "Should the member be engaged in a work setting that calls for any variation from the above statements, the member is obligated to consult with other professionals whenever possible to consider justifiable alternatives." But is the coffee shop in the mall a "work setting" *pari ratione*? And if it is, is Jonathan thereby obliged to "consult with other professionals" such as the principal or the department head, or rather with another counselor? Because the specifics of the code are either contradictory or unclear in Jonathan's case, he decides to look instead to the underlying character message of the AACD statement. Whatever decision he comes to, Jonathan is committed to living up to the highest ideals of the counseling profession. Jonathan wants to do the right thing with Sam in a way that maintains Jonathan's sense of himself as both a defender of student and community interests and as a benefactor to his friend and colleague. He wants to respect everyone's individual rights and personal dignity, but at this point he still does not know how to counterbalance the various opposing rights. Finally, Jonathan wants to be a guarantor of confidentiality, but not at the expense of hurting innocent parties.

5.   What is your decision?

In spite of the many anomalies in the ethical dilemma, Jonathan feels that he is ready to make a decision. He has found the Second Language Moral Brief to be very helpful, and, after considerable reflection, *he resolves to keep Sam's disclosures confidential.* He knows that the purpose of Second Language is not necessarily to justify or to defend an ethical decision in public, but rather to help him understand in a very personal way the moral, psychological, professional, and sociological contexts for his ethical decision-making. As a friend, he will resolve to do everything he can to help Sam, now that he knows what is bothering him. He will promise, if possible, to "be there" any time Sam needs to talk, or to relax, or even to play. If Sam agrees, Jonathan will even work behind the scenes at school to repair any damage done to colleagues and students. Jonathan will confront Sam with his moral responsibilities to take better care of himself and his students, to stop the drug overdosing, and to live up to his contractual obligations with the school. He will strongly urge Sam to continue to pursue counseling, and even to consider talking sub rosa to the principal about his problems. He will recommend that Sam take a leave of absence unless and until he begins to work actively on his personal issues. And, if all else fails, during his more spiritual moments, Jonathan will pray for Sam's healing.

Intuitions and Feelings. From the very beginning of the chance encounter, Jonathan's intuition told him to listen to Sam first as a friend. He kept hearing his mother's words that "friendship always comes first" and his father's advice that he should be clear about his "primary loyalties." On that Saturday morning at the mall, at the instant he saw Sam, Jonathan recognized an absentee friend struggling to reestablish a connection. He did not see a profligate colleague who needed to be rehabilitated, educated, or reported to the authorities, but someone who was troubled and lonely. And as he listened to Sam's woes, Jonathan's quick and ready insight was to be a sympathetic sounding board rather than a professional problem-solver. Although, at first, Jonathan experienced feelings of anger and disappointment as he listened to Sam's plight, he eventually felt great relief that finally Sam had come to him with a plausible explanation for his puzzling behavior both in and out of school. Jonathan remembers vividly his feeling of complete solicitude for Sam and his empathy for the overwhelming feeling of betrayal that Sam must have experienced when he first learned of his wife's infidelity and at her subsequent departure from their home. Jonathan trusts his initial intuitions and feelings, and he decides to do what "feels" right. His heart goes out to Sam.

Community, Story, Virtue. Jonathan lives in two major communities, and he bears the defining characteristics of each. As a member of an extended Greek-American family, he is very much a proud ethnic who respects the work ethic, loyalty to intimates and friends, and close personal relationships. As a counselor at the school for 20 years, he is very much a dignified professional who appreciates his responsibilities as a colleague, public figure, and educational leader. Jonathan actually thinks of both communities as "family"—the former a primary one, the latter a secondary one. Sam, his oldest friend, belongs to both groups, but, in this instance, Jonathan is inclined to treat him as a member of his primary family. He knows that if he had met with a relative on that Saturday at the mall, personal disclosures would have remained absolutely confidential. He considers the Greek "code of silence" on family matters to be nearly inviolable. Even if Sam is perceived by many at the school to be something of the "prodigal son," to Jonathan he is still family, and his privacy is to be protected. No good Greek ever implicates a family member in a public scandal. Jonathan has decided that even though the interests of both his "families" are in opposition in his dilemma, he will decide what to do on the basis of his primary loyalty—which is to Sam. Ideally, Jonathan would prefer to keep Sam's sad episode "all in the family." To this end, therefore, he will talk to Sam about ways they might be able to adjudicate the dilemma in-house, without going public.

Jonathan is living a continuous moral story, and he is proud of his efforts to live it truthfully and courageously. He is a person whose moral character has been largely formed by his involvement with other "actors" in his narrative, particularly his parents, wife, the principal, the department chair, and Sam. He is confident that the decision he has made is in keeping with the expectations of those who have been integral to his story. He senses that the principal, for one, would choose to support Sam in the same way, were she to be in a similar situation with a dear, close friend. After all, she is proud of the "caring community" she has built at the high school. She would be both helpful and firm with Sam. Her first instinct would be to show compassion, but she would also remind Sam of his professional obligations to students, colleagues, and the community at large. Jonathan will do this as well. Jonathan does not want to step out of character in his narrative. For him to violate Sam's trust would be to transform himself into a moral stranger in his own story. Such a deviation from character would also go against the dominant story of the counseling profession, with its cardinal virtues of trust, caring, concern, and compassion.

Jonathan thinks of the dilemma as a tragedy not without its ironic, even comic, elements. Where does Sam choose to disclose the tragic events of his life? The encounter takes place in a doughnut shop at the local mall on a Saturday morning. This is where Jonathan deliberately escapes each weekend in order to engage in the most mindless activity of his week— dunking two pistachio doughnuts into a coffee with extra cream and sugar while reading the sports page of the big-city newspaper he looks forward to receiving in the mail each Friday afternoon. On this particular Saturday morning at the mall, Jonathan is suddenly called upon to be intensely mindful of a friend's confession while mindlessly eating two very sweet doughnuts in a totally indifferent environment. The contradiction is precious and typifies the sheer ordinariness of his everyday life. But Jonathan is enough of an optimist to know that every tragedy eventually ends, and most of the time the protagonists even get to appear in another play. He is certain that he and Sam will persevere through this crisis and live to star in other real-life dramas.

Jonathan wants to be sure, however, that he can "write" this latest chapter in his story prudently, lovingly, hopefully, and courageously. This is why he has decided to keep Sam's disclosures confidential. The virtues he cherishes the most are the ones he can fulfill consistently in every sphere of his life, whether in a coffee shop or at the school counseling office. He strives to make his life a unity. To be prudent with Sam is to be "fundamentally open to the truth of things" in Sam's life. To be loving is to affirm to Sam that, in spite of his personal problems, "it is still good that you exist." To be hopeful is to know that "something good will happen" to Sam sooner or later. And to be courageous is to evince a "willingness to accept insecurity," even though Jonathan knows that the school has become a more insecure place since Sam has conflated his personal and his professional life. Jonathan will deal with Sam in the same way he deals with everyone. He will practice the same virtues with Sam. Jonathan will give Sam the benefit of the doubt, show him a "tough love" when appropriate, stick by him because he knows first-hand of Sam's inherent moral decency, and keep his disclosures a secret.

Training, Workplace Norms, Roles, Code of Ethics.

During his graduate school training, Jonathan felt more naturally attracted to the practice of empathy than detachment, even though he learned well how to draw the line between overinvolvement and prudent distance with clients. Unfortunately, this is a line that is clearer with clients than with friends. He realizes that he can never wear a professional's "bionic mask" with Sam, because this is inconsistent with his moral image of himself as someone who ought to be helpfully invested in a dear friend's life. But he has tried never to be a sermonizer or a "policeman" either in his work with clients or in his relationships with friends. Since graduate school, though, what he has learned to do skillfully with clients and friends is to confront them with self-damaging behavior. He believes he has been able to do this with sensitivity and with firmness. He has decided, therefore, to challenge Sam directly about his diazepam overdosing, even threatening, if necessary, to withdraw his support unless Sam gets "clean."

The norm at school most distressing to Jonathan is the one that places collegiality over autonomy. The pressure of the professional peer group is immense for him to align with the angry, injured majority against the "slacker," Sam. Jonathan knows that it will take courage to withstand community coercions to betray his friend in the name of collegiality. Sam is seen by others as someone who has betrayed his own community. His behavior has resulted in anarchy in his classroom, and his impact on the school and surrounding community has also been divisive and chaotic. Jonathan knows that he will receive no special rewards for protecting Sam's privacy or for defending Sam when he is attacked. Ironically, at least in this instance, Jonathan would probably be rewarded for whistle-blowing against a colleague who is considered a troublemaker. Nevertheless, Jonathan is ready to put personal reward and recognition aside. He knows he could not live with himself if he were to betray Sam. Jonathan has always reacted strongly to the biblical story of Judas, who turned his friend over to the Roman soldiers for 30 pieces of silver. He is no Judas. Moreover, Jonathan understands more clearly why he has lately been avoiding the Fireplace Lounge in town. It has become a place where normally decent human beings get a little tipsy after a long workweek and indulge in acts of public defamation. The Lounge is where those school professionals who are perceived as being most independent ("high and mighty") get publicly skewered behind their backs. He decides he will henceforth stay away from the Lounge, and let the chips fall where they may.

Jonathan is not so closely identified with his role that he is continually "on" as a counselor. He also knows how to be a friend, a spouse, a parent, a son, a Christian, and a citizen. With Sam he is foremost a friend, possibly even a "brother." Jonathan will be there in a special way for Sam, just as he is there for members of his family. He will listen lovingly, challenge unwaveringly, and maybe even offer a little advice—as he would with his own brother.

Finally, Jonathan is pleased to observe that his professional code of ethics places client protection at the center of the counseling experience and that the code is highly sensitive to the power differential that exists between professional and client. He finds much support in the code to protect Sam's right to privacy, as well as his right to full consent. While he understands that strictly speaking Sam is not a client, Jonathan reasons that if the code's moral imperatives are true for clients, then they must *mutatis mutandis* be true for friends. It seems reasonable that friends should deserve the same protections as clients. Jonathan will not use his professional role to wield power over his friend. He has no need or wish to control Sam. He only desires to help him, as he himself would want to be helped in the same situation. Moreover, Jonathan's personal code of ethics is identical with his professional code. He is striving to live a life of moral integrity, a life that is complete and undivided. Jonathan resolves, therefore, to do what is right in Sam's behalf—what he believes is in Sam's best interests—in a way consistent with the underlying character message of the code. He will keep his friend's disclosures secret.

CONCLUSION

There is no denying the mounting interest among applied ethicists in what I have been calling the Second Language of Moral Character, but this language is still a long way from being accepted by the majority of applied ethicists today. The dominant ethical lexicon is still the Language of Moral Principle, the content of the next chapter. The particular strength of the Second Language, I hope I have shown, is its "thick" emphasis on what might be called the "first-person singular" in ethical analysis. Despite its many strong points, however, Second Language analysis is vulnerable to serious philosophical criticisms (Pincoffs, 1986; Williams, 1985), a few of which follow.

Because we live in a secular pluralist society where any consensus on what constitutes "good" moral character seems fairly impossible to achieve, critics wonder who is to decide. Do we leave the specification of appropriate moral character to educators? philosophers? politicians? religionists? judges? parents? And how do we avoid ending up with conflicting, and arbitrary, notions of moral character—often the creation of religious special-interest groups—that might further vitiate any hope of reasonable consensus in a pluralist society?

As we shall see in the next chapter, one of the reasons that Third Moral Language continues to be the commanding lexicon in applied ethics today is because it attempts to correct precisely what makes moral character talk so attractive to most of my students: its subjective and concrete qualities. For the critics, these qualities make Second Moral Language seem too location-, time-, and person-bound, and too dependent on intuition and feelings. Thus it is difficult to universalize the Language of Moral Character to the "third-person plural" because of its excessive particularity and privatism. To correct this imbalance, Third Moral Language writers contend that only a process of generalizable, principles-guided, logical deductions appears realistic if we are ever going to secure ethical agreement in our diverse, secular pluralist organizations.

Furthermore, there seems to be at the core of the Language of Moral Character a disinterestedness in issues concerning social rights and responsibilities. At least on the surface, Aristotle's *Nicomachean Ethics* (1976), and his *Politics* (1982) as well, leave questions of rights and obligations completely aside. Even for some of his supporters, Aristotle appears to be mainly interested in a gentlemanly moral code for the Greek aristocrat (J. Barnes, 1982; A. E. Taylor, 1955). Third Language advocates wonder how an emphasis on moral character applies to our current society, with its deep divisions over questions of access, rights, entitlements, liberties, and obligations. The supreme good of an individual's life is not simply to locate oneself in a historical community or to situate oneself in a personal narrative in order to develop one's moral character in subjective ways.

Instead, important as these processes are, individuals need to step outside of their community, and outside of their story, in order to be able to look more discerningly and objectively at the structures of injustice in all of their communities. If a perspective on rights and obligations, based on a set of universalizable and binding moral principles, is systematically omitted from ethical analysis and decision-making, then, say the critics, there can never be any obligatory "oughts" concerning an individual's obligations to others. The duty to reform harmful social structures, including professions and organizations, thus becomes a supererogatory ideal only, morally praiseworthy to be sure, but not morally required. The outcome, as Lebacqz (1985) points out, is that existing maldistributions of power in society, and in the professions, tend to solidify.

While I am certainly sensitive to these Third Language criticisms, I for one do not believe that the Second Language of Moral Character is fatally deficient. I have attempted to show in Jonathan's case that there is still a major place in the moral life for the development of desirable qualities in moral agents and for an appreciation of the communities in which moral agents have been embedded and from which they draw their norms, narratives, and purposes. I believe that Aristotle has given us a fine account of moral character, and especially of the virtues. For him, virtue is a constituent part of happiness (the ultimate end of rational conduct); moreover, there are objectively desirable states of character, and every rational being has good reason to acquire them. These dispositions define the fulfilled rational being. Further, for Aristotle, there is a deep correspondence between the character of the citizen and the order of the polis. Aristotle is less concerned with modern abstractions such as freedom, right, and distribution than he is with the qualities of individual experiences with which they are conjoined and which generate the just political order. On this reading, Aristotle emerges as a genuine political realist, because he understands that, in the end, only just human beings will be able to produce just political orders (Nash, 1988; Neuhaus, 1986). In more specific terms, Jonathan, the high school counselor, will only be able to treat each party in his dilemma fairly to the extent that he himself is a fair person.

It is now time to proceed to the authoritative Language of Moral Principle in the next chapter.

Chapter 5

THIRD LANGUAGE: THE LANGUAGE OF MORAL PRINCIPLE

> What can I know? What ought I to do? What may I hope?
>
> Immanuel Kant, *Critique of Pure Reason*

Today, "principlism"—the word is Clouser and Gert's (1990)—monopolizes the field of applied ethics. Since the 1970s, general moral principles have provided a generation of helping professionals with a useful normative framework for ethical problem-solving (Beauchamp & Childress, 1979). Why has this come to be? I cannot think of a single contemporary moral philosopher who is as eloquent as H. Tristram Engelhardt, Jr. (1986, 1991) in developing a philosophical (and historical) rationale for what I have been calling Third Moral Language. In the section that follows, I will delineate his views in order to provide an adequate context for understanding the power of the language of moral principles in the human service professions today.

THE SECULAR PLURALIST WORLD AND MORAL STRANGERS

Engelhardt contends that the moral life is properly lived within two tiers—a secular dimension that utilizes an abstract and universalizable ethical language, and a particular-community dimension that features a personal language of virtue and vice—and both tiers must be kept rigorously separate in a secular pluralist society. The first tier offers ethical arguments that can be conclusive, because its premises are universal. The second tier is unable to secure by argument any account of the good because its premises are community-specific. Jonathan, the high school counselor in the previous chapter, lives in both tiers. The first tier includes his school and public life, and even though he and his colleagues may pursue a number of important educational goals together, they are not likely to share a common, concrete view of the moral good. This is because he and they are likely to come from a number of different face-to-face communities where some kind of moral solidarity has already been fashioned. Jonathan's second tier includes his family, church, and neighborhood, as well as smaller sentimental communities that claim his attention and fidelity. These moral communities give him concrete instruction and support regarding the meaning of life, love, goodness, right and wrong, evil, and death.

However, according to Engelhardt, even though we belong to a number of concrete moral communities, we must always come together in secular pluralist institutions. Thus we need to find a "moral grammar" that is capable of spanning these numerous, divergent communities if we are to settle our moral dilemmas peaceably. This moral grammar, of necessity, must be abstract, universal, objective, and defensible if ethical arguments are to be secured and acted upon. The Third Moral Language is calculated to achieve this agreement. From Engelhardt's perspective, Jonathan in the last chapter needs to make a *defensible* ethical decision based not only on the moral presuppositions of his various concrete communities, but also within a secular moral fabric that binds disparate individuals together in a common search for ethical solutions. I concur with Engelhardt that a good place to begin building a defensible consensus is with a set of mutually agreed-upon, general moral principles.

While I am not as inclined as Engelhardt to maintain the rigid dichotomy of moral worlds in ethical decision-making (in fact, I am arguing exactly the opposite throughout this text), I have used both his texts in my courses (1986, 1991). And while students find his descriptions of the pluralist world we live in congenial to their own views, almost to a person they are disturbed by the starkness (and "thinness") of his moral perspective. Nevertheless, his major argument is impressive to them, for all of its bleakness. In his earlier volume, Engelhardt (1986) argues that when Martin Luther nailed his 95 theses to the church in Wittenberg in 1517, he marked "the crumbling of the presumed possibility of a uniformity of moral viewpoint" (p. 3). It was this event, according to the author, that precipitated the overturning of the established Christian telos and its monolithic moral framework. And the later Enlightenment philosophy, predicated on the hope that reason and freedom alone could lead to universal agreement on questions of moral good and ethical probity, was unable to fill the void left by the dissolution of the Christian worldview.

What has evolved in the West since the sixteenth century has been a number of secular pluralist societies that feature a diversity of moral viewpoints, with no single one claiming hegemony. For Engelhardt, these secular pluralist societies are mostly "peaceable" in that no government is allowed to impose a particular religious or moral orthodoxy by force, and this includes such political heresies as Marxism. The problem, for Engelhardt, in both of his texts, is to find an ethic that is able to speak with rational authority across the immense diversity of current moral viewpoints. In his own specialization of bioethics, he is particularly concerned with understanding "what is right conduct in the health care professions and in the biomedical sciences, and [how to] justify it to others" (1986, p. 9).

Engelhardt's solution to the problem of moral diversity is to agree, in part, with Immanuel Kant, whom I quoted at the beginning of this chapter. In order to resolve ethical dilemmas, one needs something approximating an objective viewpoint. But in a secular pluralist society, all we can ever "know" regarding objective moral reality is what human beings have empirically experienced about it. This is Kant's answer to his own first question. Engelhardt, like Kant, realizes that any knowledge of reality is conditioned by the perspective of a particular historical period. He agrees with Kant that we can "at least gesture in the direction of truth" even if the "truth" is limited by our finite points of view (1986, p. 22). What we can "do" with such knowledge, in answer to Kant's second question, is to search "for common grounds to bind rational individuals in a peaceable community" (1986, p. 26). This is the nub of Engelhardt's argument.

For Engelhardt, the main way out of moral authoritarianism (a sectarian ethic) or of moral nihilism (a solipsistic ethic)—without endorsing a particular religious, metaphysical, or ideological supposition—is to secure common agreement across the diversity of moral viewpoints in any society or social institution. This can only be done through "mutual peaceable negotiation" rooted in common assent to the principles of respect for all persons and the right of each person to liberty. And the most we can "hope" for, in answer to Kant's third question, is to develop rational arguments to persuade others of the validity of our concrete understanding of the moral life. But even rational argument may not be enough to rescue us from the "brink of [moral] nihilism." Engelhardt is unrelenting in his insistence that rational arguments alone cannot definitively establish the "truth" of any concrete views of morality. Thus all we have left is "mutual agreement" built on a common understanding of moral principles. As soon as we become interested in ethical analysis as an alternative to the solution of moral conflicts through force, Engelhardt believes, we have committed ourselves to the principle of mutual respect. And sometimes the principle of mutual respect leads us to affirm the principles of beneficence (the duty to benefit others) and nonmaleficence (the duty to refrain from harming others).

In his latest text (1991), Engelhardt argues even more forcefully that we need a "rational perspective" to govern across the conflicting moral visions in a secular pluralist society. He restates his contention that a "common moral framework," rooted in the "humanistic" ideals of mutual respect, reason, and goodwill toward others, is a way out of the "moral fragmentation of the post-modern world" (p. xiii). What is especially illuminating in this latest work, I believe, is the author's remarks on "moral strangers." Students appreciate his insights on this topic, and the term is one they remember throughout the semester and long after, because it has many implications for their work in the professions. For Engelhardt, the term *moral strangers* signals the "relationship people have to one another when they are involved in moral controversies and do not share a concrete moral vision that provides the basis for the resolution of the controversies" (p. xiii). Two examples of moral strangers would be conservative Roman Catholics and atheists arguing over proper abortion policies, and protectionist and libertarian feminists disputing the appropriateness of a woman's decision to appear nude in an "adult" magazine.

Engelhardt believes that moral strangers do, in fact, share enough in common today to confront these controversies peaceably—even though individuals on opposite sides of such arguments often face each other as incorrigible antagonists who resort to misguided personal attacks, and even though, occasionally, the solution to these difficult dilemmas depends on whose religious, moral, or political vision has the most power to carry the day, because no definitive moral judgment appears possible one way or the other. For Engelhardt, the key is to find "some neutral framework" for amicable cooperation between moral strangers: This "neutral framework" must affirm the morality of mutual respect and the morality of beneficence as minimal criteria for adjudicating differences peaceably and fruitfully.

What strikes my students as especially trenchant about the term *moral strangers* is its usefulness in clarifying what goes on between professionals and clients. Frequently, the professional (who is authorized and compensated to intrude into certain elements of a person's life) and the client come together as moral strangers—as potentially adversarial moral forces. In a real sense, professionals belong to a moral and intellectual elite, whose advanced skills and understandings create barriers between themselves and the people they serve. If the barriers are to come down, according to Engelhardt, professionals and clients must share a "common view" of the good life concerning what ought to be done, what risks are prudent, and what actions should be avoided. The client will need to know the moral and professional ideals of the professional; so, too, the professional will need to know the client's expectations. For Engelhardt, the "neutral framework" that undergirds this "common view" is *a morality of agreed-upon moral principles.*

THE LANGUAGE OF MORAL PRINCIPLES
AND THEORIES

The Third Moral Language is a language of principles, and it fulfills Engelhardt's expectations that in a secular pluralist society only a "thin" moral language is capable of resolving ethical dilemmas. A thin moral language is basically procedural: It relies not on specific familial, religious, political, or metaphysical accounts of morality, but on abstract, general, and principled accounts, set within Engelhardt's formal constraints of tolerance, mutual respect, and rights of self-determination. Thus a thin-moral-language approach to ethical problem-solving requires professionals and clients to agree to ethical courses of action based on a set of general moral rules and principles. The *Oxford English Dictionary* (1993) defines principle as "a fundamental truth or proposition on which others depend; a general statement or tenet forming the basis of a system of belief; a primary assumption forming the basis of a chain of reasoning. Also, a general law or rule adopted or professed as a guide to action; a fundamental motive or reason for action." It is instructive to note that the Latin root of the word *principle* is *principalis*, first, chief, original. Thus a prince (L., *princeps*) is one who is sovereign, of paramount authority. In Third Language, a moral principle is like a prince: It functions as a kind of general lawgiver, a guide to action, a sovereign authority in ethical decision-making.

At the beginning of our work on Third Language, I sometimes ask students if they think of themselves as principled people and, if so, what it means to be principled. Most identify themselves as principled professionals, and they agree that such people have a set of moral "truths" or "beliefs" or "norms" by which they live and which they are willing to stand on and defend. Students are most likely to identify clergy, parents, and mates as examples of principled human beings, even though they may not always agree with their specific beliefs. Unprincipled people, in the estimation of many students, are without scruples, utterly devoid of moral standards or ideals. They are "sleazy opportunists" like the "inside traders on Wall Street" and the "politicians" and "advertisers" who "sell themselves to the highest bidder" in order to achieve wealth and power. Or, as one student said, "An unprincipled person is like a boat without an anchor; it flows aimlessly about, buffeted here and there by the strongest currents, until it cracks up on a rock somewhere."

Whenever I ask students what their moral principles are, however, they speak in simple maxims, which for them tend to be desirable rules of conduct: Do unto others as you would have them do unto you. Be caring. Be available when people need you. Practice what you preach. Honesty is the best policy. Keep promises. Keep secrets. Respect another person's privacy.

Accept responsibility for your choices. Treat people fairly. Respect life. Respect choice. Avoid making moral judgments. Actually, these maxims, or general moral rules, are the underpinnings for such formal principles as autonomy, veracity, fidelity, nonmaleficence, justice, confidentiality, and promise-keeping, which we explore together in greater depth as we develop the Third Language. As action guides, principles are more formal (abstract and structured) than rules, but they also function something like rules. They signal particular approaches to the solution of ethical problems. They indicate the moral rights and obligations that are at stake in a dilemma. They clarify and justify the solutions to moral quandaries because they provide the standards by which ethical actions and decisions are made. They are indeed the "princes" of the moral life.

Once again, however, because so few students want to give the impression that they are rigid in espousing their moral principles, they often describe their truths as conditional rather than categorical. The only students I have ever had who explicitly present their principles as absolute or unalterable have been some moral objectivists: for example, Christian and Jewish fundamentalists, libertarians, evolutionists, and neo-Marxists. Most other students—the moral constructivists—conceive of principles simply as general hypotheses for moral action, not as dictates or imperatives. Like Engelhardt, they are good secularists in the sense that they would never think of imposing their principles on others by force. But, unlike him, they are unaware that they sometimes camouflage their own absolutes in conditional statements; and they are not always clear about what general rules of conduct should be equally binding on individuals in the secular pluralist world, what should be done when rules conflict with one another, or how these rules can be justified and applied in diverse professional arenas.

Sometimes students will wonder where moral principles come from. Most frequently this is a question about their ontological foundations, and so we get involved in an extensive First Language discussion about the metaphysical origins of moral principles. Some objectivist students argue that moral principles derive from God or from some natural, political, scientific, or economic law. For them, principles are objectively grounded, and they are discovered rather than created. Some constructivists claim that moral principles derive from cultural evolution and that they are functions of individual and collective human behavior appropriate for specific cultures in specific historical periods. They are created, not discovered. At some point, I ask objectivists and constructivists if they think that moral principles need to be anchored in some kind of supernatural or natural foundation in order to keep them from being merely ephemeral.

Objectivists generally maintain that without an objective ground of

some sort for principles, then everything we can say about morality is subjective, and, therefore, principles can be violated with impunity. Ethical
anarchy is the catastrophic result. Constructivists are equally uncomfort-
able with moral caprice, but they believe that moral principles can survive
without a transcendent basis, because they have always been necessary for
peaceable and orderly human interactions. For the constructivists, moral
principles have a powerful sociobiological foundation, and some—such as
equality of treatment and the right to privacy—have evolved only in our
relatively recent past. Despite their differences, however, both objectivists
and constructivists are in agreement that every society needs some moral
standards for determining what counts as acceptable behavior; *a fortiori,*
they also agree that the professions are in dire need of some defining moral
principles in order to delineate the ethical parameters of living and working
together, and providing service to the public.

Whenever I ask students to explain how they think their "principles"
might generally be relevant to actual ethical dilemmas, the deontologists
and utilitarians surface, although most students have never heard of these
technical terms. Deontology (variants are nonconsequentialism, formalism,
and Kantianism) and utilitarianism (variants are consequentialism, propor-
tionalism, and teleology) are ethical theories: well-developed, systematic
bodies or frameworks of rules and principles. These two designations have
become quite common in Third Moral Language since they were first proposed by C. D. Broad (1930), and when used with caution, they neatly clarify the dominant tendencies of most contemporary ethical theories. *Rules*
are general maxims that state simple rights and wrongs. *Principles* are more
general and technical than rules in that they serve as the formal foundation
or source of justification for rules. And *theories* are the most systematic and
general frameworks of all because they serve as the ultimate justification for
rules and principles (Beauchamp & Childress, 1979).

Deontologists (*deon,* G., moral duty) such as Kant (1797/1991), and
Butler (1949) believe that there is no need to ground ethical obligations in
a hedonism, an egoism, a Divine Command theory, or in utilitarianism.
For them, right and wrong are known or perceived apart from any consideration of their consequences. Deontologists appeal to certain rules and
principles as being good in themselves. These principles are valid independently of whether or not they produce benefits or maximize good consequences. Sometimes deontologists take "conscience," or intuition, to be
their ultimate standard of morality. Most deontologists in my classes posit
the principle of autonomy (*autos,* G., self; *nemein,* G., hold sway, rule) as their
summum bonum, the ultimate moral principle. An autonomous person is one
who is self-governing, someone who has the freedom to pursue one's own
moral principles concerning right and wrong. Deontologists maintain that

because principles are good in themselves, we ought to appeal to them whenever we have questions about what might be the morally good decision to make. Identify the relevant moral principle, deontologists will say, apply it to the case, and act accordingly. Our moral principles will specify our duties, and regardless of the consequences, we will have done the right thing, because our rules have an intrinsic worth.

Utilitarians such as Mill (1861/1957) are concerned primarily with the results or purposes of an activity. Utilitarians subscribe to the principle of utility, which stipulates that the rightness of ethical conduct is judged by the extent to which it produces the greatest balance of good over evil for the greatest number of people. Most utilitarians in my classes hold that the principle of beneficence (*beneficentia*, L., doing good) is the highest good. A beneficent person is one who provides benefits to people while minimizing harms. Sometimes beneficent people go further and try to prevent and remove harm as well, although some ethicists consider these efforts to be supererogatory (*supererogare*, L., to perform beyond the call of duty). Utilitarians claim that in deciding what to do in a particular case, we need to look at the consequences of a number of possible actions. Whether people are made happier or more miserable as the result of our choices is the most important consideration for moral agents to take into account.

Third Language ethicists make fine distinctions between act- and rule-deontology and utilitarianism. I will develop these distinctions later when I apply the Third Language framework to the analysis of a specific case. But for now I want to close this section with a brief pedagogical observation about the two designations—deontology and utilitarianism. Even though students react critically throughout the semester to any author's attempt to conflate complex ethical phenomena into pat categories, almost without exception they are always intrigued by these two significations. Students readily identify themselves as either deontologists or utilitarians, and they are not the least bit reluctant to make gross generalizations on the basis of these labels. They actually delight in pigeonholing themselves and others. Some of our most heated and absorbing conversations occur around the work we do with these two theories.

With some notable exceptions in my classes, therapists, counselors, preschool, kindergarten, and elementary school teachers, pastors, law enforcement officials, and nurses see the immediate relevance of the deontological perspective. For them, certain ethical actions are obligatory, independent of their ends, because they are intrinsically right; *mutatis mutandis*, some actions are to be prohibited because they are intrinsically wrong. And, with some significant exceptions, special educators, physicians, high school teachers, school administrators, lawyers, and higher education administrators identify with the utilitarian perspective. While they may disagree sharply over what values best maximize human welfare, they agree that right and wrong can only be determined by examining their short- and long-term purposes and consequences.

Occasionally, someone in class will ask if it is possible to be both deontological *and* utilitarian in ethical decision-making. After I point out that such a position would be self-contradictory, I offer a middle position: "mixed-utilitarianism" or "mixed-deontology" (Frankena, 1973). That is, I propose that someone might have a "dominant" ethical "gene" that is deontological, and a "recessive" ethical "gene" that is utilitarian. Or vice versa. Thus, in one ethical dilemma, someone might develop a defense out of a deontological framework and, in another case, from a utilitarian perspective. Surprisingly, few students are pleased with this conceptual device, which they consider a type of deus ex machina. They usually use words like "escape hatch" or "cop-out" or "fudging" to describe the "mixed" position. They insist that they be either one or the other. It seems that students find strong explanatory and predictive possibilities in the two labels. As one woman revealed in class recently:

> Now I understand why I and my husband have been having particular problems lately in disciplining our teenager. My husband's a utilitarian who tells our son to look at the consequences of his behavior, and I'm a deontologist who constantly reminds our son that some actions are right or wrong regardless of the consequences. My husband's a businessman, and I'm a counselor. No wonder we talk right past each other when we discuss our son's automobile, dating, and homework behaviors.

Why do students give such quick assent to pigeonholing via these two terms? I believe that by the time we get to Third Language in the course, most students are more than ready for simple answers to complex ethical dilemmas. Either–or thinking can be enormously seductive after 10 or 12 weeks of strenuous ethical debate. The two designations must appear as a providential gift to students because they offer a welcome surcease to the interminable, open-ended deliberations of First and Second Languages, with their less than definitive speculations, vocabularies, and resolutions. Sometimes all that is needed for me to check this turn to dualistic thinking, however, is to frame a few critical questions about each of the two positions. Regarding deontology, I ask whether it is truly possible to make an ethical decision without considering at least a few consequences. How, after all, can we adequately explain why some behavior is right or wrong without ultimately referring to the outcomes of a behavior? Moreover, can we really live moral life in the concrete, if we are basing our ethical decisions on some a priori conception of intrinsic right and wrong? Who says that something is good or evil *in se* (in itself)? Deontology, in some respects, appears antithetical to shared decision-making in a secular pluralist society where competing and shifting conceptions of morality are the rule rather than the exception.

And in reference to utilitarianism, I challenge students to consider whether it is realistic to believe that, in making ethical decisions, all that counts are the consequences. Surely intention, background belief, character, motivation, principle, and situation must play a role as well. Moreover, can we ever know all the consequences (or even more than a few) that will occur as the result of some ethical action? How do we allow for unintended moral outcomes? Moreover, utilitarianism actually conceals an "intrinsically good" principle—utility—without which there would be no sound reason to choose actions that maximize good outcomes. Why, after all, must professionals maximize benefits and minimize harms as their first order of moral business, when other principles such as autonomy or confidentiality may be overriding? Why should I maximize good results for others and not for myself, especially when my self-interest may be in conflict with someone else's self-interest? And who is to determine what counts as good and bad outcomes? Utilitarianism, in some senses, seems indifferent to the sheer complexity of ethical problem-solving, especially when the principle of utility is in opposition to any number of other principles.

THE MORAL PRINCIPLE FRAMEWORK FOR ETHICAL DECISION-MAKING

The major purpose of the Moral Principle Framework is to justify, or defend, an ethical decision based on a logical appeal to appropriate rules, principles, and theories. Metaphysical and personal data are to be rigorously bracketed. At this point in the chapter, as in the last, I want to illustrate how Third Moral Language works in an actual ethical dilemma. My Moral Principle Framework has two parts—a Moral Brief and a Justification Schema—which I will develop shortly. As in previous assignments, students must write a Third Language analysis of a particular ethical dilemma. Sometimes they decide to reanalyze their Second Language dilemma from this different perspective; sometimes they construct an entirely new case. The choice is theirs. To show how Third Language problem-solving works, I have created a fictional case below involving a university admissions dilemma, and I have consulted an admissions officer for expert advice on this case. An additional resource for me has been an excellent ethics-driven text, Jean H. Fetter's *Questions and Admissions: Reflections on 100,000 Admissions Decisions at Stanford* (1995).

"TO ADMIT OR NOT TO ADMIT"

I [Regina] am the chief officer of admissions at "Wilson" University, a highly selective private institution in the Northeast. Not only do I have to make admissions decisions consistent with my own individual ethical beliefs, but, as a university administrator working in an organization characterized by a sense of strong collegiality, I have to make my decisions collectively with admissions co-workers. Thus, at times, I find I need to develop a strong ethical defense for my admissions decisions that will stand the test of both peer and public scrutiny.

I have just received a telephone message from the university's development office. Robert Richman, CEO of Richman International Electronics (a Fortune 500 company) and a proud university alumnus, has told the development director, Muriel, that he would be most happy to donate a gift of $10 million to the university's capital fund campaign because he wants his "favorite" nephew to be "as proud of his alma mater when he graduates" as he is. There is just one problem, however, according to the development office: We have yet to accept the nephew. "What's holding up the process?" the development director asks me. I know from first-hand experience that the development director is one of the most powerful administrators at the university, and she usually gets what she wants because of her outstanding reputation as a fund-raiser. Nobody at Wilson crosses Muriel and ever wins a political battle. Moreover, I am fully aware of my own interim status as admissions director. I am a finalist for the permanent position, and I have worked very hard to attain this promotion.

I am deeply concerned because Richman's nephew is, at best, a marginally qualified student, with only a fair high school grade-point average and passable SAT scores. His grades and SAT scores place him in the lower deciles of an average first-year class at Wilson. If the nephew were not related to a rich alumnus, the chances are great that he would be denied admission outright. What is worse, however, is that during his interview he came across as being unmotivated, spoiled, arrogant, and lazy. I fear that when Harold, our university president, asked me this morning to join him for lunch "in order to discuss an important admissions issue," he might have been thinking about Robert Richman and his nephew. I always wonder just how far the university should go to keep a potential donor happy.

I realize that Wilson does indeed have a criterion for admission called "development potential": When all else is equal, Wilson admits 10% of the entering first-year class based on a wealthy family's ability to make a substantial financial contribution to Wilson in the years following a student's graduation. If the truth be told, I have never really been comfortable with this development-potential policy, but I have gone along with it because the university in recent years has been operating with tremendous budget deficits and has been trying to add to its comparatively small endowment. But in the nephew's case, "all else" is most decidedly not equal. I want to make a fair decision, one that benefits all parties, but I also want to make a decision that will not compromise my own, or the university's, integrity. What should I do?

Third Language Moral Brief

I am grateful to a moral theologian, Daniel Maguire (1978, 1984), for the construction of what he called a "moral object," "an act with all of its attendant and meaning-giving circumstances" (1984, p. 66). For Maguire, this "moral object" is a "fact sheet" that lays out all of the essential circumstances of an ethics case. I have been influenced by this concept in developing my Third Language Moral Brief. I am not sure that Maguire would agree with my particular use of his "object" for my Third Language Moral Brief, but I am pleased to credit him, nevertheless, for the general idea. I have included some of his simple, direct questions, along with my own. The questions I include in the Third Language Moral Brief may appear obvious, but too often, in my experience in teaching ethics courses and in doing ethics consultations with a variety of agencies and professionals, the obvious gets ignored or devalued in the rush to discuss the more interesting moral complexities of difficult cases. *The goal of the Third Language Brief is to ask simple, but essential, case-specific questions, as preliminary to constructing a sound defense for taking a particular ethical action.* The Third Language Moral Brief asks the following questions:

1. Why is this case a moral dilemma?
2. What are the choices in conflict?
3. Who are the morally relevant actors?
4. Where does the action take place? Is the "where" morally relevant?
5. When does the action take place? Is the "when" morally relevant?
6. How is the manner or style of action morally relevant?
7. What are some foreseeable consequences of each decision?
8. What are some foreseeable principles involved in each decision?
9. What are some viable alternatives?
10. What does the code of ethics say?
11. What is your decision?

In what follows, as in Jonathan's case in the previous chapter, I will
respond to each of these questions in the third person while providing appropriate pedagogical commentary throughout. If Regina were actually analyzing her case, she would write in the first person as the primary moral
agent.

1.   Why is this case a moral dilemma?

Regina's case contains a number of moral issues. By "moral" I mean
any content that involves rights, responsibilities, prescriptive and proscriptive language, issues of human welfare, concerns about right and wrong,
quality of life, and best interests. And her case is a "dilemma" in the sense
that she can cite strong moral reasons to support quite opposite conclusions. She needs to undertake sustained moral deliberation and justification
in determining which course of action to take. Regina must consider the
following moral questions in thinking about her dilemma: To what extent
should she allow her candidacy for the permanent position of admissions
director to influence her decision? Is a possible conflict-of-interest a morally
relevant factor for her? Would she be willing to stand up to both Muriel,
the chief development officer, and to the president if she genuinely believed
that the nephew was unqualified to be admitted, even if this might mean
losing out on the promotion? How much weight should she give to what
she anticipates will be the president's subtle pressures to admit the nephew?
On what grounds should the president's wishes override the conflicting
claim of her personal conscience, if the two are in opposition? Is it possible
that the president knows what is in the best interests of the university, at
least in this situation?

How much weight should she give to the fact that Robert Richman is
a very wealthy man who could do much good for a university that has been
experiencing major financial difficulties in recent years? Does she have
some sort of moral responsibility to insure the long-term survival of Wilson?
After all, she stands to benefit, along with many others, if Wilson is on a
sound financial footing. If she decides primarily for academic reasons to
deny the nephew admission, she might be setting a dangerous precedent
for future cases, including underrepresented minorities. Just how important
should grades and standardized test scores be in the total admissions profile? She herself has complained about the tendency of Wilson to accept
mainly "book-smart clones," academic overachievers without noticeable
personality differences. Shouldn't nonacademic factors count as much? If
skin color, athletic ability, gender, and geographic location are fair criteria
in some admissions cases, why would it be unfair to include additional fac-

tors as well—such as development potential? Why is the latter any more arbitrary, or less meritorious, than each of the former?

Who is she to decide that the nephew is spoiled and arrogant? Perhaps, when interviewing the nephew, she, or he, was just having a bad day, or maybe she had a prior disposition to look unfavorably on the relative of a wealthy white male. Was she unfairly stereotyping the nephew because of his connections? How can she retain her integrity as a professional if she is straight-jacketed by the demand to accept a less-than-qualified student, simply because he comes from money? If Wilson has a "need-blind" admissions policy, why can't it also have a "wealth-blind" admissions policy as well? And, yet, isn't it true that admissions standards are rarely, if ever, applied as absolute, across-the-board prescriptions for everyone? Shouldn't academic standards be responsive to personal circumstance, unique contribution, and idiosyncratic difference? Shouldn't she consider the good that admission to Wilson might do for the nephew over the long term, as well as the good that admission might do for the university? Doesn't she have many clients in this case, each of whom has justified claims to make regarding rights and welfare? How can she be fair to all parties while making a decision that will properly benefit the institution as well as benefit particular individuals?

2. What are the choices in conflict?

Actually, Regina faces many conflicting sets of choices. Among them are the following:

- To accept the nephew, all things considered.
  To reject the nephew, all things considered.
- To accept the nephew but only provisionally.
  To accept the nephew without provision.
- To convince the uncle that the nephew is academically and emotionally unsuitable for acceptance.
  To convince the uncle that the nephew has promise, and despite his problems, he will be suitable for acceptance.
- To confront the development director once and for all about the unacceptability of her interfering in the admissions process.
  To go along with the development director's active involvement in the admissions process.
- To seek additional supportive data for the nephew's admissions portfolio.
  To let the nephew's portfolio stand on its own without additional data.

- To tell the president she has already made up her mind.
  To refrain from telling the president she has already made up her mind.
- To go public with her misgivings concerning a development-potential criterion for admissions.
  To keep her concerns low-key and in-house.

Regina determines that the most important *ethical* set of conflicting choices is *to accept the nephew, all things considered, or to reject the nephew, all things considered*. These conflicting choices represent her ethical "bottom line." She believes that the other sets of choices are possible courses of action she might take before, during, or even after she has made the "bottom-line" choice, but none of them seem ethically central to her. Some of them, however, could be viable alternatives that might release her from having to make a difficult ethical decision in the first place. She will consider some of these alternatives later in the Moral Brief.

3.   Who are the morally relevant actors?

The primary moral agent is
Regina. She must make the ultimate decision. Even though she makes admissions decisions conjointly with her five colleagues in the office, as interim director she has a great deal of professional discretion. She can persuade, cajole, argue, negate, and override her committee, all within the acceptable boundaries of reasonable, collective decision-making, of course. She is proud of the fact that, even though some decisions have been difficult and emotionally charged, the admissions committee has been unanimous in every admissions decision it has made in the past year.

Secondary moral agents include
The university administrators—president and chief development officer. Their opinions about the case will have an impact on Regina's ultimate decision. Each party has unique interests and responsibilities to protect and discharge. These leaders will also be making a decision about Regina's promotion to permanent director of admissions, as both are members of the search committee. Whether or not they will exert pressure on Regina to make a particular choice remains a moral decision each of them must make.
Robert Richman. Although he has not come right out and said it, he has made his expectation very clear: Accept the nephew and receive the financial contribution, the largest gift ever made by a single donor in Wilson's history.

The nephew. While he is something of an academic underachiever, he has shown some intellectual promise. He enjoys creative writing and has been editor of his high school's literary magazine. He does like the university's creative writing program enough to have applied to Wilson. He could be very happy at the university, if only he could get in. His life is going to be significantly influenced by the admissions decision, because he has not applied to another college. He either goes to Wilson, or he goes into the job market at a time when satisfying and profitable work is scarce.

The admissions staff members. Their universitywide reputations, as well as their personal integrity, are on the line as well in this case. Whatever the outcome, they will be seen as directly colluding in the admissions decision. They will bear full professional responsibility, along with Regina, for any action taken in this case.

The university itself. Its reputation as a highly selective institution is at stake. But its financial future is also at stake. Students and alumni are implicated in the decision, because their lives are directly affected by the intellectual quality of students who are accepted each year at Wilson. Currently, a Wilson degree is considered an asset to graduate schools and corporations all over the world. *U.S. News & World Report* rated it number 3 in its region in the latest issue of college rankings. If, however, too many marginal students are accepted in the future—and the nephew could well be an entering wedge—the worth of the degree will diminish considerably. But unless the university bolsters its endowment fund considerably, its financial future will be very unstable.

4. Where does the action take place? Is the "where" morally relevant?

Sometimes location is morally relevant to a case; sometimes it is not. Regina believes that, in her dilemma, the "where" is morally significant, but perhaps not morally decisive. If she actually makes the decision in the president's dining room over lunch, then she has acted unethically, because admissions decisions should be made in the admissions office in collaboration with professional peers. If she makes the decision in a private telephone conversation with the chief development officer, then she has effectively preempted the give-and-take with her admissions peers that is necessary to make consensual admissions decisions. And, worst of all, if she makes a decision "over drinks" in the alumni lounge with Robert Richman, then she is acknowledging that "back-room" decision-making is ethically appropriate in controversial cases. *Regina resolves to make the final decision with her colleagues in the office in an open and public manner.*

5. When does the action take place? Is the "when" morally relevant?

Often the time when an action takes place evokes morally relevant information in a case. Regina is convinced that timing is essential in this case, if she is to behave ethically. Should she make the decision with her staff *before* she goes to lunch with the president? Or *before* she confers with other interested parties? Or are these prior deliberations perfectly appropriate given the seriousness of the decision? Should she keep the nephew waiting on a decision beyond the official mailing date, in order to collect more information and to engage in additional sub rosa consultations with key players around the university? Or is she obligated to make a punctual decision out of respect to the principle of equal treatment? Does the nephew have a justified right to know as soon as possible whether or not he has been admitted, rather than having to wait beyond the official date for her office to make up its mind? *Regina decides that, whatever the decision, the nephew will be notified of his status in early April, along with every other student in the pool.*

6. How is the manner or style of action morally relevant?

Regina is convinced that *how* she makes the decision is as important as the decision itself. She can do a lot of behind-the-scenes campaigning, or she can be open-and-above-board in her decision-making. She can equivocate and vacillate, or she can be clear-cut and resolute with administrators and colleagues. She can be honest with Robert Richman, or she can be diplomatically duplicitous. She can be evasive with the nephew, or she can be candid. She can accept full responsibility for whatever decision she makes, or she can put all the blame on her staff. She can publicly express her doubts about the development-potential policy, or she can whine about it behind closed doors. *Regina decides to act openly, honestly, and responsibly, whatever her decision, even though the personal costs may be high.*

7. What are some foreseeable consequences of each decision?

If Regina decides to *accept* the nephew, some foreseeable *good* consequences might be: Richman would donate $10 million to the university's capital fund campaign. The university would reach its capital fund goal. The university's endowment would increase significantly, thus making the university more financially solvent in the years ahead and enlarging the diversity pool by providing more financial aid for needy students of color.

Corporations would likely be impressed with Wilson's ability to attract large corporate donors such as Richman International Electronics, and they would increase their donations in turn. Regina would forge closer professional ties between her office and Muriel's development office. Because Muriel would "owe" her something professionally, perhaps in the future the two offices could work more effectively together to benefit students of need. A positive admissions decision in this case certainly would not hurt Regina's candidacy for the permanent position of director of admissions. She could be seen as "flexible" and as a "team player," someone willing to put aside her preconceived ideas in order to benefit the entire university community. For one, the university president would be indebted to her, and his support for her promotion could prove invaluable. The nephew might benefit greatly from the opportunity to develop his intellectual potential, especially in creative writing. The development-potential criterion would remain intact in the admissions process, in spite of the controversy it has stirred up around campus.

If the nephew is accepted, some foreseeable *bad* consequences might be: The Richman donation would be seen as tainted. The temptation would be even greater in the future to compromise admissions standards in order to assure sizable financial support from outsiders. The precedent of allowing outsiders to determine admissions policies is a dangerous one. While the sum of $10 million is substantial, in real-dollar terms it would really make very little short- or long-term difference to the enhancement of the university's endowment fund and any consequent increase in financial aid for underrepresented groups. The Richman gift would actually be earmarked for several projects, the endowment being just one. Corporations might think that Wilson is doing quite well financially, given the Richman gift, and would refrain from making donations in an economically tight market. Muriel might, in the future, make even greater demands to have marginally qualified students admitted if they also demonstrate "development potential." Regina could be seen by her peers as a person who "bends" too easily, as someone who "buckles" under pressure, as someone who is "unprincipled." This might threaten her relationships with powerful, but principled, people around the university, including the president, Muriel, and the vice president for student affairs. Regina's promotion could be endangered if she is seen as a person who makes expedient compromises. The nephew might think that he can get whatever he wants in life without much effort because of his connections. He might "coast" through his studies, grow even more arrogant and lazy, and possibly even flunk out along the way. The development-potential principle would be seen as receiving official university support at a time when campus activists are questioning its "elitist" and "greed-driven" features.

If Regina *rejects* the nephew, some foreseeable *good* consequences might be: Robert Richman could donate $10 million anyway. Muriel and the university president could have a new-found respect for Regina as a person who acts on principle, regardless of the consequences. And Regina would have shown the community that she is able to stand up to the political pressures of three key administrators in order to make what she thinks is the morally right decision. Of no little personal consolation would be the fact that, for once, Muriel would not get what she wants. Regina would have upheld the autonomy of the admissions office and the integrity of the admissions process. And because she would be viewed as a person of unimpeachable integrity, she would be promoted. She would be seen as a salient symbol of the moral ideals Wilson stands for: courage, earnestness, integrity, and honesty. The message would be sent clearly that achievement, motivation, and intellectual and leadership potential are still what Wilson values most in prospective students: Money will not buy an unqualified student an admission to Wilson. Regina would be able to make a decision that does not compromise her professional integrity. She would get her promotion because she demonstrates by her adherence to principle that she deserves to be a member of the university's "leadership team." The nephew could realize that only merit and effort, rather than an avuncular connection, are likely to get him what he wants in life. And Regina would have a pretext for calling an open, university-wide forum on the development-potential issue. Perhaps now she would gain credibility among those faculty who want to abolish the criterion.

If Regina rejects the nephew, some foreseeable *bad* consequences might be: Richman would not make the $10 million donation. In fact, out of bitterness, he could turn other potential corporate donors against making donations to Wilson. And he might lobby actively to subvert Regina's promotion to admissions director. Muriel could become an antagonist who makes life miserable in small and large ways for the admissions office and for Regina as well. Regina might not get the promotion, because she is viewed as an "inflexible prima donna" who would probably undermine the leadership team's decision-making process with her intractability. The president would no longer favor her with key committee memberships or with trips to professional enrichment conferences. He might even begin to challenge her unit's budget requests. The nephew, in a fit of retaliatory anger, could appeal the decision to the highest levels, getting his uncle and his father—a prestigious lawyer—involved in his behalf. The nephew could accuse Regina of negatively prejudging his case on the basis of his relationship to Robert Richman. Those students who are marginally qualified because they do not test well, but who are otherwise qualified in important respects, might turn their backs on Wilson, thereby creating a declining admissions cohort in coming years. Worse, potentially gifted students might never get an opportunity to fulfill their talents at Wilson, because their "paper-profile" is unconventional. Because the Wilson leadership team feels rebuffed, it could undertake a strenuous, campus-wide initiative to convince the Wilson community that a development-potential policy makes excellent sense in a financially strapped institution. Regina would be no match against the well-paid experts who visit the campus to defend the policy. And, sadly, Regina would have to live with the nagging feeling that while she may have won the short-term moral battle, she lost the long-term political war.

8.   What are some foreseeable principles involved in each decision?

If Regina *accepts* the nephew, key moral principles she might appeal to are: fidelity, gratitude, nonmaleficence, and beneficence. *Fidelity* is the duty to be faithful or loyal to others, especially those to whom one is contractually bound. Fidelity is a kind of promise-keeping that, legally, is commonly expressed in terms of contracts, trust, and fiduciary relations. Regina could argue that she has an overriding duty to be faithful to the institution that employs her, and, in the Richman case, fidelity means doing what the university believes is in its long-term best interests. *Gratitude* is the obligation to be thankful for benefits bestowed by a donor. While this duty is more flexible than contractual or promissory duties of fidelity, Regina could make the case that she owes a debt of gratitude to the institution that has given her the greatest "gift" of all: a well-paying, prestigious position. Accepting a marginally qualified student at the institution's behest is actually a minimalist way for Regina to show her gratitude for her donor's (Wilson's) beneficence over the years.

Nonmaleficence is the principle that establishes a duty not to harm, injure, or impose risks without compelling justifications to do so. Regina could claim that rejecting the nephew might put Wilson at great financial risk. Future financial aid for needy students might be jeopardized because of the depleted endowment fund. Also, future building projects could stall, and corporate matching funds could dry up. And Regina could appeal to the principle of beneficence to defend the nephew's acceptance. *Beneficence* is the obligation to maximize benefits and minimize harms. It is active welldoing. What better way to maximize benefits for Wilson, Regina could reason, than to accept the nephew—negatives and all—in order to produce a greater financial good, one that would advantage everyone in the Wilson community. Regina could ground each of these principles in the *theory of utilitarianism:* Each of the principles would insure beneficial outcomes for the university.

If Regina *rejects* the nephew, key principles she might appeal to are:

autonomy, nonmaleficence, beneficence, and justice. *Autonomy* is the principle that respects independence, internal self-rule, and self-determination. Regina could defend her decision to reject the nephew on the grounds that her duty to act in such a way as to respect her own rights and responsibilities as a self-ruling, competent professional is a compelling one in this case. She could also reason that Wilson is an institution whose autonomy she respects. It has a right to be independent of outside coercion to accept poorly qualified students. Regina could argue, in behalf of the principle of *nonmaleficence,* that she must reject the nephew for his own sake, as well as for the institution's. To admit the nephew could conceivably injure his self-esteem if he is unable to perform according to Wilson's high academic standards. A decision to admit could also tarnish Wilson's reputation as an elite academic university.

The decision to reject would be *beneficent* because it would actually produce greater benefits over the short and long term than the decision to admit, in that Wilson's reputation would remain secure and the entering wedge of admitting more and more poorly qualified students on the basis of their family's ability to make sizable financial contributions would be prevented. Regina could also make the case that a decision to reject would benefit both the nephew and the institution over the long term. The nephew might learn that merit and hard work are what actually pay high dividends throughout the life-course; and the institution could benefit because it would be seen as uncompromising on high academic standards. This principled position might attract even better students in the future and result in even larger corporate gifts and government support for research grants. Of no small achievement, perhaps the uncle would learn that he cannot "buy" an admission to a proud university. This could result in new-found respect for his alma mater. *Justice* is the principle that deals with the comparative treatment of individuals and with the fair distribution of benefits, burdens, and scarce resources. Regina could claim that rejecting the nephew is the fair thing to do, because to admit him would possibly be to deny someone else who might be better qualified to come to Wilson. She could argue that the promise of a large financial contribution is not a relevant enough reason to justify admitting an undeserving student. Neither is it fair to deny a space to a student who, on the basis of more relevant academic and nonacademic criteria, may be eminently more qualified to attend Wilson than the nephew.

9. What are some viable alternatives?

Alternative courses of action that Regina might take that could preclude her having to resolve the case as an *ethical* dilemma are: She could offer the

nephew provisional acceptance for the following year on the condition that
he take an extra year of study at a prep school to stengthen his application
portfolio. She could go out of her way to seek additional information regarding the nephew in the hope that some compelling new school achievements
will emerge. She could reinterview the nephew with a more empathic mind-
set, allowing for the possibility that neither of them may have been at their
best in the initial interview. She could talk to Robert Richman privately about
her professional and ethical compunctions in admitting the nephew, taking
her cue for future action from his response. And she could talk to Muriel, either telling her to stay out of the admissions process or asking for her off-the-
record advice as a respected colleague of many years.

   She could also decide not to jump to conclusions regarding the president's motivation in extending an invitation to lunch. She could confess to
the president at lunch her serious misgivings in this case and "feel him out"
regarding the complex professional and ethical ramifications of her dilemma. She could seek additional advice from trusted and respected colleagues around the university, while trying to win sympathetic allies in the
process. She could withdraw from consideration as permanent admissions
director in order to make a decision without the slightest suspicion of
conflict-of-interest. She could call for a campuswide debate on the development-potential policy and wait for the results before making the decision
regarding the nephew. She could reexamine her beliefs about professional
integrity, equal treatment, and meritocratic admissions standards in order
to determine whether, in fact, her ethical principles could justifiably be set
aside in this case. Regina decides that, while some of these viable alternatives are constructive, they serve mainly to delay the inevitable: *She must face
the issue as an ethical dilemma and make a well-informed, ethically and professionally
defensible decision this semester either to admit or to reject the nephew.*

10. What does the code of ethics say?

   Regina consults the National Association of College Admission Counselors' *Statement of Principles of Good Practice* (1989). She determines that if she
follows the code's principles, she must do the following: Keep the nephew's
personal data strictly confidential and within the jurisdiction of the admissions office (Part II. A. 2). Notify the nephew as soon as possible if he is
inadmissible (Part II. A. 5). She must be mindful of her obligations to the
entire university community (Part II. A. 13). She must use the nephew's
test scores and related quantitative data "discretely" and for purposes that
are "appropriate and validated" (Part III. A. 1). She must "refrain from
using minimum test scores as the sole criterion for admission" (Part III. A.
3). She must use test scores in conjunction with other relevant data and

encourage the use of all pertinent information in making her decision (Part III. A. 4, 5). She must maintain the confidentiality of the nephew's test scores (Part III. A. 10). Finally, she must specify in a published "subgroup population" profile where the nephew belongs due to his "unique character or special circumstances" in being admitted, if he is admitted (Part III. A. 12). *While the code does not give Regina specific substantive advice as to whether she should admit or reject the nephew, she does resolve to follow the procedural recommendations to the letter, even though some of the procedural strictures are in apparent conflict.*

11. What is your decision?

At this point in her decision-making process, *Regina is leaning toward rejecting the nephew.* The Moral Brief has been a preliminary examination of the relevant ethical data in the case, and it has been a valuable exercise. But Regina has one additional step to take before she can make a final decision in her case. Although she finds some of the viable alternatives in the Moral Brief helpful—she will probably even act on a few—she does not believe she can forestall a decision beyond the April 5 deadline. She realizes that she is more of a deontologist than she might have thought before constructing the Moral Brief, as she finds the possible good and bad consequences of her eventual decision to be less compelling than the consideration of such principles as autonomy, nonmaleficence, and justice for their own sake. But Regina also knows that because there are many moral agents whose lives will be affected for good or bad in her case, she must take into serious consideration at least some of the possible key consequences of her ultimate decision. Perhaps she is a mixed-rule-deontologist.

Before making her final decision, however, Regina will undertake one final check: She will subject both choices—to accept or to reject the nephew—to a bit more rigorous analysis. She will run the two choices through the Third Language Justification Schema, taking great pains to be as even-handed as possible not to load her defense in favor of either decision. She will wait until she has made a defensible case for each choice before making a final decision. And she will consult her Moral Brief for relevant data whenever appropriate in the analysis that follows.

Third Language Justification Schema

My Justification Schema follows the Moral Brief and is a variation on the one devised by Beauchamp and Childress (1979), although I have taken considerable liberty with their structure. *The goal of the Third Language Justification Schema is to prepare a step-by-step, principled defense of a particular ethical deci-*

sion. The Third Language Justification Schema asks the following questions:

1. What is your decision A? What is your decision B? (A and B are neutral designations, for the sake of analysis only, and not a rank ordering.)
2. What *rules* do you appeal to in order to justify (support, give reasons for) each of the decisions?
3. What *principles* do you appeal to in order to justify each of the decisions?
4. What theories do you appeal to in order to justify each of the decisions?
5. What conclusions do you reach regarding your final decision after you compare both justifications?
6. What afterthoughts do you have now that you have made your final decision?

In what follows, I will respond to each question as Regina might, and I will add appropriate pedgagogical commentary. I will go through questions 1 through 4 for decision A, and then for decision B, before considering them together for questions 5 and 6.

1. What is your decision A?

Regina decides to accept the nephew.

2. What *rules* do you appeal to in order to justify decision A?

Students seem to enjoy talking about their moral rules in class. I ask them to recall the earliest moral maxims they can remember hearing in their families, schools, or peer groups. We have great fun reminiscing about who said what, when and why, and what unspoken moral agendas might have been operating for the speaker. I have given some examples of these maxims earlier in the chapter. In Regina's case, she can remember the following rules that she learned at home—primarily from her parents—that might be morally relevant to the decision to admit the nephew: "Give the underdog a chance." "Accentuate the positive. Look for what a person can do well." "Don't fight a battle you know you are going to lose. Over the long run, this is suicidal and helps nobody, not even your enemy." "In order to get what you want, you must make compromises. But know where to draw the line." "You get only one shot at success. Don't blow it when it comes." "You can't always tell the worth of a person by his credentials. Look at his moral character as well." "Never look a gift horse in the mouth." "The love of money may be the root of all evil, but money wisely

spent can be the root of much good." "Treat people fairly. Don't play favor-
ites." "Do unto others as you would have them do unto you." "Sometimes
a bad decision can become a good decision over time."

The general thrust of these rules appears to favor admitting the
nephew on the grounds that he may be an underdog who needs this chance
to prosper. Moreover, the rules seem to carry the message that Regina
would be impolitic in resisting the requests of a powerful, wealthy alumnus
and the university's administrative superstructure, which will make the
eventual decisions about her career. Certainly, if she were in the nephew's
place, she would want to be given a chance, wouldn't she? But the nagging
question for Regina still remains: Where exactly should she draw the line
in order to avoid fatally compromising her personal integrity? Her rules do
not appear to offer unequivocal support for the decision to admit the
nephew.

3. What *principles* do you appeal to in order to justify decision A?

Regina can appeal to the principle of *fidelity* to defend her acceptance
of the nephew. Paul Ramsey (1970) believed that fidelity is the most fundamental of the moral principles, because it is the one from which all of the
others are derived. For him, fidelity is like promise-keeping; when someone
agrees to work with an organization or a client, an implicit promise is made
to be faithful. A fiduciary trust is established. From that point on, fidelity
(or faithfulness) to the institution and to the individual becomes a moral
obligation. For Ramsey, this duty is "covenantal," because it emphasizes
mutual belongingness, loyalty, and enduring responsibility. Regina could argue that her primary moral duty in this case is to remain faithful to the
university. After all, Wilson hired her as an admissions officer with the expectation that she would live up to the contractual obligations of the position; and these obligations include keeping promises to her employer to be
loyal and trusting the institution to know what is in its own best financial
interests. It is entirely possible that Robert Richman's contribution is in Wilson's best financial interests. Shouldn't she, therefore, give the leadership at
Wilson the benefit of the doubt and trust them to make prudent judgments
regarding the utility of a development-potential policy in admissions?

Regina could also appeal to the principle of *gratitude* to defend her acceptance of the nephew (Ross, 1930). Duties of gratitude usually take two
active forms: grateful conduct by the beneficiary toward the donor, and
grateful use of the benefits received from the donor (Tournier, 1963). And
even though no donor has an inherent moral right to demand particular
acts of gratitude, the beneficiary is still morally required to fulfill "gift-

based" obligations in some way. Regina could reason that she has been the beneficiary of an extraordinary gift—a prestigious, lucrative, and powerful administrative position in an elite American university. Because this gift is continually identified with the donor—Wilson—Regina's "use" of the gift is thereby qualified and limited. Thus she has at least a minimal moral obligation to listen seriously to the arguments made by the university in behalf of the nephew's admission. Regina, in principle, cannot use the gift to make decisions completely independent or disdainful of the donor's wishes, no matter how morally compelling her reasons. It may be that accepting the Richman nephew is a well-intentioned way for Regina to express her thanks to Wilson University for the gift it has bestowed on her.

Regina could also appeal to the principle of *nonmaleficence,* which, in many ethical theories, is considered to be stronger, *ceteris paribus,* than duties of autonomy, beneficence, and justice (Hart, 1963). That is, our obligation not to harm others is seen as more morally stringent than our duty to respect others' rights to self-determination, or our duty to take active steps to benefit others, or our duty to insure that all individuals receive equal treatment and a fair share of benefits and burdens. As important as these other principles are to the ethical life, we are, at the very least, morally required not to injure others (Rawls, 1971; Ross, 1930). This obligation is contained in the Hippocratic (ca. 460 B.C.–ca. 377 B.C.) prescription in the *Epidemics* (*Primum non nocere,* L., First, do no harm). Nonmaleficence is a duty of forebearance, often formulated as a series of prohibitions: Do not harm. Do not deprive another of opportunity. Do not treat someone unjustly. Do not bear false witness. Do not put anyone at unnecessary risk. Regina's decision to admit the nephew could prevent several kinds of serious injury: She might be able to forestall the university's possible, catastrophic financial collapse. She might avert a potential lawsuit by the nephew. She could keep the uncle from experiencing feelings of anger, bitterness, frustration, betrayal, and possibly retaliation, all of which would be damaging to Wilson. She could effectively counter in-house political opposition to her promotion. She might thwart a downward turn in corporate giving. She might be able to stave off the threat of the university's having to borrow from the endowment fund in order to pay its bills. And she might be able to arrest a pattern of decreasing financial aid, especially to minorities.

Finally, Regina could appeal to the principle of *beneficence* to justify accepting the nephew. Beneficence is the duty to confer benefits and prevent harms; it is also the duty to balance possible goods against possible harms. Thus beneficence entails the provision of benefits as well as a balancing of benefits and harms (Beauchamp & Childress, 1979). According to at least one contemporary ethicist, Paul Kurtz (1988), the principle of beneficence is "deserving of the highest praise." It derives from the "positive desire to help others, to improve their lives, to confer benefits, to reduce misery, to spread happiness . . . to alleviate pain, suffering, and deprivation, and to increase the sum of the goods a person can attain" (p. 90). While it is difficult to know precisely which beneficent actions are morally obligatory or merely supererogatory, ethicists are generally in agreement that, under certain conditions, beneficence is an obligation for all, at least in some minimal respects (Frankena, 1973; Ross, 1930).

Regina could argue, in behalf of beneficence, that accepting the nephew would produce many goods and would also bring about the greatest balance of benefits over harms. Her action would produce greatly improved financial benefits for Wilson, not the least being the uncle's $10 million gift. The capital fund's goal would be reached. The endowment would be substantially increased, signaling to other corporate donors that Wilson is alive and well economically. Financial aid would become more substantial, because interest on the endowment would grow and a percentage of it could then be earmarked for grants-in-aid, especially for needy minorities. Wilson might be able to fulfill its dream of becoming a mecca of cultural diversity in the university world. Regina's action could result in improved teamwork between her office, the development office, and financial aid, because internecine rivalries between the offices might possibly cease or at least become less intense. Her promotion could be assured, and she would be able to continue with fresh leadership initiatives to diversify the campus, while maintaining the high academic quality of the institution. The nephew could benefit from the decision, because he would be able to major in creative writing, maybe find himself intellectually, and go on to become a responsible adult. And, finally, Regina's decision would mean that the development-potential criterion would undoubtedly survive, in spite of militant efforts on campus to abolish it.

4. What theory do you appeal to in order to justify decision A?

Regina could appeal to a *rule-utilitarian* theory to justify her decision to admit the nephew. As a utilitarian, she could ground her rules and principles in the belief that an admissions decision is right only when it produces good consequences for everyone who is involved: the student, the university, the student body, the alumni, the faculty and administration, the admissions office, and herself. And as a rule-utilitarian, she would consider the good and bad consequences in general, rather than in particular, of her decision to admit the nephew. Moreover, she would probably refer to one or more moral rules in order to justify her decision, which she would then attempt to generalize to other similar situations. If Regina were to appeal to an act-utilitarian theory, she would consider the good and bad consequences that are likely to arise from this particular admissions decision in this particular circumstance. The act-utilitarian skips the level of rules and defends decisions by appealing directly to the principle of utility: Maximize good outcomes. As a rule-utilitarian, however, Regina would appeal to rules and principles of ethical conduct that themselves determine which decisions are right and wrong, and which she would then generalize to similar situations in which ethical judgments must be made.

If Regina admits the nephew, it will be on rule-utilitarian grounds. The general rule that an admissions director should make decisions that will advantage the greatest number of constituencies, while disadvantaging the fewest, has always been a stabilizing and indispensable guide for her. So, too, the principles of fidelity, gratitude, nonmaleficence, and beneficence have been vital moral lodestars in her work, which she simply cannot disregard. She would appeal to these principles again and again when facing a similar kind of admissions dilemma, just as she would appeal to the same kinds of informal and formal rules. Regina is interested in ethical precedents and generalizability in her decision-making, because she strives for consistency across specific situations. And she is determined to make a decision in this case by appealing to those rules and principles that will have the greatest utility. If Regina decides to admit the nephew, it will be because it makes sound economic sense *and* because it makes generalizable moral sense as well.

1. What is your decision B?

Regina decides to reject the nephew.

2. What *rules* do you appeal to in order to justify decision B?

Regina could appeal to the following rules to defend rejecting the nephew, rules she often heard from a revered mentor when she was in college. The mentor, a director of admissions, and the main reason why Regina chose her current profession, hired Regina to work for her office on a part-time basis when she was an undergraduate. The mentor used to say at various times: "Follow your conscience." "Stand up for what you believe, even when it is unpopular." "Once you have an opinion, you are automatically a minority of one. If you don't like being a minority, don't have an opinion." "All you've really got is your personal integrity. When you compromise it, you're left with nothing." "It's not who you know that will get you into the Big University in the sky; it's what you've done with your life that will get you admitted." "Be loyal to yourself, and everything else will follow." "Keep grades in perspective in the admissions process. They are important, but only one measure in the larger scheme of things. Who ever asks successful people what grades they got in high school?" "It's true that money talks; but it's up to you to turn down the volume." "When in doubt, check it out. Every applicant is deserving of a second look." "Speak truth to power."

The general intent of these sometimes contradictory maxims appears to support the rejection of the nephew. Regina remembers vividly the importance to her mentor of personal integrity, commitment to principle, and acting courageously as an individualist. But she is still troubled. Her mentor rarely spoke of how an admissions decision might benefit or harm key players outside the admissions office. Certainly Regina does not want to compromise her own personal integrity, but she must also weigh the integrity of the applicants, alumni, families, colleagues, and the welfare of the entire university as well. Nevertheless, the mentor's moral rules provide strong deontological reasons for rejecting the nephew.

3. What *principles* do you appeal to in order to justify decision B?

If Regina decides to reject the nephew, she might appeal to the principle of *autonomy*, the ne plus ultra of deontological theory. As a moral principle, autonomy has a long history, as it was first used to denote self-rule in Greek city-states. In later centuries, the Church taught that autonomy is severely impaired, because human beings are finite and sinful creatures who are incapable of full self-determination without God's special grace. Yet individuals are also created in God's image, and this confers a special, albeit limited, autonomy on them. This autonomy is meant to constrain earthly rulers from committing harmful actions toward individuals and to allow them to exercise free will in working out their eternal salvation. Kant (1797/1991) maintained that autonomous beings respond not only to their appetites and desires but also to self-imposed moral commands in the form of universal laws. And these universal moral laws are internal. Kant taught that free choice requires independence from "heteronomous" structures such as the Church; hence autonomy is independently living by one's own laws.

Today, the term tends to combine political, moral, and psychological meanings. John Rawls (1993) speaks of "rational" political autonomy as a person's having the moral power to "form, revise, and pursue" a particular conception of the good and to take full moral responsibility for entering into an agreement with others in accordance with this good. Beauchamp and Childress (1979) contend that autonomy actually represents a "family of ideas," including rights of individual liberty, freedom of choice, being one's own person, shaping one's own morality, and accepting ultimate responsibility for one's moral views (p. 59). And Kurtz (1988) argues that an autonomous person is one who is able to control one's own private life through "choice and decision" and that this involves "courage, audacity, and verve." We must not "seek to flee to a mythological deity for help" (p. 112).

Interestingly, Scruton (1982) is one of the few contemporary political philosophers to talk about *institutional* autonomy in a moral context. He maintains that an institution is autonomous when it has the capacity to make its own statutes and bylaws, when it is outside the control of some higher political body, and when it has its own special aims and purposes that no other institution could have. Universities would seem to possess at least some degree of autonomy in each of Scruton's senses. Regina could defend her decision to reject the nephew on the grounds that Wilson University possesses an autonomy every bit as significant as the uncle's and nephew's autonomies. She could argue that a university such as Wilson has a right to be free of interference from external forces, no matter how wealthy or politically powerful, because it is an autonomous entity. Moreover, it has a right to establish its own admissions criteria free from outside influence, because it is an independent, self-governing institution whose identity depends on the maintenance of its rights to intellectual self-definition and academic freedom.

Regina could also claim that because she is a professional who is capable of independent judgment, internal self-rule, and moral accountability, she should be able to reject the nephew, providing she has made a fully informed, impartial decision to do so. If she genuinely feels that the development-potential criterion is antithetical to the university's egalitarian ideals, and if she believes that admitting the nephew would seriously compromise the academic standards for which Wilson has become famous, then the university must, at the very least, respect the integrity of her decison. Regina could even argue that the nephew's autonomy might be impaired; thus the university would have a right to deny him admission on the grounds that he is incapable of deliberating rationally about his choice to attend Wilson. During his interview, the nephew gave little evidence of having developed his own life-plan with much forethought. He seemed detached and distracted, and unmindful of the consequences of his decision to attend Wilson. Neither did he seem to do much autonomous thinking for himself. In fact, his inclination to attend Wilson appeared to be a tepid one, shaped mainly by his uncle's wishes to have a member of his family attend the university.

Regina might also appeal to the principle of *nonmaleficence* in rejecting the nephew. Concerning this principle, some ethicists tend to interpret the injunction to avoid harming others so broadly as to include injuries to reputation, self-esteem, and liberty. They also point out that the obligation of nonmaleficence encompasses both actual and potential harm; thus the principle requires that moral agents be deliberate and cautious in their decision-making, because harms can occur unintentionally. In this sense, negligence can be defined as the failure to meet the moral obligation to guard against the possible, unintended risk of harming someone. Regina could argue, in light of the principle of nonmaleficence, that rejecting the nephew would avoid injuring the reputations of Wilson, the uncle, and the admissions office. If the nephew is as weak as his academic history suggests, then an admission based exclusively on a development-potential factor could irreparably damage the prestige of the university.

Moreover, if Regina were to admit the nephew—who does not appear to have the proper intellectual background, preparation, or talents—to a high-powered, prestigious university, she could be vulnerable to the charge of negligence. Whether or not she intended it, the nephew might flunk out of Wilson somewhere along the way. This could conceivably injure his academic self-esteem so badly that he might be unlikely to pursue a college education again. Finally, Regina could reason that, if the university accepts the nephew because of a corporation's implied threat to withhold a generous subsidy, then it has established an alarming precedent: It has endangered its right to be free of outside controls. This could result in major damage to the university's reputation and to its liberty.

Regarding the principle of *beneficence*, Regina might make the case that rejecting the nephew would actually enhance his, and the university's, welfare. Beneficence involves comparing the relative weights of costs and benefits in ethical decision-making; consequently, a beneficent decision is one in which the risks are outweighed by the probable benefits. A risk refers to a potential future harm; a benefit refers to anything that promotes human and institutional welfare (Beauchamp & Childress, 1979). Regina could assert that rejecting the nephew would actually result in far greater benefits than risks to every constituency at Wilson. The university would maintain its academic integrity. Thus academically gifted high school students would continue to apply each year, and Wilson alumni would continue to earn the respect of the corporate and university worlds. The development-potential criterion from now on would apply only to those students who are fully qualified to be admitted. The message would be sent that wealth alone is not sufficient for admission to this proud university. Corporate opportunists who might be prone to quid pro quo giving would stop the practice. And wealthy alumni would hesitate before tendering the applications of marginally qualified relatives and friends.

Furthermore, the nephew would understand that while money might purchase privilege in other universities and social settings, merit and effort are what ensure access to a principled institution such as Wilson. Thus the nephew might choose to attend a prep school, or to take a number of courses in the university's evening division, in order to strengthen his academic credentials. He might even learn that intelligence, hard work, motivation, and character are what really count in living a praiseworthy life. The uncle could become an even more loyal, and generous, alumnus, because his university has chosen to take a nonconciliatory approach that makes it virtually incorruptible when making admissions decisions. And finally Regina herself might gain from denying the nephew admission to Wilson. She could strengthen her candidacy for permanent director of admissions, because she has demonstrated a moral probity that sets her apart from all of the other candidates. She has said no, when it would have been much less risky to say yes.

Finally, Regina could appeal to the principle of *justice* in denying the nephew admission. It was Aristotle, in Book V of the *Nichomachean Ethics* (1976), who wrote one of the most influential treatises ever on the principle of justice; but his understanding of justice was more formal than normative. Aristotle argued that whatever respects are being considered, individuals who are equal in those respects should be treated equally. This is to assert no more than the rule that equals should be treated equally, because all people should get their due. Unfortunately, Aristotle's theory of justice does not give us substantive criteria for determining equality, even though it does appear to presume in favor of the principle of equal treatment of individuals. Left unanswered, however, are difficult "material" questions about equality: Who is equal and who is unequal? What morally relevant factors ought to justify differential treatment—merit? kinship? social position? wealth? skin color? gender? Which moral rules ought to govern the allocation of scarce resources? Is it possible to arrive at a fair scheme for distributing society's benefits and burdens to its members? Even though Aristotle's analysis provides no material properties of justice, all subsequent work on this principle has had to take account of his early thinking on this topic.

Certainly, Regina agrees with Aristotle that, in the admissions process, equals ought to be treated equally, and they ought to get their due. But in what senses can the nephew be considered an equal with all the other applicants? Academically, he is below the norm. Is it just for him to benefit from the "happy" accident that he is related to a wealthy uncle who is a graduate of Wilson and who "happens" to be considering the donation of a substantial gift to his alma mater? Is it just that the nephew's "right" to pursue a degree at Wilson is predicated exclusively on a policy of preferential treatment for the scions of wealthy alumni? Regina speculates that it seems to be a basic violation of justice to regard the nephew as a priori

deserving of equal treatment solely because his admission would guarantee
Wilson a major economic return.

Regina could argue that rejecting the nephew is the fair action to take
because she believes that a policy of preferential treatment for a few individuals, based on a development-potential standard, is unjust. Such a policy
seems unfairly to advantage those students, such as the nephew, who, because of a sheer accident of birth, stand to gain unearned access to an elite
university. Moreover, the policy seems to unfairly penalize all those qualified students who, because of an unlucky happenstance of birth, do not
bring with them the promise of huge corporate benefactions after they
graduate. At least 10% of those students who may be fully qualified to attend Wilson in every relevant academic respect will be disadvantaged by
the policy, simply because there are no prosperous financiers anywhere in
the family pedigree. Regina could claim that the development-potential
factor results in an unjust admissions policy that actually treats equals unequally. In justice terms, she does not understand how a financial-promise
factor could ever be a morally relevant admissions yardstick.

4. What theory do you appeal to in order to justify decision B?

Regina could appeal to a *rule-deontological* theory to justify her rejection
of the nephew's application to Wilson. As a rule-deontologist, Regina could
argue that a respect for autonomy and the right to equal treatment are
intrinsically good rules in admissions decisions, regardless of the consequences. Therefore, if the rules apply in one case, they apply in all cases.
Respect for autonomy, a Kantian concept, entails the right of self-
determination, choice, and mutual regard. The right to equal treatment,
an Aristotelian concept, calls for giving people what they deserve and distributing benefits and burdens on the basis of fair criteria. These rules are
both binding and generalizable for the rule-deontologist. Unlike an act-
deontological theory, rule-deontology offers a generalizable standard for
determining what is right and wrong in all relevantly similar situations. Regina's two admissions rules obligate her to be consistent in like circumstances.

Regina might make the case that to admit the nephew because the
uncle will contribute to the university's capital fund campaign is to treat
both individuals as mere means, in order to achieve the self-aggrandizing
ends of Wilson. The uncle and nephew thus become conditional moral
agents who exist only to serve the university's self-interested needs. This is
a violation of the rule that respects autonomy, because the university ex-
ploits the uncle and nephew without regard to their own unique interests,

needs, strengths, and weaknesses. Regina's decision to reject the nephew could actually protect both the nephew's and uncle's autonomies, because the university would be making a judgment based on what the nephew has accomplished on his own merits, not on his uncle's. And if the university supports Regina's autonomous right to make a fair and impartial decision to reject the nephew, in spite of all the adverse outcomes, then Regina demonstrates to others that her office is free of external control and is in charge of its own internal affairs. Regina's professional right to make independent judgments in her area of competence is thereby assured.

Regina could also argue that the rule of equal treatment requires a basic equality of opportunity in admissions decisions. To deny the nephew admission would be to give him what he rightfully deserves. Her decision would be based on the equal-opportunity rule that all individuals who seek admission to Wilson have the same right to be evaluated according to their motivation, prior effort and accomplishments, and future potential. In these respects, the nephew is clearly deficient, and Regina could contend that he deserves to bear the burden of nonadmission when his record is compared to other equals. Also, the nephew's rejection would be a fair allocation of a scarce resource: Because more students seek admission to Wilson than there are places to accommodate them, a positive admissions decision is considered to be an achievement of great worth. What is needed are educationally relevant factors for making comparative judgments about who is to be admitted and who is not. The meritocratic criteria of productivity and promise provide Regina with educationally relevant standards for making fair allocation decisions in the admissions office.

5. What conclusions do you reach regarding your final decision after you compare both justifications?

After looking carefully at the ethical pros and cons of each of the two possible courses of action, *Regina decides to reject the nephew.* She starts at the first level of justification, the moral rules. While the rules Regina learned at home are compelling, in this case they seem in fundamental conflict with the moral rules she learned from her college admissions mentor. The mentor's maxims stress self-determination, prudent decision-making, commitment to principle, respect for one's own integrity, and courage—rules Regina takes very seriously both in her personal life and in her professional work. Conversely, as she gets older, Regina has become increasingly critical of her parents' moral rules, because these seem too deferential to authority, too utilitarian, and too calculating to be effective guides to ethical action in the world of admissions. Regina believes that she needs to be more morally independent in the work she does, more ethically self-regarding than perhaps her parents would recognize. Consequently, Regina chooses to fall back on the mentor's rules as her first line of ethical defense in deciding to reject the nephew.

The mentor's rules are morally cogent in her professional setting, because they stress the significance of respecting a number of conflicting autonomies, especially Regina's own. Moreover, they encourage her to act out of her deepest moral convictions, particularly in those most difficult admissions cases when an unpopular decision could very well incur the obloquy of some powerful people. On principle, Regina truly wants to give the nephew the benefit of the doubt concerning his poor high school transcript, test scores, and unsatisfying personal interview, but her every professional instinct says that he is an underachiever of major proportions. Moreover, he is the worst kind of underachiever: undisciplined, arrogant, self-righteous, and indolent. It is clear to Regina that he does not deserve to be admitted to Wilson on the basis of the demonstrable evidence. The special advantage of the mentor's rules is that they urge her to trust the wisdom of her own best judgments: She should follow her conscience, stand up for what she believes, and be loyal to herself. She does not know how she could ever live an authentic life if she were to flout these simple moral maxims.

At the second level of justification, Regina is particularly moved by the obligations imposed by the principles of autonomy and justice in this case. She is steadfast in her belief that a university must be maximally free of interference from outside forces if it is to remain a truly independent institution. At the very least, Wilson needs the autonomy to establish its own admissions standards and control its own admissions process. Any consent on her office's part to external influences on decision-making, no matter how beneficial to the university on fiscal grounds, could seriously undermine Wilson's integrity by compromising its rights to determine its own fate. For Regina, nothing less than Wilson's rights to academic freedom and intellectual self-definition are at stake here—rights she regards as fundamental to a university's identity. Regina has always placed the highest value on the educational sovereignty of a university.

Regina knows that the admissions office is the first line of entry to Wilson, and it must retain the rightful authority to act as the gatekeeper. Just as medical and law schools assume the right (and responsibility) to determine the fledgling membership of their respective professions—consistent with the highest standards of each discipline—so too, Regina believes, university admissions offices should have the same prerogative to decide the membership of their incoming undergraduate classes. To compromise this prerogative because a wealthy corporation resorts to "bribery" is to allow an extraneous force to violate what she believes is the university's near-absolute right to self-governance. Regina would certainly agree that the uncle has a defensible right to contribute a large gift to the university's fundraising campaign. But she would argue that the university has no correlative responsibility to accept his nephew simply because of the contribution. In fact, Regina believes that such a responsibility is basically indefensible on every ground save one—financial expediency—and, in this case, both the urgency and ethical relevance of financial exigency at Wilson appear to be tenuous.

Regina is adamant that one of the most fundamental professional rights a university guarantees to an admissions officer is the right to make autonomous and responsible decisions about which students to accept and which to reject. Regina knows she has a moral responsibility to ground these decisions in an impartial, rigorous, and fair analysis of all the relevant educational and personal data of each applicant. Obviously, a prudent balancing of each candidate's strengths and weaknesses is an integral part of any admissions decision, and trade-offs are likely to occur with every decision. But Regina feels that she and her colleagues have been hired to perform these official duties based on their qualifications and that she should be allowed to carry out these responsibilities with the full support of the university. She understands that no admissions decision is ever made in a vacuum, and, at the very least, she has an obligation to listen to any relevant party who wishes to advance a case beyond the objective portfolio data in behalf of some candidate's admission. But ultimately it is her office's primary obligation to make the final decision, and Regina believes that it is the correlative responsibility of the university administration to respect the autonomy of her office and support the decision.

Regina is certainly sensitive to the costs that she and the university must bear if she rejects the nephew. But in terms of simple justice—all of the risks to the university notwithstanding—she is convinced that denial of admission is the fair action to take in this particular case. While she knows that a beneficence argument can be made to show how either an acceptance or a rejection could actually produce many benefits for all parties, she prefers to make her decision primarily on the grounds that the nephew has not fairly earned an admission to Wilson, by any stretch of the admissions criteria. To advantage the nephew with an admittance on nonacademic grounds would be de facto to treat certain other students unequally, especially when they fulfill all the standard criteria for acceptance to Wilson. Thus the nephew would receive the benefit of a scarce resource—a place in the incoming first-year class—at the expense of someone who may be an equal, or a superior, in every relevant respect save one, development potential.

The principle of justice is a highly compelling one for Regina. She is simply unable to accept development potential as an academically, or morally, relevant distribution criterion in admissions. She is unwilling to use this measure alone to justify differential treatment in acceptance decisions. Occasionally, she has been willing to make an argument for the moral and educational relevance of other characteristics such as skin color and gender—characteristics for which the bearer is not directly responsible—on the grounds that justice is done when radical inequalities are diminished and when historically disadvantaged minorities have been advantaged by such a system of conferring benefits. She feels that a strong case can be made that gender, ethnic, and racial criteria are directly related to the overall educational well-being of Wilson. But, in this particular dilemma, development potential seems a crassly expedient indicator, devoid of any pertinent educational or moral content. The nephew would appear to be undeserving of preferential treatment, simply because he has never been disadvantaged by radical inequalities.

Finally, at the third level of justification, Regina considers herself a mixed-rule deontologist because she predicates her decision to reject the nephew on the rules of respect for self-determination and the right to equal treatment—regardless of the good and bad consequences that might result. However, she is acutely mindful of the possibility that her decision could actually produce more benefits than harms for Wilson. While these beneficial outcomes are pleasing to her, they are not critical factors in the rejection decision, which she feels she has made primarily on principle. Regina also realizes that if these rules are morally cogent in this particular case, then they are equally cogent in similar admissions cases as well. She holds to the belief that either respect for self-determination and the right to equal treatment are good rules everywhere, or they are good rules nowhere. She wants to be sure that Wilson does not simply "use" her office, the nephew, and the uncle to promote the university's capital interests. And she wants to assure that Wilson treats all candidates equally on the basis of their prior efforts and achievements, motivation, and future potential, except in those very special cases where historical inequalities need to be redressed and additional criteria may be necessary. Regina is more than willing to generalize these particular rules to like cases in like settings.

6. What afterthoughts do you have now that you have made your final decision?

Regina is not fully satisfied with the decision to reject the nephew, although she is prepared to defend it strenuously on rule-deontological grounds. Regina has chosen to override the principle of beneficence with the principles of autonomy and justice in rejecting the nephew. But she knows that countermanding beneficence with autonomy and justice entails serious ethical risks, because she has a stringent moral obligation as admissions director to make decisions that will maximize benefits and minimize harms for the entire university. She is concerned that the decision to deny the nephew an admission might actually bring more harm than benefit to Wilson. During her more reflective moments, she is even willing to concede the wisdom of the development-potential standard, especially for financially strapped institutions. She wonders if it might not be permissible in some special circumstances to lower entrance standards for a few wealthy students in order to produce benefits for the many who are fully qualified but not so well-off. Regina is not entirely oblivious to the possibility that there might even be times when an admissions officer is morally obligated to set aside principle-driven actions for the sake of institutional survival. She knows that a strict adherence to ethical principles during periods of severe crisis can just as easily destroy an organization as benefit it. The task for Regina in this particular case is to discern whether Wilson has actually reached this crisis point and, if so, to decide the extent to which she should compromise her tenaciously held moral principles.

Regina would be less than truthful if she did not consider the possible damage to her own career as a result of her decision. She knows that some of her superiors will perceive her to be both disloyal and ungrateful. A few might even wonder why she is so self-destructive. They will point out that, in the past, Wilson's central administration has looked with favor on every funding request made by Regina's office. They will argue, therefore, that Regina "owes" something to an institution that has never failed to be responsive to her budgetary entreaties for publicity, travel, recruitment, and salaries. Moreover, they will ask Regina if she can even remember the last time the university president made a direct personal request of the admissions office to accept a student. Regina does not want to be seen as professionally suicidal. Neither is she comfortable with the perception that she is intransigent or morally high-handed. Perhaps she could have met in a genuine spirit of dialogue with more key leaders around the university in order to reexamine her personal beliefs about professional integrity, autonomy, equal treatment, meritocratic admissions standards, and preferential admissions policies based on development potential.

Finally, Regina is upset that she did not take two important steps at some early point in the decision-making process: Offer to withdraw her application for permanent admissions director in order to avoid conflict-of-interest charges, and call for a campuswide debate on the development-potential policy. Both actions would have been more in keeping with her self-perception as a person of integrity, courage, principle, and fair-mindedness. She also wishes that she had reconsidered some of the more viable alternative courses of action she could have taken with the nephew. Perhaps offering him a provisional acceptance, or reinterviewing him, or going out of her way to gather additional data in his behalf, or meeting with him *and* his uncle in a less formal setting where she could sensitively discuss her several reservations about the case, might have enabled the nephew and the uncle to preserve their individual integrities. Despite the validity of these misgivings, however, Regina resolves to deny the nephew an acceptance to Wilson University. And she will offer to explain her reasons for the decision to any administrator who is interested, within the ethical bounds of a meticulous respect for the nephew's privacy, of course.

CONCLUSION

Louis P. Pojman (1995) effectively summarizes the major weaknesses of a Moral Principle approach to ethical thinking. Among its flaws, Third Moral Language appears unable to motivate people to aspire to high ideals or to perform supererogatory actions. Principles by themselves are but pale copies of the virtues, in that they seem incapable of inspiring individuals to live them out in their day-to-day lives. Another concern is that Third Moral Language is so legalistic that it reduces ethical problem-solving to a series of casuistic, hair-splitting exercises. Also, moral principles seem arbitrary because they are devoid of an explicit religious dimension, and in those cases where principles may be in conflict with each other, it is left exclusively to a person's intuition to find a resolution. Any ultimate appeal to religious authority or even to natural law is out of the question because of the stringent secular requirements of Third Moral Language. And, finally, with its emphasis on action, Third Moral Language is deficient, because, according to Pojman (1995), "It is not enough to do the right thing, even for the right reason; it is also important to do it with the right attitude and to have the right attitude and dispositions even when no action is possible" (p. 180).

In spite of these criticisms, however, Regina finds the Third Moral Language useful because it provides her a clear theoretical framework to sort through her sometimes conflicting ethical duties and obligations as an admissions officer. Although, admittedly, she finds the language of principles, rules, and theories somewhat abstract, Regina is, nevertheless, able to apply them to her specific case in a very helpful way. She is careful to use the principles and theories less as intractible norms and more as general ethical guidelines that she interprets and applies to her specific professional context. Because the stakes are so high, she is more than willing to undertake the detailed, almost laborious process of analyzing her dilemma via the

Moral Brief and the Justification Schema before coming to a final ethical decision. In this case, Regina is less interested in religious solutions, high ideals, or even the "right attitude," than she is in being able to arrive at a publicly defensible and fair decision regarding the nephew's admission to Wilson University.

Like Pojman (1995), some students find the Third Moral Language to be weak, because it appears to be utterly destitute of those qualities that make the First and Second Moral Languages strong. But they rarely dismiss the Third Moral Language outright. Instead, students marvel at its precision and its ethical utility, even while they criticize moral-principle language for being uninspiring, masculine, linear, abstract, impersonal, formulaic, pat, and legalistic. Like Regina, most students who live and work in secular, pluralist organizations appreciate learning how to defend an ethical decision with a discourse that is quasi-legal, lucid, and comprehensive.

In the final chapter, I will examine several alternatives to the Three Moral Languages I have discussed so far, and I will recommend an integrative, trichotomous ethical language more fully suited than any single one of these others to the complexities of ethical decision-making.

Chapter 6

ETHICAL BRICOLAGE: INTEGRATION AND DISCERNMENT

> All great works of creative ethical thought . . . involve moral *bricolage.* They start off by taking stock of problems that need solving and available conceptual resources for solving them. Then they proceed by taking apart, putting together, reordering, weighting, weeding out, and filling in.
>
> Jeffrey Stout, *Ethics After Babel*

The *Oxford English Dictionary* (1993) defines *bricolage* as the "construction or creation from whatever is immediately available for use; an assemblage of haphazard or incongruous elements." A moral bricoleur, according to Stout's (1988) definition, is someone "who engages in selective retrieval and eclectic reconfiguration of traditional linguistic elements in hope of solving problems at hand" (p. 293). Moral bricolage, in his sense, is "the process in which one begins with bits and pieces of received linguistic material, arranges some of them into a structured whole, leaves others to the side, and ends up with a moral language one proposes to use" (p. 294). Stout has helped me to understand that, as a teacher and writer, I have actually been doing moral bricolage in regards to my understanding of ethics pedagogy and moral language. I have borrowed key terms and concepts from a number of moral systems in order to assemble something that I hope is useful for educators and human service professionals and the people who teach them ethics. I have engaged in "selective retrieval and eclectic reconfiguration" of various moral philosophies in attempting to develop a Three Language system of applied ethics. And I have stressed those particular "linguistic elements" I believe are most salient to the "problems at hand" that professionals face almost on a daily basis. My overall goal has been to help each of my students to create a useable ethics "text": one that "weaves" together a functional "moral language" from among the "bits and pieces" of traditional moral vocabularies.

What I wish to achieve in this final chapter is to tie up some assorted odds and ends in the best spirit of moral bricolage. My aim here is not to say the final word on the teaching of applied ethics, or to present the "ultimate moral reconfiguration" for seekers of ethical truth. I leave such heroic concinnity to others more able (and daring) than I. The truth is that, as yet, my flawed First Language is simply not up to the task of providing ultimate ethical closure on anything. I am a cautious hermeneuticist, after all. Rather, my goal is a far more modest one: I simply want one last opportunity to make some tentative concluding comments on a few issues I have only touched upon in earlier chapters. I want one more chance to reflect on some of the pressing concerns facing ethics educators today.

INTEGRATING THE THREE MORAL LANGUAGES

I have argued, in the spirit of moral bricolage, that ethical decisions are shaped by the interrelationship of several elements: personal philosophies, metaphysical beliefs, the virtues, communities, narratives, rules, principles, circumstances, consequences, feelings, intuitions, codes of ethics, training, and workplace norms. In previous chapters, I have presented a trichotomy of moral languages in my efforts to capture these variegated elements. In pursuit of an integrative model of applied ethical analysis in my teaching, I am continually trying to blend the bits and pieces of several moral languages into a functioning whole, with the purpose of ending the isolation of each of the several ethical systems. Sadly, too many First, Second, and Third Language writers tend to treat their own systems as self-sufficient and complete, and they miss few opportunities to disparage their rivals. Proponents of Third Language often dismiss the other ethical languages as subjective, imprecise, and unsystematic. Advocates of Second Language frequently criticize the others as excessively abstract, metaphysical, and pseudo-legal. And devotees of First Language tend to challenge the other languages for being superficial, ungrounded, and relativistic. At this juncture, however, I simply wish to reiterate my belief that *good ethical decision-making incorporates all three moral languages,* including the increasingly popular moral language of caring, which I would subsume under my Second Moral Language.

I maintain that Jonathan and Regina, the two primary moral agents whose cases I discussed in previous chapters, need to draw from all three Moral Languages, including the language of caring, if their ethical deliberations are to be comprehensive and percipient. Jonathan must explore the moral impact of his Background Beliefs, as well as the influence of his guiding rules and principles, if he is to enlarge his understanding of possible courses of ethical action with Sam. I always try to treat the Jonathans in my classes as multidimensional moral agents who are potentially trilingual in their ethical decision-making. In addition to speaking the Language of

Moral Character, Jonathan is also someone who holds significant Background Beliefs and who adheres to ethically relevant rules and principles. He must master these Moral Languages as well. Questions of confidentiality, disclosure, informed consent, and promise-keeping in Jonathan's case have as much to do with his Third Language principles as they do with his Language of Moral Character. And his convictions about friendship, the family, private and public line-drawing, responsible teaching, and the school's rightful role in the community touch profoundly on his Christian and communitarian First Language beliefs.

Likewise, Regina must add First and Second Language components to her framework if she is to explore to the fullest moral extent her decision to reject the nephew's request for admission to Wilson. Issues of preferential affirmative action, diversity, equal treatment, meritocracy, social justice, and the American university's proper role in advancing larger sociopolitical agendas belong to the province of First Language. And a Second Language analysis could shed much light on Regina's particular personal preoccupations with autonomy, integrity, fairness, and preferential policies based on a wealth criterion. These additional moral languages would round out Regina's Third Language analysis because they present a larger picture of all the factors at play in her decision to deny the nephew admission to Wilson.

Unfortunately, *there are very few integrative models of applied ethical analysis in the professional literature today.* In fact, in the very early years of teaching ethics courses, I found no synoptic or systematic models. During the 1950s and 1960s, approaches to ethical problem-solving were largely improvisational and often popularized and exhortatory. Joseph Fletcher (1966, 1967) exemplified this type of applied ethical analysis *in extremis.* He advocated in a series of very influential and controversial works a single approach to moral decision-making—a situational ethic grounded in the theory of rule-consequentialism, although he rarely used this type of technical language. For Fletcher, no action was ever good or right in itself. Rather, people needed to make ethical decisions about such topics as sex and business practices depending "on whether [an action] hurt or helped people, whether it served love's purpose . . . *in the situation*" (1966, p. 34, emphasis in the original). Fletcher based his morality of love on *agape*, the love of which only God is capable but which each one of us must strive to emulate. He gave readers a simple formula for determining ethical courses of action regarding lying, premarital sex, abortion, adultery, and even killing: First of all, examine personal motives and circumstances. In the privacy of their hearts, according to Fletcher, moral agents must love their neighbors, carefully consider the circumstances of particular behaviors, rise above the rigid, narrow moral codes of the hidebound traditional institutions, and boldly act.

In the 1970s, ethical problem-solving became more theoretical. Beauchamp and Childress's pioneering applied text for the healthcare field, *Principles of Biomedical Ethics* (1979), introduced a systematic, logical-deductive procedure for analyzing ethical dilemmas. The authors taught that healthcare providers could resolve moral dilemmas "only by examining moral principles and determining how they apply to cases and how they conflict" (p. ix). Their widely used text was dominated by a Third Language perspective, in spite of an end-of-the-book, one-chapter nod to "Ideals, Virtues, and Conscientious Actions." And Sissela Bok's (1978) seminal way of handling the issue of lying was exclusively Third Language. She looked mainly to deontological and utilitarian writings in order to develop "a theory of moral choice which [could] help [professionals] in quandaries of truth-telling and lying" (p. xix). Her advice to physicians on truth telling, for example, came out of a justification model of ethical analysis, grounded in a final appeal to the principle of patient autonomy. Most recently, Ruth Macklin (1987) followed the example set by her predecessors: She, too, urged a Third Language solution to an astounding variety of ethical dilemmas in modern medicine. The reader looks in vain throughout Macklin's text, however, to find even one reference to First or Second Language considerations.

At the present time, I believe three approaches to teaching applied ethics typify the most popular alternatives to First, Second, and Third Language orientations, and not one of them is truly integrative. I call these contrasting ethics pedagogies the *self-help model;* the *political-analytical model;* and the *consultancy model.* I readily admit that I have drawn from the strengths of each of these models in my own work as an ethicist, but because my pedagogical approach is both analytical *and* systematic (a trichotomous Moral Language model of applied ethical analysis), my sympathies are more likely to lie with the political-analytical model than with the other two. Despite its strengths, though, I believe that the political-analytical model is deficient *suo iure,* because it relies on only one paradigm for ethical problem-solving—a minimalist Third Language focus—and because it subordinates ethical analysis to larger political purposes. The other two models are somewhat atheoretical, and their advocates actually engage in very little systematic ethical analysis. In truth, one of them, self-help, is openly critical of discursive systems of applied ethical analysis as a way to teach ethics.

The Self-Help Model

Briefly, the self-help model teaches a private and individualistic ethical decision-making. Some exponents of this model tend to write self-help, even self-improvement, ethics manuals for popular consumption. A few of these have become best-sellers (Halberstam, 1994; Kidder, 1995; Kreeft, 1990). Following in the footsteps of the original ethical self-helper, Joseph Fletcher (1966, 1967), self-help ethicists today predicate their teaching on a belief in individual responsibility and an independence from formal analytical systems. They are the radical libertarians of ethics pedagogy, because they assert that all individuals must decide for themselves what is right and wrong. Common sense is the major prerequisite for ethical living. For some of them, cooperative ethical problem-solving is likely to lead to "group think" (Kreeft, 1990). They also argue that referring to canonical rules and principles in order to legitimize moral behavior deprives moral agents of their freedom. In their estimation, systematic ethical schemas are artificial, legalistic, and patriarchal (Noddings, 1984). In their place, the self-helpers pursue a "practical ethical wisdom for everyday moral decisions" (Kreeft, 1990).

Self-help ethicists today represent a diversity of background beliefs, including among their ranks secular humanists (Kurtz, 1988), Christian theists (Kreeft, 1992), libertarian philosophers (Nozick, 1989), and even some privatist feminists of caring (Noddings, 1984). What they all share in common, though, is the understanding that while ethical decision-making may require a method, it does not require a system. By and large, the self-helpers emphasize *pragma* not dogma, concreteness not abstraction, persons not principles, and personal experience not academic reflection. At first glance, those students who favor a more subjective way of thinking about moral dilemmas find the self-help model to be highly attractive. The moral constructivists in particular like thinking in the "first-person singular" about ethical issues rather than adverting to formal philosophical systems to solve problems. They like the injunction to rely on their consciences for the practical ethical wisdom needed to resolve everyday dilemmas.

While I have never been able to win over all of the subjectivists to the point of view that a systematic and analytic integrative model is the most functional and responsible approach for decision-making in the professions, I do get many of them eventually to acknowledge the serious limitations of ethical self-help in the work they do. Many accept that, even though they strive to be individualists, they are also public persons who must be in command of a number of moral languages in order to secure external support for their ethical decisions. Subjectivists end up agreeing with me that the self-helpers have much to teach us about the value of moral independence and good common sense, but ethical justification in a secular pluralist world must never be solipsistic, exclusive, or hidden. Ethical justification must be made public, and it must transcend what is merely subjective. When necessary, it must win a consensus. For all of their inspiration and persuasiveness, the self-helpers preach what is essentially a private ethic. I maintain that because a self-help ethics pedagogy will frequently have difficulty meeting the test of public statement and defense, it will be unlikely ever to secure a wide-ranging agreement on the most effective ways to address controversial ethical dilemmas in the professions.

The Political-Analytical Model

The political-analytical model has a few things in common with the self-help model, including a healthy suspicion of formal ethical systems and a predisposition to take a practical, casuistic approach to thinking about ethics. But it is here the similarities end. Most political-analytical ethicists have very clear social and professional purposes in their teaching, and they promote collaborative decision-making in the classroom as well as frequent group discussion about controversial policy issues (Purpel, 1989; Singer, 1993; Strike & Soltis, 1992). They eschew a purely private, ad hoc problem-solving process. For example, ethicists Kenneth R. Howe and Ofelia B. Miramontes (1992)—two special educators—are advocates for the rights of students "with exceptionalities"; thus the subtext for much of their ethics teaching is political. The authors' highly meritorious purpose is to secure social justice and fair treatment for special-needs students.

My difficulty with the political-analytical model is twofold: It is only minimally integrative, and it has a tendency to underplay ethical reasoning in favor of political special pleading. For example, Howe and Miramontes (1992) assert at the outset of their text that they are not interested in doing "applied ethics" if this means "mere mastery of a given set of principles and precepts" (p. xix). Instead, they encourage their students to engage in ethical reflection by examining a number of concrete cases and by collaborating on solutions to "ethically problematic situations." Their ethics pedagogy is grounded mainly in group discussion about special education issues, and while they do talk about principle-based and virtue-based ethical theories in an introductory chapter, the authors make it clear that ethical inquiry is mainly about process, negotiation, and compromise. Their central question is, "What, all things considered, ought to be done in a given situation?" (p. 98).

I have used this text on two occasions, and although my students and I appreciate the clarity of its writing style and its unabashed commitment to the rights of special-needs children, most (including special educators) feel that the text is mainly an extended apologia for PL 94-142—a public law that requires education for all handicapped children. While they respect—and most even share—the authors' devotion to PL 94-142, students are at a complete loss as to how they are supposed to "reason and collaborate about ethical issues" on the authors' terms. Not a single student is able to identify the authors' "framework for reflection and deliberation" (p. xx) after reading the text, but everyone is able to articulate, without hesitation, the authors' political presuppositions. And a few students do express resentment over the authors' attempts to propagandize a mainstreaming position under the guise of teaching a "deliberative framework."

The truth is that because there is no clear reflective framework to be found anywhere in the text, students are desperate to locate a "set of principles and precepts," in order to provide them some assistance in grappling with the several provocative cases the authors present. The text gives them little help in "considering all things" from a coherent theoretical perspective. For *my* purposes, however, the authors do succeed in whetting students' appetites for a more substantive and systematic Second and Third Language analysis of many of the excellent cases in the back of the text. In spite of my difficulties in using their text, however, I will continue to make it a required reading for the foreseeable future, because I believe my problem-solving approach effectively complements theirs.

The Consultancy Model

The consultancy model is becoming a popular alternative to formal ethics courses and seminars at the university. This model seems to have gained in popularity in recent years, because of the legal need for both novices and professionals to increase their ethics awareness in the workplace (Rion, 1990; D. D. Welch, 1994). The temptation is overwhelming for ethics consultants to turn into moral "circuit riders"—traveling experts who conduct regular tours through the professional organizations that desperately seek their expertise. Sometimes these peripatetic experts do brief "guest shots" in a variety of courses in medical and law schools where there may be no formal, semester-long ethics offerings. Or they may present one- or two-day workshops in applied ethics at the actual worksite. On rare occasions, an organization may even hire an ethics consultant on a full- or part-time basis to provide on-the-job advice and training. Macklin (1987), for example, is a bioethicist on the staff of Albert Einstein College of Medicine and its affiliated hospitals, where she makes daily rounds with physicians and other healthcare professionals. And Rion (1990) heads a corporate consulting firm—Resources for Ethics and Management—that works directly with businesses in order to train ethically responsible managers.

I, too, have done much private consultancy work through the years with organizations, ranging from providing one- or two-day, on-site ethical training to staff at private schools, hospitals, universities, and ski lodges, to brief speaking appearances in courses and at regional and national meetings of many professional associations. In almost all cases, I leave these sessions personally unsatisfied, even though, in most instances, participants' evaluations of my work have been quite good. I sometimes feel that the "invention" of applied ethics consultants has become the "mother of necessity." While I continue to consult with organizations on the principle that some ethics training is probably better than none at all, I am always conscious of the limitations of this type of ethics teaching. At its best, the consultation model of pedagogy can be inspiring, pragmatic, and clarifying for working professionals. At its worst, it can be superficial, hurried, atheoretical, and exhortatory. In fact, I feel ethically obligated early in the contractual-agreement stage to inform potential clients of the serious drawbacks to a brief ethics consultancy compared to a more methodical, semester-long, academic exposure. This disclosure rarely discourages potential consumers, however, because, at the present time, the market for applied ethics consultancies in the professions is virtually inexhaustible, in spite of the obvious deficiencies of "one-shot" presentations.

I believe the defects to be grave indeed. Because time is at a premium, at best I can only skim the moral surface of troublesome professional dilemmas. At times, I am called upon to be more the entertainer or the preacher than the teacher. Even with smaller groups, my "moral conversation" (Nash, in press) becomes ancillary to the lecture, to the homily, and to the performance. I feel I am never able to do justice to my Three Language approach to ethical decision-making, because I am so rushed in the typical on-site consultancy format. Rarely can I assign preliminary readings that are more demanding than a very brief article or a one-page handout, and then I have no assurance that the designated piece will even be read by workshop participants by the time I appear. Hence the teaching I do in this mode is distressingly atheoretical, in that I am forced to rely mainly on my practical experiences and on anecdotal information in order to make my presentations professionally credible and engaging. The temptation to make intellectual compromises in a consultancy is almost irresistible, because, by and large, my audience has no theoretical frame of reference with which to process and assess my observations.

In some cases, clients are merely content to rely on my putative expertise in the content I am teaching them, and they receive the material pliably but unenthusiastically. And in some other instances, because I speak mainly to captive groups who are required by their employers to be in attendance, resistance from a few sneering recalcitrants in an audience can be particularly irritating. At this stage in my career, I must confess that I am starting to find an audience's belligerence more bothersome than intimidating or challenging, and, at times, I have to struggle not to become sardonic or detached as a teacher. Most of the time, however, I transcend my own worst tendencies, and what I end up doing in my consultancies is less systematic inquiry than professional prodding.

I encourage groups to consider the "ethical tone" of their organizations and offices and to create a moral climate characterized by mutual respect for ethical differences. I urge the creation of "ethics support groups," whereby time can be set aside on a regular basis for talking about and resolving particularly vexing ethical dilemmas. I dare practitioners to develop procedures for recruiting ethically responsible colleagues and for holding each other morally accountable in the workplace. And I challenge an organization to construct a code of ethics if it does not have one, and, if it does, to become a true "community of conscience" that tries to live by the principles its code espouses. But all the while I am goading people, I am also wondering if the consultation model serves any real, long-lasting ethical purpose in organizations. I can enjoin and exhort professionals with the best of them, but I continue to have serious doubts that the consultation model is the most effective means for delivering problem-solving ethical instruction.

The Integrative Model

In my role as an integrative classroom teacher over the many years I have been teaching ethics courses, I have come across only one applied text that attempts a fusion of moral languages in actual problem-solving— Karen Lebacqz's *Professional Ethics: Power and Paradox* (1985), which I have referred to in Chapter 4. Unlike my framework, however, Lebacqz's includes a separate language of political and professional structures rather than a language of background beliefs, and she writes to the clergy as her focal professional group. Another ethicist I have mentioned frequently, William K. Frankena (1973), develops a framework somewhat similar to my own, but his presentation is strictly philosophical rather than applied. Nevertheless, I believe that since 1963, when Frankena published his first edition of *Ethics*, very little has appeared that has substantially improved on his brief introduction to the field of ethics. Furthermore, I am amazed that so few applied ethicists today even bother to reference Frankena's text. Simply speaking, we have all stood on his shoulders in the work we do as ethics educators. I and my students find Frankena's concise technical treatment of ethics to be an invaluable propaedeutic for our more practical explorations.

More recently, John W. Glaser (1994) attempts to integrate three "realms" of ethics—individual, institutional, and societal—in a slim volume comprised mainly of bioethical case studies and checklists. Because the text is concerned exclusively with creating an ethics of beneficence, however, and because there are only 39 pages of exposition in the entire volume, my students find the work virtually useless as a methodical presentation of ethical decision-making. Finally, whenever I use Betty A. Sichel's *Moral Education: Character, Community, and Ideals* (1988), my students immediately see the extent of her influence on my development of Second and Third Moral Languages. Like Sichel, I also critique the caring ethic, although my concerns are somewhat different from hers, as the reader will see below. What is missing in Sichel's excellent text for my particular purposes, though, are two elements: an elucidation of what I have been calling First Moral Language, and a systematic concern with the analysis and resolution of everyday ethical dilemmas.

Lebacqz's text is the paradigmatic work for a professional course such as mine. My students are deeply indebted to Lebacqz for her efforts to produce a pioneering text of applied ethical fusion, but because the text is written from an unapologetic political (feminist, liberation theology) perspective, it ends up being implicitly critical of what I have been calling the Third Moral Language. Although Lebacqz does not come right out and call the Third Language inferior, many of my students are left with the impression that a language of rules and principles is "sexist, oppressive, and unliberating," because it ignores the impact of personal character, gender, and political structures on ethical reasoning. Fortunately, however, even though Lebacqz writes out of a mild neo-Marxist perspective, she is not entirely dismissive of the languages I teach. She does use the Third Language, in addition to her other two, in analyzing the case of a minister who must deal with a young parishioner who is in the process of deciding whether to have an abortion. In contrast to Lebacqz's explicit political and theological approach, I try to be more even-handed in the presentation of my Three Language framework in my teaching. I take great pains to emphasize equally the strengths and weaknesses of each system and to minimize, whenever I am able, the influence of any covert political agendas I might bring to the framework.

I am often asked by my colleagues why any student would bother spending so much time learning three philosophical languages in order to analyze a single case. They wonder why one cannot suffice. I can remember an economist, a fellow panel member, warning me before a two-hour presentation to a group of 300 hospital administrators that I should "keep my presentation extra simple or else I would drown the audience in an ocean of philosophical effluvium." He added, "I know these people quite well and they just want answers, not philosophy." I must admit that I was a little more pleased than usual when the presentation actually took the better part of three hours, so engaged were the members of the audience in trying to learn, and apply, all three languages to some of their most obstinate ethical dilemmas. And not once did anyone in the hall ask me for an "answer." I

was especially surprised at the enthusiasm the group had for learning something about First and Second Languages, even though neither lexicon is as
immediately practical as the Third Language.

At the university, some of my colleagues will inquire, "How do you
convince students that all the conceptual work is worth it? After all, aren't
they on the firing lines every single day, with very little time to think about
the complexities of moral philosophy?" While I cannot honestly report that
every student is thrilled with the work we do in class, I can state that people
like Jonathan and Regina accurately represent the majority of students in
my courses. Like these two, sometimes even the most skeptical of my students will give themselves over to the daunting task of learning three new
languages, especially if they can see the "cash value" of their efforts in the
workplace. And although I have presented only one approach that Jonathan and Regina took in the preceding two chapters, many students actually apply all three languages to their cases. Thus, they are able to examine
their cases from three different moral frameworks in order to arrive at comprehensive, richly detailed, fully reasoned conclusions.

AN ETHIC OF CARING

Howard Brody (1987) argues that the richest ethical language for medical practitioners should include "decisional, relational, and philosophical"
elements. Brody makes the case throughout his *Stories of Sickness* that when
individuals are unable to make healthcare decisions on their own and have
not left advance directives, then "caring" decision-making by professionals
should emphasize the "relational" elements of each patient's "life-
narrative": Each patient should be viewed as a human being with needs
to be loved, supported, and understood within the unfolding of a very personal lifelong story. Brody goes to great lengths not to polarize the decisional, relational, and philosophical dimensions of ethical decision-making,
but his implicit critique of an "ethic of universal principle" dramatically
points out the deficiencies of the Third Moral Language. According to him,
a "rights-based universal ethic" is inadequate unless it is grounded in an
ethic of "narrative and relationship."

Brody's most recent work (1991), like its predecessor, features the telling of powerful medical stories whereby healthcare professionals and their
patients are involved in complex, enmeshed relationships that are caring in
nature. The opening chapter describes the moral comings and goings of a
veteran chief of medicine in a teaching hospital. The reader looks in vain
to find even a single reference to Third Language rules and principles as a
way to resolve an array of very upsetting, everyday ethical dilemmas in a

hospital. Instead, one gets a lecture by the chief that is highly critical of the practice of "scientific" medicine, along with an exhortation for young physicians to exercise a "caring authority" with their patients in making ethical decisions. Brody talks throughout the first chapter about the need for a physician to respect the "magic and mystery" of the physician–patient relationship by becoming a "loving" and "authoritative" parent who is willing to confront the patient openly about health risks. This type of "paternalistic" intervention is ethically appropriate, according to Brody, only when the "relational" component of the physician–patient relationship has previously been established.

Brody is actually one of the latest in a growing line of caring ethicists who criticize the domination of a Third Language approach to ethical decision-making in the professions. He is not nearly as strident as some others, however. Because he actually seeks some kind of rapprochement between Second and Third Moral Languages—between the "relational" and the "decisional" approaches—Brody is less prone to pit the two languages against each other than are moral thinkers such as Carol Gilligan (1982) and Nel Noddings (1984), whom I have discussed in an earlier chapter. Let me say emphatically at this point that, despite the criticisms that follow, as an applied ethicist, I have the greatest respect for Gilligan's and Noddings' writings. I have used their work in my teaching and scholarship for years, and I will continue to do so. Moreover, I cannot say enough about the impact that Noddings in particular has had on my thinking through the years about a number of issues in moral philosophy. She is a careful, inspiring writer. Notwithstanding these qualifiers, however, the Gilligan Noddings approach to caring presents certain difficulties in my ethics pedagogy.

Gilligan and Noddings make the argument that gender differences in ethical thinking stem from the early childhood years and that continuous nurturance by the mother leads women to seek interconnections and responsiveness throughout their lives. In contrast, when men separate from the mother in order to assume a male identity, they tend to repress their early nurturing emotions and become abstract and legalistic in their thinking. Both Gilligan and Noddings stress repeatedly the superiority of a "feminine" language of connection and nurturance over a "masculine" language of rights and principles.

Even though he is a male, Gilligan and Noddings are likely to applaud Jonathan's decision in Chapter 4 to keep the secret of his friend, Sam, because Jonathan, above all else, shows a profound regard for caring. He decides on a final course of action in his ethical dilemma only after appealing to his intuitions, feelings, community, and personal narrative. At least in part, Jonathan discerns his dilemma through a feminine language of caring, in contrast to the dominant masculine language of juridical rules and principles. For Gilligan and Noddings, Jonathan's decision would be laudable because it demonstrates a heightened sensitivity to context, relationship, and emotional nuance that is strikingly missing in Third Language deliberations. In their view, Jonathan's decision would represent a genuinely caring one because he deliberately subordinates such principles as autonomy, beneficence, and nonmaleficence to themes of mutuality and relatedness. He recognizes that ethical problems are not simple case exercises in deductive logic. Rather, they are profoundly relational and have to do with the human need for support, love, and reciprocity. They require for their resolution a basic faithfulness to those he loves and nurtures. Jonathan resolves to remain loyal to his friend Sam, even though he might have a compelling logical justification based on principle to break Sam's confidence. Jonathan does not want to risk the loss of his friendship with Sam, and so he chooses to keep the relationship intact. He searches his heart for reasons to sustain the bond.

But Gilligan and Noddings would find much that is distressing in the way Regina thinks about her ethical dilemma in the preceding chapter. For them, Regina's ethical vision would be seen as constricted, because she thinks exclusively in the "masculine language" of autonomy and justice, rules and principles. If Regina is to make a truly "just" decision about the nephew, she must encounter each of the secondary moral agents in her dilemma within a web of complex and interdependent relationships, as Jonathan does. These persons are not mere philosophical abstractions. The feminist perception of justice is that it is primarily a problem of care and mutual responsibility in relationships (Carmody, 1992; Kittay & Meyers, 1987; Noddings, 1984). Regina is connected, indeed immersed, in a series of enduring relationships with many individuals at Wilson, and for her to predicate the resolution of her dilemma solely on an appeal to decontextualized principles and theories is to sunder the intimate connections that naturally exist between herself and others. This is to act unjustly, because, for many feminist ethicists, "right" relationships must precede any serious concern for individual rights. Before she can resolve her dilemma on principled grounds, Regina must first determine whether she is in right relationship with Wilson University's development officer, her staff, and even the president. The basic rule of caring is that no norm is more important than the maintenance, and strengthening, of these concrete connections.

Certainly, an ethic of caring does present an important counterbalance to the impersonality of Third Language logic. The feminists of caring are right to point out the unidimensionality of Regina's ethical reasoning when it deliberately screens out references to context, feeling, and affiliation. But try as I might, I am unable to convince the majority of students—*especially the women*—in my classes that an ethic of caring is a plausible replacement for, or even a valuable addendum to, First, Second, or Third Languages. In recent years, students have raised several critical concerns about an ethic of caring, concerns that an emerging cadre of revisionist feminist writers are also expressing (S. Callahan, 1991; Grimshaw, 1986; Kaminer, 1990; Sichel, 1988; Weiler, 1988; S. D. Welch, 1990). In what follows, I will briefly reiterate in my own language some students' more serious questions.

Category Confusion

The first set of questions gets at the tendency of some writers on caring to confuse categories. Students ask these sorts of questions because they are unclear as to whether caring is an ontology, a product of biology or culture, a virtue, or a moral principle. A few examples of these types of questions are the following:

- Is caring a general feminine orientation toward reality? If so, why do women, and not men, possess this state of being, and why is this orientation necessarily good? Why is it that some women are not caring, and some men are?
- Is caring actually rooted in what Noddings calls "deep biological and psychological structures"? How does she know for sure? Is it possible to derive any normative statements about caring from what is alleged to be a natural biological state? Or is caring mainly a product of enculturation and socialization, with no real "deep structural" properties? With her vocabulary of "natural" and "deep structures," is Noddings—and others who use this language—actually a natural law thinker who has yet to come "out of the metaphysical closet"?
- Is caring a moral disposition like empathy and compassion, two virtues that appear to be synonymous with caring? How exactly does caring improve on the cardinal theological virtue of love? Why multiply ethical terms needlessly when one would seem to suffice? Or is caring simply another general action guide—a principle like autonomy or beneficence—dressed up in gender-correct language?

Gender Stereotyping

A second set of questions has to do with gender stereotyping:

- To what extent does an ethic of caring unwittingly reinforce the worst kind of feminine "essentialism" by relegating the realm of nurturance and feelings to women, and reason and logic to men? Isn't it more than likely

that both genders are capable of what Martin Buber (1923/1958) called
"I–Thou" and "I–It" relationships?

- Why should the sexes be polarized even more than they are? Isn't an ethic
  of caring likely to solidify gender stereotypes between the sexes, precisely
  at a time when gender inequities must be redressed in this society?
- Moreover, why should men and women be exempted from the responsibility to cultivate desirable moral characteristics, simply because these
  characteristics are alleged to be more "natural" to one gender than the
  other?
- How can women avoid the temptation of "gender despotism," the assumption that because only they are capable of cultivating an ethic of
  caring, then women are more ethical than men? Haven't men practiced
  a "gender despotism" for centuries, rooted in the belief that they alone
  are the "rational" sex, and therefore the superior one? Are women merely
  rewriting men's despotic history for themselves?

The Private/Public Dichotomy

A third group of questions confront the private/public dichotomy in
some of the caring literature:

- While an ethic of caring seems to make some sense in the private domain,
  where individuals are engaged in intimate, proximate relationships with
  each other, how exactly does it apply to large-scale, secular pluralist organizations, which usually lack the intensity and intimacy of close affilia-
  tions?
- How does an ethic of caring speak to the problems of disenfranchised
  people of the world? With its emphasis on private emotional states and
  concrete primary relationships, how can an ethic of caring avoid being
  asocial and apolitical? In what specific ways can an ethic of caring be
  responsive to the need to reevaluate and transform unjust social policies?
- How can professionals keep from reducing all ethical language to the private world of affect? If it is true that the "masculine" moral language of
  the public world has been driven by an overemphasis on abstract cogni-
  tion, how then can professionals prevent a "tyranny" of private, affective
  language just as vicious in its own way as the "tyranny" of a rules/prin-
  ciples language?
- Why does the literature in behalf of caring include so many hard-edged,
  sometimes incensed, characterizations of "patriarchal" religion, masculine logic, male-dominated hierarchies, Western male "canons," and
  Third Language approaches to ethical dilemmas? Why aren't these characterizations more caring? Why does a private, affective, gender-

particular ethic tend to result in indignant opposition to traditional systems of morality? Is this angry dismissal of tradition caring?

The Impracticality Dilemma

A fourth set of questions challenge the capacity of an ethic of caring to settle real-life ethical dilemmas. While an ethic of caring is intuitively appealing, it alone does not appear to offer much concrete help to professionals in dealing with complex, or even everyday, moral problems.

- If in trying to resolve moral problems, women eliminate all references to rules, principles, rights, even virtues—because these are "patriarchal," abstract, and nonrelational—how then do they avoid ethical decision-making, which is exclusively situational, emotive, subjective, and arbitrary?
- Isn't there a time when women, and men, must resort to a more abstract and universal Third Language analysis in order to adjudicate ethical conflicts among competing interest groups in the professional workplace? Because an ethic of caring is so amorphous in impersonal, secular pluralist institutions, how else can contesting professional parties be expected to reach consensus if not around rules and principles?
- How precisely can an ethic of caring resolve "big" moral dilemmas such as abortion, capital punishment, euthanasia, and unequal treatment, or even "little" moral dilemmas such as cheating, lying, incompetence, violations of confidentiality, and whistle-blowing?

Sidney Callahan (1991) has remarked that even though the notion of gender difference in moral reasoning has gained a following in recent years, there is simply no empirical evidence to substantiate sex differences in moral judgment. She cites a spate of recent psychological, philosophical, and cross-cultural studies (Flanagan & Jackson, 1987; Harding, 1987; Mednick, 1989; Okin, 1989; Stern, 1984; Wilson, 1993) that cast serious doubt upon the claim that men and women actually reason differently, or that they approach such concepts as love and justice from contrasting moral perspectives. Some of these studies claim that class, race, religion, culture, age, social power, and education have a far greater impact on ethical thinking than does gender. According to Callahan, "Alas, it is a myth of female chauvinism that women, by their gender alone, could be counted upon to be more moral and caring leaders or administrators of any sort" (S. Callahan, 1991, p. 197). Most students I have taught through the years readily recall professional women in their lives—"iron ladies"—who have been anything but moral and caring leaders. In fact, the women in my classes are more likely to mention particular nurturing and "maternal" men than women who have been their mentors, even though they might have preferred the latter.

In my courses, the majority of students of both sexes tend to agree with Callahan. They find value in all three Moral Languages, and when necessary, they, like Regina in the aforementioned Wilson University case, turn readily to a language of rules and principles in order to work through ethical dilemmas in their work settings. And I believe they try to do this in a caring way. I also believe that every moral language has its unique purposes, and the language of caring is no exception. An ethic of caring can be an important palliative to formal principles of moral reasoning, especially when these are stretched to excess. But I likewise hold that there will never be a "magic bullet" for ethical problem-solving, no single, all-encompassing ethical language to decide all of our moral fortunes. Morality is too complex and differentiated to be approached through a single category such as gender. In order to make sound and satisfying ethical decisions, the professionals in my classes will need to learn how to reason, feel, intuit, care, philosophize, defend, and act in character. Unless they develop all of these specific capacities, their search for magical short-cuts in ethics deliberations is likely to lead to frustration and, worse, to tyranny.

CHARACTER EDUCATION AS A SUBSTITUTE FOR APPLIED ETHICS

In Chapter 4, I referred in passing to those character educators who urge that public schools and universities must begin to cultivate a certain kind of moral character in their students (Bennett, 1988, 1992; Bloom, 1987; Hirsch, 1987; Honig, 1985; Kilpatrick, 1992; Lickona, 1983, 1991; Ravitch, 1985; Wynne & Ryan, 1993). The virtues these writers mention most often as worthy of educators' sustained attention are diligence, civility, responsibility, self-restraint, prudence, honesty, self-respect, and compassion. Prominent in these writers' texts is the assumption that for ethics education to be truly effective, it must exclusively be character education. Reasoned analysis and systematic problem-solving are unnecessary. In fact, these skills are distracting, because they give the false impression that knowing how to think about ethics is all that is required to be an ethical person. In a nutshell, what bothers character educators about "applied ethical analysis" and "moral reasoning" is that teachers such as I assume that students "can learn to make good moral decisions without bothering to acquire moral habits or strength of character" (Kilpatrick, 1992, p. 18).

The character educators most likely would see what I do as completely misguided, because I accentuate a type of reasoned decision-making in my teaching. To them, I am spending too much time talking about moral languages, systems of analysis, case studies, and ethical dilemmas, while ignoring my chief responsibility to shape moral character. The character educators would remind me that in order to "do" good, students must first "be" good, and when they acquire the right virtues, then their ethical dilemmas will take care of themselves. I stated in Chapter 4 that while I essentially agree with the overall goals of the character educators, I am deeply concerned that they overemphasize one element of moral character—virtue—at the expense of other essential elements: intuition, feeling, intention, communities, personal narratives, and language. Virtue inculcation is their Rx for every educational ill. I also pointed out that character educators leave themselves open to the charge of anti-intellectualism because they neglect the cognitive dimension of character development: reflection, critique, analysis, and justification. For them, training, exemplification, imitation, and practice are sufficient for instilling moral character.

I am also disturbed that so much writing in this genre smacks of ultra-conservative special pleading. Authors' worries about the degraded state of American schooling tend toward apocalyptic extremes. Moreover, their political views and cross-references are often identical. For example, among the factors Edward A. Wynne and Kevin Ryan (1993) most frequently mention as causes of "moral decline" in education are a relaxing of academic standards; a proliferation of elective courses; an overemphasis on postmodernist, revisionist, and neo-Marxist studies that are generally critical of American culture; the trend toward moral relativism in the social sciences; a loss of respect for authority; preoccupation with self-esteem, personal decision-making, and cultural diversity in the schools; and a demeaning of such traditional values as patriotism, discipline, intellectual rigor, and respect for law. William J. Bennett (1992) and Bill Honig (1985) use virtually the same language in their respective analyses of "moral decline" in the nation's schools.

For William Kilpatrick (1992) and Allan Bloom (1987), any departure from traditional education is demonstrably evil because it is calculated to overthrow the moral status quo. Both writers, for example, see Friedrich Nietzsche's fingerprints all over the "decay" of Western culture and democracy. In their view, Nietzsche is to blame for iniquities as far-ranging as Western relativism, nihilism, fascism, Nazism, anti-Semitism, radical feminism, rock music, values clarification, self-esteem education, and even the rejection of such principles as "sacrifice," "service," "duty," "obligation," and "responsibility" (Bloom, 1987; Kilpatrick, 1992). By implication, anyone who may be a supporter of self-esteem and values clarification in the schools is, to these writers, a Nietzschean and ergo a relativist, even a fascist.

What exactly is character education, and why do its proponents think it is a worthy substitute for formal ethics training? For Kilpatrick (1992), character education is "based on the idea that there are traits of character children ought to know, that they learn these by example, and that once they know them, they need to practice them until they become second nature" (p. 15). Bennett (1988) would supplement the "three R's" by teaching the "three C's"—"content, character, and choice." He would have teachers articulate "ideals and convictions" to students because they "know the difference between right and wrong, good and bad, and [they] exemplify high moral purpose" (p. 18). Thomas Lickona (1991) would have the schools teach "respect and responsibility," two virtues that "constitute the core of a universal, public morality" (p. 43). And Wynne and Ryan (1993) advocate that educators should stress "character, academics, and discipline" in order to foster such virtues as "diligence, acuity, and prudence" (p. 68). The educational imperative in all of these writings is that teachers must stress "traditional moral values" if the schools are "to be put back on track."

Kilpatrick (1992) identifies "two approaches" to teaching morality—"character education" and "decision-making"—and he spends an entire text extolling the former and ridiculing the latter. I have used his text on several occasions in my classes, and, unfortunately, the author's acerbic, polemical style succeeds mainly in infuriating those students who disagree with him and in playing to the fears of those who concur with his disparagement of "decision-making" in the area of applied ethics. Kilpatrick typifies the writing style of many character educators, in that he tends to undermine many of his own best insights by the "slash-and-burn" tactics he employs to dismiss those with whom he is at moral loggerheads. At times, he resorts to mordant caricature in developing the positions of "liberals," "progressives," and "romantics" who are in philosophical opposition to his own views. His characterizations of Jean Jacques Rousseau, Carl Rogers, Friedrich Nietzsche, and John Dewey, for example, amount to little more than character assassination, so savage and simplistically drawn are his analyses of their works. Kilpatrick polarizes my students because he draws the line so sharply between what he calls "moral reasoning" and "character education," the latter of which, for him and other writers of his ilk, is actually virtue training.

Kilpatrick (1992) reserves his most intense scorn for "decision-making" or "moral reasoning" in moral education. He is critical of the "dilemma method" that ethicists such as myself use in our teaching, because he claims our classroom discussions become "bull sessions" in which nobody ever reaches definitive conclusions; our students are encouraged to be "nonjudgmental"; we teach questions of right and wrong as "subjective" and relativistic; we deliberately sabotage traditional religious beliefs; we replace virtues with "values" and abstract rules; we elevate feelings over background beliefs and subject matter; we obliterate the distinction between "reasonable moral arguments [and] mere rationalizations"; and we deprive students of reading texts that express "larger purposes . . . that give meaning to existence" (pp. 16–17). All we appear to be doing in our applied ethics courses, Kilpatrick alleges, is teaching students how to clarify their values. We have become preoccupied with developing critical-thinking strategies. According to Kilpatrick, it would be wiser for us to assign works of fiction that allow students to "identify with models of courage and virtue in a way that problem-solving does not," and then get out of the way and let the novels work their ethical magic (p. 28).

I for one plead *not guilty* to all of Kilpatrick's criticisms. And I know many of my colleagues do as well. He and other character educators grossly misrepresent the work that applied ethicists do. My classes are not "bull sessions" that fail to reach conclusions. In fact, the reverse is probably more true. As a student once indelicately put it, my classes "could stand a little more bullshit, because people seem so anal-retentive, analytical, and decision-driven." For me, the ultimate purpose of ethical analysis is to reach fully informed, grounded, defensible conclusions. The major weakness of an ethic of moral character, I believe, is that, for all its self-illumination, it is fundamentally indefensible in a secular pluralist society. Its aretaic "conclusions" are far too arbitrary and subjective for consensual decision-making in secular organizations. Because the language of character education tends to exclude rights and obligations from consideration of what actions to take in ethical dilemmas, right and wrong seem entirely dependent on the motives, intentions, and dispositions of the primary moral agents. This, of course, is appropriate as far as it goes, but because there seem to be very few obligatory oughts or rights issuing from the virtues, then all moral standards appear merely as subjective ideals. Thus, while it is an important part of the whole framework, the Language of Moral Character *by itself* is unable to determine the rightness and wrongness of an ethical decision.

Furthermore, while I acknowledge the ubiquity of nonjudgmental, subjective, and relativistic moral views in today's professional world, I also make it a point to expose the fallacious assumptions in these views whenever we undertake our First Language studies. This is the reason why I often assign texts written by theologians and classical philosophers. Rather than intending to depose anyone's religious beliefs, as Kilpatrick charges, I want my students to consider seriously many of the best arguments against relativism and subjectivism. If anything, our First Language explorations challenge students to reconsider their overly facile, sometimes reflexive, dismissals of conventional religious teachings. These explorations also force my students to examine their relativistic leanings with much closer philosophical scrutiny. And, *totidem verbis* (in so many words), these First Language texts expose the subjectivist as well as the absolutist leanings in the writings of the character educators as well.

Also, I very rarely mention the term *value* in my teaching, except to distinguish it from *morality* and *ethics*. I am not a values clarifier, as Kilpatrick claims. Throughout my course, I define a value as a nonmoral good. Actually, the word *value* came into the English language in the fourteenth century as an economic term to denote the "material or monetary worth of a commodity." Thus economists arbitrarily assigned a value to something on the basis of its marketable price (*OED*, 1993). In class, we treat values as personal commodities or preferences (such as books, cars, and ice cream) that certainly make our lives pleasurable but, of themselves, have little to do with morality or with resolving ethical dilemmas. I stress that while values can make a major contribution to the happy life, they offer little to the morally good life. As I pointed out in Chapter 3, it is through background beliefs that one can *know* the good life. And in Chapter 4, I maintained that it is through the virtues, the moral goods, that one can *lead* a good life. As I argued in Chapter 5, it is by rules and principles that one can *defend* the good life. And it is by values, the nonmoral goods, that one *has* a good life. In the first case, life is comprehensible; in the second, it is virtuous and moral; in the third, it is justifiable; and in the fourth, it is happy and satisfying.

Finally, in reaction to Kilpatrick's charges that I am "Rogerian" in my teaching, I must emphasize that I do not teach applied ethics courses from a "therapeutic" perspective. I have as many problems with "nondirective," "nonjudgmental" styles of teaching morality as Kilpatrick does. In fact, my whole purpose in teaching ethics is to help students to understand the difference between "reasonable moral arguments" and "mere rationalizations." This is precisely what my Third Moral Language is all about. I insist that students approach ethical decision-making in the spirit of Aristotle's intellectual virtues: commitment to learning; objectivity; respect for the truth; and humility in the face of the facts. Ironically, these are also among the virtues that Kilpatrick praises, but nowhere in his text does he instruct us on how to employ these intellectual dispositions most effectively in order to read the great character-building works of fiction he so enthusiastically recommends. I attempt to teach texts according to the principles of my Moral Conversation. He is content merely to warn the reader that "adults should be careful not to treat [the great books] like doses of moral medicine" (p. 268).

The truth is that character education can never be a substitute for applied ethical analysis. While I am quick to admit that the Second Language of Moral Character is an important component of "reasonable moral argument" and defensible ethical decision-making, I am even quicker to assert that, by itself, it is incomplete. Regina in the previous chapter could certainly benefit from a Second Language approach to her dilemma if she is to remain true to her image of her own best self, but she requires First and Third Language insights as well. Also, both she and Jonathan in Chapter 4 need to undertake a First Language examination in order to recover those Background Beliefs that are foundational to their thinking about the appropriate principles and virtues in their respective cases. And Jonathan needs to have some Third Language recourse to relevant rules and principles if he is to establish what his moral obligations to others in the case might be. It is my contention, contra Kilpatrick and other character educators, that Jonathan and Regina need to know what they *believe*, and how they can *defend* their actions, as well as who they strive to *become*, before they can be said to have fully developed their moral capacities. Virtue inculcation and imitation alone are not enough to produce good human beings who are also good ethical problem-solvers.

BEYOND ETHICAL BRICOLAGE TO MORAL DISCERNMENT

In conclusion, I have learned over a quarter of a century of teaching preprofessionals and professionals that solving ethical dilemmas is always complicated, often ambiguous, and rarely final. I have met few students who do not agonize over, and continually second-guess, their ethical decisions. I do as well. Most students, I find, are willing, even eager, to spend an entire semester thinking through all the intricacies of ethical decision making, and they remain grateful for the opportunity to polish their ethical skills. But not all. There are always some students who wonder why we go to all the trouble. They challenge me to tell them what to do. I have come to understand this skepticism, this need to have quick, clear-cut answers to very difficult—at times, even Sisyphean—moral problems. Some students are just not ready to confront the nightmare of moral ambiguity and ethical uncertainty.

The most I can do is to remind students that decisions always leave "moral traces"—doubts about the ethical road not taken, the other choices not made. No matter how thoughtful the analysis of a dilemma, or how authoritative the grasp of what I have been calling ethical bricolage, or how defensible the ultimate decision, students and instructors must always be cautious when making a final ethical judgment. No decision will ever be absolutely indisputable. No single moral language, even in ingenious combinations with other languages, will ever be totally satisfying. In the end each one of us must find a way through the thickets of difficult ethical cases with thoughtful deliberation and with considerable humility. This is why I have chosen to teach my subject matter with "cool passion"—with a great deal of personal enthusiasm balanced by strong doses of critical detachment and modesty.

When all goes well, however, my greatest hope as an ethics educator has always been that more than a few of my students will reach the kind of moral discernment James M. Gustafson (1981) writes about:

> The final discernment is an informed intuition; it is not the conclusion of a formally logical argument, a strict deduction from a single moral principle, or an absolutely certain result from the exercises of human "reason" alone. There is a final moment of perception that sees the parts in relation to a whole, expresses sensibilities as well as reasoning, and is made in the conditions of human finitude. In complex circumstances it is not without risk. (p. 338)

I happen to believe the risk involved in that "final moment of perception" is worth taking. In fact, Gustafson's "final discernment" is the culmination of all my work as an ethical bricoleur.

Chapter 7

A QUESTION-AND-ANSWER EPILOGUE: SIX YEARS LATER

Since *"Real World" Ethics: Frameworks for Educators and Human Service Professionals* was first published in 1996, a number of readers have sent me letters and e-mail messages with their reactions to the book. I find, as usual, that I have learned the most from listening to various students' critical reactions to my work (always presented in the spirit of respectful moral conversation that I discuss in Chapter 2), as well as from the specific tactical questions they raise about the implications for their own work vis-à-vis my ethical frameworks, my pedagogy, and my own personal moral beliefs. Many of these students, like my colleagues, have taken the time to offer me helpful, concrete suggestions as to how to improve the book. One of these suggestions actually gave me the idea for organizing this final, new chapter as an epilogue.

Rather than radically revising the entire manuscript by incorporating these recommended changes throughout (no respondent thought this to be necessary, and neither do I), I have decided to add an incisive question-and-answer epilogue, as my way to provide further reflection, commentary, interpretation, and clarification on the original content and format. What follows, then, is a series of questions that I have found to be recurrent among readers—colleagues, reviewers, and students. I am well aware that my answers will not resolve all the problems that readers raise, but at least, I hope, they represent an honest, non-defensive attempt to come to terms with much of the instructive feedback I have received. I am grateful to get another opportunity to make *"Real World" Ethics* a more reflective book. I direct my responses to both teachers *and* students of ethics.

QUESTION: Your intended audience for the book includes professors, teachers, and students interested in, or directly involved with, *all* the helping professions. Have you cast too wide a net over your audience? What relevance, for example, do your teaching strategies as a professor have for students who do not plan to become teachers themselves? What do they care about your reflections on your own teaching, or your many concrete suggestions for teaching this material in secondary schools and colleges?

RESPONSE: These are questions that touch directly on my reasons for wanting to write *"Real World" Ethics* in the first place. My original intention was to create an applied ethics text for educators and other human service professionals that was unique; a text that spoke not only to students but to the teachers of those students as well. While each of the applied ethics texts that I have used in my courses over the years had their considerable strengths, every single one of them was directed exclusively to students and practitioners. The authors themselves remained shadowy, omniscient figures, very careful not to reveal their own struggles with the complex ethical material they were trying to clarify for readers. It was as if these scholars had mysteriously emerged onto the scene as full-blown ethics educators, as experts who themselves never experienced a single misgiving or doubt about either their content or their teaching methodology. Because I am first of all a teacher educator, and then a moral philosopher, in all that I do in the classroom, I want my students also to consider the *teaching-learning* implications of the subject matter they are studying. This, in my opinion, is even more necessary when the content is as controversial and complex as ethics and morality.

More than once in the early years of teaching my course, I yearned for a book that would speak to *my* needs as a teacher to construct an intellectually tenable, pedagogically creative, and professionally relevant ethics experience. Furthermore, I was convinced that my students, all of whom were striving to become educators and/or teachers themselves (either in schools, colleges, or human service settings), would gain as much from learning about my own successes and failures in shaping and delivering an applied ethics course as they would from the content itself. More to the point, I wanted to make a "real world" ethics truly real by writing candidly and personally about the *why* and the *how*, as well as the *what*, of my ethics teaching.

What better way to model ethical practice, I thought, than to muse reflectively and honestly on all the problems that a teacher faces in constructing a new course, particularly one that purports to be about morality. Moreover, what better way to illustrate a "real world" ethical dilemma than to present the teaching of ethics itself as an ethical dilemma, one that I, and others like me, must confront every single day that we step into a classroom. The chapter title that I love the most in my book is the one that names Chapter 2: "Teaching Ethics Ethically." This is also the chapter that speaks loudest to ethics educators, according to their feedback.

I long ago lost count of those students from a variety of human services who have taken my courses over the years, who then went on to become ethics educators themselves—at every level of schooling, and in every human service venue. Year after year, there is a common ethical ground that seems to bind together all of the pre-professionals and professionals who take my ethics courses. Despite their different settings and situations, they all face similar ethical challenges in working with human beings; they all need training in the specialized moral languages that will help them to grow in ethical discernment; they all will eventually need to justify their ethical decisions to a number of constituencies; and many will themselves become ethics educators, either as trainers, consultants, advisers, workshop facilitators, or as full-fledged classroom teachers. Frequently, they will say to me that watching me trying valiantly to teach ethics, blunders and all, and listening to me talk openly about the ethics of teaching ethics while exposing myself to constructive criticism, was what encouraged them to take on the formidable task of teaching this material themselves.

In this regard, I have recently come across an excellent text, *Ethics and the University*, which deals with both ethics content and teaching methodology, written primarily for college teachers. The author, Michael Davis (1999), makes the following statement that is germane to the point I am trying to make regarding the possible usefulness of the dual approach I am describing here—teaching about *teaching* ethics, as well as teaching about *resolving* ethical dilemmas:

> Teaching professional ethics . . . can itself generate questions of academic ethics . . . . For example, if teaching medical ethics is a kind of inculcation of proper values, how can an academic committed to freeing the mind of mere inculcation ethically teach medical ethics? (p. vii)

Davis is saying that an ethics educator cannot help but generate ethical questions by the very act of teaching ethics. In one sense, an ethics educator needs no other content. I wanted to write a book that confronted these issues head-on, one that constructed ethical questions explicitly rather than implicitly. I found it impossible to disentangle the subject matter of ethics from the problems of the subject doing the teaching of ethics. For better or worse, *"Real World" Ethics* was meant to be that book. I stand today on the merits of my initial choice to write that kind of book.

QUESTION: In your desire to make your book applicable to both teachers and students, is it possible that your technical vocabulary, your reading lists, and your penchant for moral philosophy and ethical theory might to be too ambitious, particularly for undergraduates?

RESPONSE: My dual approach—writing both to teachers of ethics and to pre-professional and professional students learning about ethics—is not without its difficulties. Whether undergraduate or graduate, students without a philosophical background find my technical language daunting. Professors of ethics presumably know the technical language, and so my use of such terms as *deontology, utilitarianism, autonomy,* and so forth, represents familiar nomenclature to them. But most students who happen upon this material for the first time labor mightily to make sense of what they often consider to be impenetrable jargon. They sometimes feel the same way about the assigned specialized readings that I frequently mention throughout the book.

I initially considered including a glossary of technical terms in my book, but decided against it. In my experience, students rarely go to the back of a book to consult a glossary, or even a bibliography or an index, for that matter. More importantly, I wanted to avoid isolating the technical language by challenging myself to define the words in the immediate context in which I was using them. Overall, I think I did a fair job in this respect, although some of my respondents thought otherwise.

Having said this, however, I think it is important for educators to remember that undergraduates take courses outside their majors all the time, and these courses require at least a basic knowledge of highly specialized languages. Whether it is a course of study dealing with the arcane argot of literary or linguistics theory, or the intimidating terminology of any number of science or economics courses, I contend that when students are motivated, they will learn the language; in fact, many will master it. Notice how quickly and easily most students command what, to me, is the indecipherable speech of computer technology. The truth is that students of all ages want to be multilingual, if they are able to see the immediate and long-range practical payoff of new language acquisition.

Many students tell me that at the end of my course, after having worked with *"Real World" Ethics,* for a semester, they took great pride at how fluent they had become in using the moral languages which initially they felt were insurmountably technical. I was aware of this all along, of course: During the semester I often point out to them how terminologically wise they are becoming. I also point out to them that *fluency* in their use of ethics nomenclature need not be synonymous with *arrogance.* The technical language that professionals use, sometimes haughtily, for better or worse, often shapes reality for the people we serve. This realization itself is a significant ethical burden for practitioners, and it must be borne responsibly.

My strategy is to acquaint beginning students with the technical ethical language that professional communities use (Bruffee, 1993). If students are to become proficient professionals, then they need to start using the customary language of their professional guilds early and often in order to master it. This needs to happen from day one. Moreover, I often invite students in my courses to make their own unique contributions to the specialized language of applied ethics. I am no longer surprised whenever students come up with a more resonant ethical term on their own where before there might have been none, or only an inadequate or imprecise one.

Today, for example, ethical languages in the bio-sciences, as well as in the fields of medicine and computer technology, are changing rapidly as unprecedented moral dilemmas arise almost daily. My students have taught me what is ethically acceptable as a matter of computer etiquette, for instance, and what is not. I have learned from them, somewhat painfully, that a term like *flame*— sending off a hastily conceived, angry e-mail—has specific ethical implications both for sender and receiver alike.

Students quickly understand that all of us—veterans and neophytes alike—are together in the process of making professional ethical languages mean something useful to both practitioners and clients. No single professional or profession has a monopoly, or the last word, on an ethical language or an ethical code. Moral languages, like codes of professional ethics, are continually undergoing changes as new and challenging situations arise. When I first became a member of the National Association of Student Personnel Administrators in the late 1960s, for example, this organization did not even have an official code of ethics. Now it has a well developed one, albeit one that is constantly in flux, as is the American College Personnel Association's code. The moral languages in both of these professional codes have changed over the years as new, often daunting, ethical dilemmas emerge to challenge student affairs administrators in the nation's colleges and universities.

I make it a point to let students know that moral language, like all other languages, is a living, evolving thing. A word such as *autonomy*, for example, has signified different moral meanings for different eras. The Ancient Greeks developed the term so that it would stress communal responsibility over individual rights without losing sight of the importance of the latter. Christians, for 2000 years, have construed the concept of autonomy to be the logical moral consequence of each person's being made in the image and likeness of the Creator, and, therefore, wholly responsible for choosing their eternal salvation or damnation. Christians also believe that because people are made in the image of their God, they have a sacred right to be treated with respect and dignity.

Most postmodernists today think of the principle of autonomy as being primarily a functional social construct, more useful to some cultures than others, with no need for a divine backup (Rorty, 1999). In the postmodern sense, then, the principle of autonomy is a kind of cultural adaptation that confers survival benefits on some societies where democratic individualism is a core value. In contrast, autonomy imposes risks on other cultures where communitarianism and tribalism are pivotal religious or political values.

Most students rise to the occasion. They enjoy mastering a new language because they understand that language competence is intimately connected to competence in professional practice. The more ethical language that they are able to command the more morally discerning they will become in the day-to-day practices of their workplaces. Discernment is all about getting below the surface of everyday professional life. Ethical discernment is knowing how to look deeply into the ways that professionals might be violating a client's rights, treating a student unfairly, unconsciously discriminating against a member of a minority group, unwittingly breaking a promise, or subtly manipulating a patient in order to secure an informed consent. Mastering appropriate ethical language is a prerequisite for improving moral discernment. Without a finely honed sense of how to separate out the morally serious from the morally trivial elements of an ethically challenging situation, professionals can easily come across to the people they serve as paternalistic, or worse, ethically negligent.

It is true that for many practical-minded students moral philosophy and ethical theory can be very challenging, and may, at times, even appear to be beside the point. But without an in-depth understanding of these disciplines, there will never be a sound moral scaffolding for any profession. More pragmatically, without this knowledge, it is unlikely that professionals will be able to construct a closely reasoned, defensible rationale for what they believe, and what they must do, as ethical practitioners. While all of this reading, analyzing, and appropriating of specialized language is hard work, its long-range value for the workplace is immeasurable. The acquisition of First, Second, and Third Moral Languages provides not just a handy problem-solving strategy; these Languages also deepen personal moral understandings by enlarging the professional's ethical range of vision. We have seen all too frequently in recent years how a politician's or a corporate C.E.O.'s ethical myopia has seriously harmed constituencies and irrevocably destroyed personal reputations.

QUESTION: You talk a great deal about teaching ethics with "cool passion." Certainly your syllabus in Chapter 2 reflects this attitude. But what are some examples of your own background beliefs, your own moral character ideals, your own principles that undergird your ethical problem solving? And how do your biases shape the way that you conduct moral conversation about ethics? When (if at all), and how, should teachers disclose to students what they themselves think is morally laudatory or repugnant? Can ethics teachers ever get "hot" about their content, or is it only about being "cool" and detached?

RESPONSE: This question is packed—both complex and slippery, and, thus, impossible to answer in any genuinely satisfying way in such a short space. I agree, however, that one of the dangers of a pedagogy rooted in "cool passion" is the temptation for the teacher to strive for a pedagogical impartiality that is simply unattainable. In the interest of achieving some nonjudgmental distance from the material, some external moral perspective beyond the fray (is this ever possible?), even some sense of postmodern moral irony regarding ethical dilemmas, the cool, dispassionate teacher can end up being woodenly non-committal on all the truly important ethical questions that challenge the helping professions. The question implies that there are some ethical issues, after all, that cry out for teachers' and students' passionate moral judgments, perhaps even necessitating their strong moral censure or approval when the time is right.

Therefore, where is the place for the kind of moral outrage in my system, present, for example, in the work of an educational activist I admire greatly such as David Purpel (1999)? Is moral conversation on ethics only about promoting a kind of impartial philosophical understanding? A watery, feel-good tolerance for different ethical points of view? And what appears to be a fairly formulaic problem-solving technique? My answers to this last set of questions are no, no, and no. As an ethical pragmatist, I hope that I am neither detached, watery, nor formulaic.

I believe unequivocally that intentionally causing unnecessary pain and suffering is bad, as is treating others unjustly and exploiting them for personal gain. These actions are guaranteed only to produce unhappiness, strife, and, at times, even violence. Needless to say, whenever human service professionals treat their clients in these ways, they contribute to the ultimate moral degradation of all the helping professions. And, when they do, the rest of us are ethically obligated to summarily condemn these abuses in the strongest terms. We must do this, not only because such abuses are wrong, but because they contaminate the public's perception of *all* human service professionals, and this includes each one of us. This is why a professional closing of ranks in order to protect wrongdoers is always morally questionable.

Richard Rorty (1999) aptly describes the work of ethical pragmatists:

> What matters for [ethical] pragmatists is devising ways of diminishing human suffering and increasing human equality, increasing the ability of all human children to start life with an equal chance of happiness. This goal is not written in the stars, and is no more an expression of what Kant called "pure practical reason" than it is of the Will of God. It is a goal worth dying for, but it does not require backup from supernatural forces. (p. xxix)

The upshot of what Rorty is suggesting for an approach to ethical decision-making is this, and I completely concur: The kind of conversation on ethics that must take place in a secular pluralist society is one where no single person is seen as having an irrefutable corner on ethical truth. The ideal for professionals is to settle their ethical differences without imposing their metaphysical or political absolutes on others. Ethical problem solving, in my estimation, is most effective whenever it emerges from an honest exchange of opposing points of view in a free and open encounter. I believe that all of us—professionals, professors, and students—must learn to live with the fact of moral plurality, and with the understanding that we must never demand absolute validity in our ethical conversations with each other. In fact, in over three decades of teaching ethics to all types of pre-professionals and professionals, I have never found an "absolute moral validity" that every professional could ever agree on. Nor would I want to.

Absolute validity notwithstanding, however, I believe that it is important for teachers to be up-front with their students about their own ethical presuppositions regarding what they believe to be right and wrong. This includes making a full public disclosure about the evaluative criteria that the teacher will use to assess the effectiveness of a student's ethical decision making. In my own case, I explain the core beliefs in my own First Moral Language, and I try to point out how these will influence the way I approach, analyze, and resolve ethical dilemmas. I am also very clear with students and clients that in the time we will spend together, I plan to teach them a number of different moral vocabularies as tools to help them to become more ethically discerning, as well as to solve their concrete ethical problems.

I am candid that it is highly unlikely that they will ever be fully satisfied with any single one of my moral languages, nor I with theirs. But I will urge them to do the best they can with the flawed languages and problem-solving techniques that they and I have at hand. For those who might be interested, I always suggest reading a very practical, frequently cited article that I wrote on a technique that I call "moral conversation" (Nash, 1996). This piece spells out how educators might talk about ethical issues with students at all levels of schooling, as well as how to disclose their own positions on the thornier issues that come up in discussion. In fact, I often make this article the first required reading of the course. Despite its deficiencies, it does manage to set a conversational tone in the classroom that encourages all participants, including the teacher, to put their ethical cards on the table early and often.

QUESTION: Why is it that, disclaimers to the contrary, there seems to be a distinct undertone of moral relativism and values clarification in your pedagogy, even though you are openly critical of both in Chapter 6 of your book? You claim to be a postmodernist. Is a soft ethical relativism, and a deliberate moral neutrality, the logical consequence of a postmodern moral philosophy?

RESPONSE: I am *not* a relativist, if relativism implies that I think all resolutions to ethical dilemmas are of equal moral worth. This is to say that I am not a relativist, if the term means that because those background beliefs which ground ethical decision making so often appear to vary from culture to culture, from organization to organization within the same culture, and from individual to individual, that, therefore, there can be no truly defensible ethical conclusions that might hold for all professionals caught in similar moral dilemmas. Context is everything, or so this version of relativism goes; therefore universality of ethical agreement is neither possible nor desirable. I think that the twentieth-century atrocities committed in the Nazi death camps; the mass slaughters at My Lai, Hiroshima, and Nagasaki; the continuing practice of slavery and genocide throughout the world; and the imposition of a system of apartheid on South African blacks, completely destroy the pretensions of a non-judgmental moral relativism. (See Jonathan Glover's powerful and sweeping *Humanity: A Moral History of the Twentieth Century*, 1999, for a similar critique of moral relativism.)

Also, I am *not* a relativist if the term implies that because a considerable aspect of ethical decision-making appears to be a function of personal taste and perspective, then moral judgments are mainly subjective and idiosyncratic, and ought never to be binding on other professionals. According to this view, subjectivity is everything; what is right or wrong depends exclusively on what feels right or wrong to the professional. Moral reason, therefore, is always influenced by emotion and preference, and, as David Hume once said, matters of taste are beyond disputation. Thus, when all is said and done, moral judgment, like personal taste in food, clothing, or sexual attraction, is essentially non-rational, hence, unarguable.

In this view, ethical decisions can never be rationally defended; they can only be exclaimed. This is the philosophical stance of the emotivist, and in a secular pluralist democracy, it will always be found wanting. While it is true that feelings are an important, at times crucial, resource to tap in ethical problem solving (I will say more about this later), much more is needed. Defending an ethical decision simply on the basis of how the practitioner feels about an issue is to invite from students and clients accusations of professional elitism, arbitrariness, and worse, malfeasance.

In reaction to these particular types of moral relativism, I hold that some ethical decisions in the professions are indeed better than others, in spite of the special circumstances, contexts, and individual tastes and preferences of practitioners (although, at times, all of these are important factors to consider in arriving at well thought-out ethical solutions to complicated dilemmas). As I have repeatedly said throughout the book, ethical decisions are most valid when they are defensible: That is, they must meet the test of publicity in the sense that the problem-solving process, along with its results, need to be communicated and shared—and, when necessary, tested and verified—with others, both inside and outside the professions.

These decisions must also be guided (not predetermined) by both the codified ethical standards, and by the customary practices, of the professions. Moreover, they must be based on carefully constructed arguments that are intellectually convincing to reasonable people. And, most important, they must be consistent with the professional's particular background beliefs, moral character, and guiding principles. If these last elements are missing, then the entire ethical decision-making process is nothing more than a shell without a core.

I *am* a relativist, however, if the only alternative to relativism is what I sometimes see as an extreme form of moral objectivism among my students. This is the view that in ethics there are moral absolutes (universal, unchangeable, and exceptionless), which are said to be grounded in the unquestioned law of God, or the inexorable law of human nature, or the iron-clad law of reason, science, or politics. I can only ask: Who is qualified to proclaim these absolute "laws," and what do we do when they are in conflict? While I am more than willing to listen respectfully to staunch moral objectivists both in and out of the classroom, I just do not believe that any appeal to immutably divine or natural laws as the "final" justification for resolving an ethical dilemma has a useful role to play in a secular pluralist democracy. Too often in my experience, both in seminars and in professional consultancies, extreme objectivist appeals to transcendent authorities of one kind or another tend to be conversation-stoppers when it comes to ethical problem-solving. Either intentionally or unintentionally, objectivists end up short-circuiting all the hard work that I believe is necessary in order to secure agreement on controversial ethical decisions in the professions.

I must admit that I greatly respect those students and professionals whose background beliefs are rooted in a sense of divine transcendence, or in some other kind of metaphysical or political ultimacy. They can be torridly passionate in their moral convictions, and, at times, I admire them for this. I have met far too many blasé or jaded postmodern professionals who think that possessing strong moral convictions worth fighting, even dying, for is an illness to be cured rather than an ideal to be celebrated. But even though I make it a point to encourage objectivists to openly articulate their most cherished beliefs to the rest of us as they, and we, sort through our ethical options, I also push them to try to make their case, if at all possible, in the Second and Third Moral Languages as well.

These moral languages are the lexicons more calculated to speak to professional colleagues of a secular bent who might hold contrasting background beliefs. Along with the First Moral Language, these vocabularies are more likely to stand up to John Rawls's (1971) test of publicity in a secular pluralist democracy that I mention in Chapter 3 and in an earlier paragraph in this chapter. I do not want objectivists to water down their beliefs; instead, I want them reframed in a public language that is both morally compelling and rationally persuasive to all the rest of us. I am also sensitive, however, to the retort that, sometimes, reframing private background beliefs, particularly those of a more metaphysical leaning, in a public language is to compromise and dilute their meaning.

Actually, there is a moderate philosophical view that stands between absolutist expressions of relativism and objectivism, and it is the one to which I subscribe. Let me call it an *ethic of pragmatic moral consensus.* I start with the assumption that, though personally I am dubious (but open-minded) about the existence of a universal human nature (I do accept a universal human biology, however), or a beneficent Divine Being who alone is the Author of all morality, I still believe that people share much in common, despite their obvious cultural, philosophical, religious, and political differences. For one, most people want to achieve some semblance of the good life, and they want to solve their everyday problems, preferably by their own efforts, but also, when necessary, by seeking the advice of professionals.

What most religious, political, and social moral codes throughout the world seem to agree on is that the best way to create the good life for everyone—what philosophers call the promotion of human flourishing—is to display a respect for self and others, to practice compassion, to act responsibly, to work with and on behalf of others, and to insist on social justice for all (Johnson, 1997; Smart, 1983; Smith, 1991). It should go without saying that these traits are also the essential prerequisites for all the helping professions whose mission is to enhance human flourishing in some way.

These are universal moral ideals because, in my opinion, they are useful and life-sustaining. They set the stage for people to live together productively, happily, and peacefully. Our moral obligations to keep our word, tell the truth, respect the rights of others, prevent harm, honor due process, and strive for social justice are the inescapable requirements for constructing mutually fulfilling social orders. They are also the sine qua non for solving concrete ethical dilemmas in the professions. These are the moral principles that, despite their abrogation in many cultures, serve to forge a common bond among all human beings.

Am I a postmodernist? I am in this sense: I believe that none of us can ever prove conclusively that our favorite ethical language is the one that all others will need in order to adjudicate their dilemmas in the most moral way. It is impossible for any one of us to step outside of our personal histories, cultural contexts, and interpretive frameworks in order to gain a "God's-eye" view of the perfect way to settle moral disputes and to solve ethical problems. The best that we can do, and this is difficult enough given our human limitations, is to strive together to reach some kind of a moral consensus on how we ought to treat each other. A good first step is to learn to respect each others' ethical languages, that we try to understand them on terms other than our own (this alone is nearly an insurmountable challenge, according to a postmodernist like Joseph Natoli, 1997); that we practice empathy when we do not understand them; that we challenge them in a nonviolent way whenever we disagree with their assumptions and conclusions; and, when a compelling case has been made, that we even adopt them and make them a part of our own ethical lexicon.

How else, I ask, might we be able to achieve some kind of human solidarity across our many differences as a people; to find some way to stop inflicting pain and humiliation on each other, whenever we display our different moral languages, our different background beliefs? All of this, I submit, is not to be dismissed as mere values clarification or as encouraging only an insipid appreciation for moral difference. Neither is it meant to relieve us from the professional obligation to call others to account whenever they act immorally. When my system is working well, "real-world" ethical decision-making is a rigorous exercise in engendering authentic moral discernment. Moreover, while it shows a healthy respect for the reality of moral pluralism, it also pushes us to take ethical positions and defend them, and it requires others to do the same.

QUESTION: What exactly do you mean by "zero-level" beliefs? And how can we ever get to the "zero-level" anyway? Doesn't this suggest that there are ultimate foundations (a "down" down there) to our ethical assumptions? Isn't this in conflict with your own often-reiterated background belief, inspired by Richard Rorty, that interpretation and perspective go all the way "down," and that what might be a "zero-level" to one person might be a level-five or even a level-ten to another?

RESPONSE: A zero-level belief is the most basic assumption that any of us can articulate at any given time about the morals and ethics that we hold to be true. It is the "down" down there, but it is not the final "down," nor is it an unconstructed, context-independent "down." Our zero-level beliefs are always subject to modification, and, sometimes, even to drastic transformation, as our experiences, languages, and personal narratives continue to change and evolve. A zero-level moral belief, whether metaphysical, scientific, or political, is a controlling supposition that each of us makes in order to begin the process of thinking through and adjudicating complex ethical dilemmas. It is a fundamental starting point for moral discernment; for sorting out what might be morally relevant or morally irrelevant to the ethical dilemma at hand.

I try never to impose my own First Moral Language assumptions on students, although this is always a delicate balancing act. Even when I unintentionally err in pushing a pet belief a little too intensely, most students are willing to forgive me this uncharacteristic (I hope) transgression. They know from previous experience with me that I hold no zero-level moral belief to be politically sacrosanct, metaphysically unyielding, or resistant to critique. As I continually emphasize, a zero-level belief is, at best, a working hypothesis, a tool in the ethical toolbox, and it is only as good as it is useful. In fact, this last assertion of mine is itself a zero-level belief, and I want my students to understand its direct relevance to how I think about, and solve, my own ethical dilemmas. Often I will ask them the following type of questions: "Given what I have just said, what unspoken assumption(s) do you think I am making about the subject at hand? What am I taking for granted that I need to state explicitly in order for you to understand my reasoning? Why do you suppose that these 'unmentioneds' are important to my ethical problem solving process?"

Students receive very little training throughout their schooling in how to get to the zero-level of their most cherished beliefs. They are far more comfortable in responding to what might be called second- or third-level moral questions that are similar to the content of my Second Moral Language. They find it very easy to locate and identify the personal, psychological, and communal influences on their moral belief system. Most of them, with a little coaching, are able to talk profusely about the impact of a variety of mentors, face-to-face communities and institutions, and defining texts on their moral and ethical development. Students relish telling stories about who said and did what to them when they were very young that might have left an indelible mark on their formation as moral beings. They also cherish the opportunity to recall particular memories of those favorite teachers and professors, relatives, and friends who might have taught them right from wrong, good from bad, more often by informal, lived example than by formal, moral declaration.

In order to move students from second- and third-levels of moral thinking to zero levels, I need to get them comfortable asking the kind of philosophical questions that I formulate in the question-and-answer section immediately following this one. In recent years, I have deliberately assigned commercial texts that might be featured on the *New York Times'* Best-Seller List, as well as more academic texts. An example of the former is *Tuesdays with Morrie* (Albom, 1997); the latter, *The Trouble with Principle* (Fish, 1999). Some texts might have a slant that is religious or political; others a psychological or biological leaning. The work that I want these readings to do, no matter how different in genre and perspective, however, is to push students to ask the necessary "why" questions, to get them to travel to the deeper levels of moral understanding and justification.

Two texts that have done this extraordinarily well in my courses during
the last 5 years have been commercial bestsellers. Their content, while only
obliquely moral on the surface, always manages to fire the ethical imaginations of most of my students. These books force them to examine more
carefully what might be called their "dormant moral habitus." I am talking
here about Anne Lamott's *Bird by Bird* (1994) and Sara Lawrence-Lightfoot's
Respect (2000). Easy to read, enjoyable to contemplate, and disarmingly
wise, both texts, nevertheless, make it nearly impossible for students not to
think profoundly (and explicitly) about what constitutes sustainable moral
meaning in their own lives.

QUESTION: I find that the First Moral Language is the most difficult
of the three languages to understand and to apply. Your "probes" in Chapter 3, though helpful, are somewhat abstract, particularly to non-philosophy
majors. Are there other probe questions that might also prove effective in
getting at the "zero-level" of background beliefs?

RESPONSE: Yes, I have developed some additional First Language
probes, including some religiously oriented ones that I owe to the influence
of James W. Fowler (1981) and Warren A. Nord (1995). The seemingly inexplicable, tragic events occurring throughout the world during the closing
years of the twentieth century, and on into the twenty-first, have resulted in
a palpable, public turn toward religion and spirituality in the search for
greater meaning. In particular, events such as the falling stock market
worldwide, wars of ethnic cleansing and genocide throughout the globe,
the increasing social class distance between the haves and the have-nots
in many first-world and third-world countries, rampant religious bigotry
everywhere, and the devastating horrors of terrorism in events such as the
destruction of the World Trade Towers on September 11, 2001, have jolted
the feeling of well-being and security that Americans seem to think is their
natural entitlement.

I have since written two books on religion, spirituality, and education
(Nash, 1999, 2001), and in both I try to make the case that what many
practitioners value religiously and spiritually always plays a part in their
approaches to ethical problem solving, *whether they know it or not.* The challenge, however, is to construct First Moral Language questions in such a
way as to allow for religious and spiritual exploration whenever appropriate, without obliging students to do this kind of self-examination. Some
students will always be religious skeptics or even apathetic about matters of
religion and spirituality, and this is to be respected. They should not be
made to feel that the best zero-level assumptions are, of necessity, religiously
based ones. I find that the questions below tend to succeed more often than
they fail in evoking students' deeply held moral and spiritual convictions. I

have used the following questions for the past several years in a variety of venues (e. g., workshops, courses, publications, public lectures, syllabuses) in order to evoke the kind of zero-level self-examination that First Moral Language requires:

- What gives your life meaning? What makes life worth living for you?
- Have you read any books (fiction or non-fiction) in the last several years which you can honestly say have changed the way you think about (or live) your life? Which ones? How so?
- What beliefs, morals, or ideals are most important in guiding your life at this time? What ones would you pass on to your children? Or to your clients or students, if they asked?
- Do you believe that your life should have a purpose? If yes, what is your purpose? If not, why not?
- Can you give some specific examples of how your important beliefs, morals, or ideals have found actual expression in your personal and/or professional life? If you cannot, why not?
- Whenever you must make an important personal/professional decision, what pivotal moral beliefs or ideals do you sometimes fall back on?
- Do you think that there is a "plan" for human lives? Is there one for your life? If yes, where does the "plan" come from?
- When your personal/professional life appears most discouraging, hopeless, or defeating, what holds you up or renews your hope?
- What does the concept of death mean to you? What does failure? What does success? What does happiness? What does justice? What does morality? What does evil? What does good?
- Why do you suppose some persons and groups suffer more than others? Why do some persons and groups experience more success and happiness? Why is it that some persons and groups act more ethically or unethically than others?
- Will human life go on indefinitely, do you think, or will it ultimately end? If you do not care for the question, why not?
- Some people believe that without religion morality breaks down. Do you agree or disagree? Why?
- What do you think of this statement? Ethically, we are all egoists, because, if we are completely honest with ourselves, we must admit that we act out of enlightened (or unenlightened) self-interest in everything we do.
- Or this statement? Egoism is ultimately a selfish philosophy. Without a commitment to altruism, people's actions would be unimaginably self-centered, cut-throat, and hopeless.
- Or this statement? There are no moral absolutes, because morality

is totally relative to a particular culture, group, belief system, or personal preference. We are all inescapably different.

- Or this statement? There are indeed moral absolutes, because regardless of cultural or personal differences, people do, in fact, agree on a number of core moral principles. In some ways, we are all very much alike.
- If I were to ask you the following questions, how would you answer me? Why should I treat you fairly, when it might be to my advantage to treat you unfairly? Why should I tell you the truth, when it might be to my advantage to tell you a lie? Why should I keep a promise to you, when it might be to my advantage to break the promise?
- Why should anyone bother about being moral at all? Why should you try to act ethically in an organization that seems inherently unethical? Why not just do what feels good, or what you can get away with, or what suits your fancy at the moment, or what gets you promoted?
- Under what conditions would you ever be willing to impose a moral judgment on anyone, or to hold anyone morally accountable in the work you do?

QUESTION: The overall tone in your approach to ethical problem solving, your good intentions notwithstanding, particularly regarding the Third Moral Language, is overly secular. Don't you know that some professionals find it very difficult to think about resolving ethical dilemmas when the languages you teach them—yes, even the First Moral Language—are so radically de-coupled from religious language?

RESPONSE: It is true that I have failed to provide a systematic analysis of exactly how religious faith might influence ethical decision-making. Even though I have implied in Chapter 3 that I am something of an existential, postmodern agnostic, and even though, in large part, I want to keep organized religion (but not a private spirituality) out of the public domain, I do see a substantial role for religion, spirituality, and the language of faith in doing ethical analysis. The main reason that I wrote *"Real World" Ethics* in a non-religious or non-sectarian language, however, is because we live in a secular, pluralist society where no government-established religion rules the day. This is both a boon and a bane in doing ethical problem-solving in a democracy rather than in a theocracy.

While it can be considered liberating that there is no enforceable, ultimate moral authority to which all of us must appeal in making moral decisions in this country, it is also frustrating that ethical problem-solving is, at best, such a tenuous and uncertain activity, mostly up for grabs, according to which parties make the most persuasive, public arguments for their decisions. Despite its messiness, however, I for one come down on the side of a no-holds-barred, secular conversation regarding the best ways to resolve challenging, unprecedented, ethical dilemmas. Reaching a workable ethical consensus in politically, religiously, and philosophically diverse human service organizations will be impossible if one or another version of absolute religious truth is allowed to control, and eventually to stop, the moral conversation.

Having said this, however, I will also take this opportunity to state clearly that for many students religion and morality, spirituality and ethics, are philosophically inseparable. I have met hundreds of students in my courses through the years who find it nearly impossible to de-couple their ethic from their religiosity or their spirituality. For many Christian, Jewish, and Islamic believers, being good without a belief in an omnipotent, all-loving God is unimaginable. For those of an Eastern bent, being compassionate, kind, and caring without a profound sense of the sacred interconnectedness of all forms of life is unachievable. And for others who consider themselves privately spiritual without being religiously affiliated, acting ethically is inextricably bound up with their personal sense of transcendence. Rather than debunk these orientations (which I have no right or desire ever to undertake), I believe it is my professional responsibility to fully grasp the influence of my students' religious and spiritual beliefs on their moral and ethical convictions. In my opinion, to do anything less would be to engage in professorial malpractice.

Where, then, do I stand personally on the issue of being good and being either a believer or disbeliever? Philosophically, I hold that it is entirely possible for people to be good without God. So too is it possible for people to believe in God and not be good. In this regard, I am always struck by the sheer brilliance of Socrates's question in the *Euthyphro:* Is something good because the gods love it, or do the gods love it because it is good? Plato would have Socrates side with those who believe that something is valuable or good on its own terms, not on the gods' terms.

This is to say that the gods love the good precisely because it is the good. Thus, a concept of good necessarily precedes the gods. It would make no sense to say that a god is good, if there were not first a preconception of what good means. If good is something that the fickle gods can ordain at any given time, then good is, by definition, a concept that is ephemeral. This would make morality thoroughly dependent on a god's (or gods') whims, something constantly changing, as it frequently does in the Jewish and Christian bibles (see Gomes, 1996; Spong, 1991). Therefore, it is my contention that we can be good without a priori believing in, or appealing to, those gods.

Tolstoy once said somewhere that just as there can be no real flower without roots, so too can there be no genuine morality without religion. I disagree strongly with Tolstoy. In my estimation (and in Aristotle's in his *Nicomachean Ethics*), morality needs many roots, in addition to the religious, in order to survive. Among these roots is the continuing support of the secular society in which morality is located. Morality, like religion, needs the root of utility value if it is to endure. It also requires the roots of constant habituation, modeling, and reinforcement, both inside and outside such social institutions as churches, families, work sites, schools and colleges, government, business, and media. Morality and ethics, like religion and education, are as much time-bound, social constructs as they are timeless creations of the gods.

All of this is not to say, however, that ethics ought to be a completely autonomous endeavor. Unlike an ethics scholar like J. L. Mackie (1977), I refuse to close the religious frontier on ethics. To do this is to impoverish our moral consciousness. It is to render anachronistic such perennial, First Language moral questions as "Why should we bother being moral anyway?" and "In the event that my self-interest and yours collide, why should I sacrifice my interests in order to do what might be right?" These types of zero-level questions are unanswerable in the absence of an appeal to metaphysical truths of one kind or another or to moral universals.

For many of my students, appeals to utility, egoism, or secular principles that are arrived at through group consensus fail to get at the moral core of what is most important to them. There seems to them to be a more stable and enduring sense of purpose, transcendence, and the tragic in the religious stories of Hinduism, Buddhism, Sufism, Christianity, Judaism, Islam, or Taoism than there ever will be in the pallid worldviews of science, or in the secular philosophy of pragmatism. These students prefer to consult the sacred texts in their religious traditions in resolving moral conflicts because they find them to be more ethically persuasive than mere secular documents.

The challenge for me and for teachers everywhere in secular institutions, once the doors are opened to religious and spiritual factors in ethical problem-solving, is to keep the inquiry open-ended, non-judgmental, and non-coercive, and to find ways to get people to agree as well as disagree. It is to work hard to locate the more resilient, *common ground* of religious morality that transcends individual differences, while still striving honestly to acknowledge the intractable, *hard ground* of irreconcilable religious and secular differences.

I have discovered a few irrefutable truths in all my years of teaching, and here is one: There will never be simple, cost-free compromises when people believe with all their hearts and minds that their moral, religious, or political truths are superior to those held by others. Any attempt to arrive at an easy, conflict-free, moral consensus around religious difference is doomed to fail. As recent terrorist activity of all kinds throughout the world has repeatedly shown, militant believers and disbelievers sometimes maim and kill over their differences. And they do this with the full certainty that their religious and moral convictions supercede all others' in their absolute truth claims.

One goal of moral conversation that I suggest in Chapters 2 and 3 is to encourage students to talk honestly about their most deep-seated, religious (or non-religious) beliefs, whether these are theistic, pantheistic, atheistic, or agnostic. In ethical dialogue, the almost insurmountable challenge for teachers and students alike is this: How can we as a community find ways to engage with intellectual integrity in a postmodern, pluralistic morals-ethics conversation without asking people to voluntarily annihilate a significant religious-spiritual piece of themselves in the search for common ethical ground? This challenge can be resolved, I am convinced, only when students and educators confront it openly, publicly, and without fear. It is a problem whose solution requires genuine group empathy and generosity, as well as a willingness to mix it up in the spirit of respectful, intellectual give-and-take.

For my part, I always say something like the following to students in my ethics courses at the beginning of the semester:

> I want you to know that First Moral Language appeals to religious and spiritual truths are more than acceptable in this course. I must warn you, however, that not everyone will agree with your zero-level religious beliefs, if you do, in fact, have any. We will always respect these beliefs, of course, but at times we might feel the need to gently challenge or disagree with them. Neither I nor anyone else are here to reinforce particular religious or spiritual beliefs when it comes to justifying our ethical decision-making.
>
> But neither are we here to destroy them. The overall goal of our work together in this seminar on ethics is to get us to talk with one another about difficult ethical issues in a spirit of mutual vulnerability and regard, respect and support. The intellectual virtues that I hope to foster in this class are not carping, conversion, or confrontation; they are the virtues of connection, caring, and compassion. In my estimation, these latter virtues are genuinely religious in character. They are also eminently useful as one basis for ethical decision-making.

QUESTION: Your critiques of character education and an ethic of caring in Chapter 6 are harsh. Is this consistent with your emphasis on a moral conversation that is always respectful of opposing points of view?

RESPONSE: Yes, my critique of character education and an ethic of caring in Chapter 6, as these orientations relate to ethical problem-solving, is pointed, but not, I hope, unfair or intemperate. I have since written a book on character education—*Answering the "Virtuecrats": A Moral Conversation on Character Education* (1997a)—that spells out my concerns at greater length. Because I do not want to simply reiterate the criticisms that I made in *"Real World" Ethics* or *"Virtuecrats"*, I will try to try to cover some new ground in the remarks that follow.

What I find intriguing is that while few readers tend to disagree with my criticisms of character education—they tend to concur that in its worst manifestations in the public schools, character education can be indoctrinative, reactionary, and redolent of a Judeo-Christian outlook on the world that is both overly prescriptive and inattentive to the religious and philosophical differences of students—many more think that my analysis of an ethic of caring is decidedly uncaring and off the mark. Some students tell me that it looks as if I am deliberately picking on women (even though my criticism of character education is equally pointed and aimed mainly at males who are its chief spokesmen).

Some also claim that my "overly rational" dismissal of the caring perspective for ethical decision-making merely validates the view that men are incapable of moving beyond a rules/principles perspective in their ethical constructions (although I am critical of those who employ only a logical Third Moral Language approach in their ethical thinking). And some feel that I tend to engage in critical overkill, in the sense that theorists like Nel Noddings and Carol Gilligan never expected their caring frameworks to be used as the sole tools for concrete, ethical problem-solving in the professions. For what it is worth, I think there may be considerable validity in this latter observation.

These students go on to make a very effective case that the caring advocates are really more interested in constructing a generic philosophy of caring (an all-purpose, ethical meta-language, if you will) that could effectively inform my three moral languages than they are in simply creating a practical strategy for ethical problem-solving. As an aside, if this is true, then many in the nursing profession do not agree. Even a quick perusal of professional nursing and bioethical journals demonstrates that at least some of the allied health professions attempt to base their policies predominantly on an ethic of caring. But the point is still salient: The proper function of a caring ethic might very well be to form an overall moral disposition in caregivers—one that I would still argue is necessary but not sufficient in preparing ethical professionals—rather than to do the nitty-gritty analytical work of ethical-dilemma adjudication.

More important to me, however, is the assumption, often made by some advocates of an ethic of caring, that honest critique is somehow inconsistent with the best principles of moral conversation that I elucidate in Chapter 2. I could not disagree more strongly. Unlike some of these people, I believe that challenge and compassion are not mutually contradictory. In fact, there are times when, precisely because I care, I have a moral responsibility to speak my own truth to another's truth, and I must trust that both of us can find a way to express our disagreements in such a manner that our dignity and integrity remain intact. Diana Eck (1993), the renowned comparative-religions scholar at Harvard, advocates a "culture of dialogue" in higher education that echoes my own views on moral conversation:

> We do not enter into dialogue with the dreamy hope that we will all agree, for the truth is we probably will not. We do not enter into dialogue to produce an agreement, but to produce real relationship, even friendship, which is premised upon mutual understanding, not upon agreement . . . . a culture of dialogue creates a context of ongoing relatedness and trust in which self-criticism and mutual criticism are acceptable and valuable parts of the . . . exchange. (pp. 197, 225)

I do attempt to enter into a genuine dialogue with proponents of caring and character education in Chapter 6. I have had many public exchanges with passionate adherents to these two ethical approaches since I first published my book in 1996, and although we have rarely left the dialogues unscathed, we always manage to enter into a new and better type of relationship with each other. We set the rules beforehand that we are not discussing our positions in order to produce any kind of factitious agreement or fractious debate; rather, we are seeking mutual understanding, clarification, and the type of dialogue that might result in self-criticism of our own strongly held views. We acknowledge at the outset that respectful, carefully conceived criticism is both acceptable and desirable.

Most significant, we understand that genuine dialogue, built on a foundation of respect, trust, and mutual exploration, of necessity invites candor and critique. It does this because it conveys the message that a "value-neutral" approach really does not take the other's point of view very seriously. Conversation about ethics is superficial without criticism and challenge. In my classes, it is frequently the ethical absolutists (of all political and religious stripes) who are unable to tolerate sincere criticism in dialogue. I have found that conversation about ethics without the opportunity to engage in critical questioning (I do not mean contrarian academic caviling or sniping) narrows rather than widens the search for ethical truth.

I would argue that the extent to which teachers and students are able to construct a conversational environment in the classroom which fosters a spirit of genuine, open-ended moral inquiry, affects whether we and they will feel safe enough to consider, and to express, all points of view. We should be able to do this no matter how controversial or out-of-step with the conventional ethical wisdom our views might be, and no matter how much critique, deserved or undeserved, will come our way.

QUESTION: What responsibility do professionals have for providing a kind of moral compass for their students and clients? Is the study of applied ethics only about professional problem-solving? Why can't it also be about how to exemplify the moral behavior we would like to see in the people we serve and with whom we work? In what ways will your three languages make me, and others, better human beings, in addition to helping us to become better ethical analysts?

RESPONSE: I hope that the tone in which I wrote *"Real World" Ethics,* as well as the principle of teaching ethics ethically that I espouse throughout the book, exemplify the type of "moral compass" I think it is possible for applied ethics educators to become. My intention in constructing the text was not to do a work of character or moral education. I leave this task to others far more sure of themselves in knowing how to draw up exact blueprints for the production of moral exemplars in the professions. No, my goal was far more modest, yet no less daunting. I wanted to teach students how to understand, and to work through, all the intricacies of defensible ethical decision-making.

I have never had an intention to become anyone's moral mentor, if by this phrase it is meant that I want to replicate my best moral self in the professional practice of others. I am too dense a mass of moral inconsistencies and compromises ever to want these things cloned. I ask only that my students read my words on the printed page, and observe my behavior in the classroom, with the following questions in mind: Is the professor working hard to translate his theory into his practice? Or, in the words of Chapter 2's title: Does he teach ethics ethically? If not, is he at least trying to do so, to the best of his ability, and how can he improve? As I said in Chapter 1, the primary purpose of a course in applied ethics is implied in the phrase itself: an opportunity for students to learn how to apply the three moral languages to the ethical dilemmas that all professionals must eventually address and resolve.

Admittedly, I am a pedagogical minimalist when it comes to teaching ethics. I just do not believe that the art and craft of ethical decision-making have much to do with instilling grandiose moral visions in students. I do not want to lose the individual in a transcendent moral or political scheme. Neither do I wish to run the risk of choosing inconsistent means (coercion, indoctrination, shame) in order to bring about laudable moral ends. I am on the side of those postmodernists who see it as their duty to foster a kind of incredulity toward all-embracing ethical narratives that require an unthinking acquiescence on the part of their adherents as to their ultimate truth.

Karl Marx once said that his favorite intellectual rule of thumb was *de omnibus disputandum* ("everything must be doubted"). While I would never go as far as Marx as to doubt everything at all times (I wonder, for example, if he himself ever doubted the principle of dialectical materialism), I do believe that on issues of ethics and morality, much is a matter of individual, and group, taste, training, and temperament. Thus, whenever someone's moral opinions are presented as irrevocably binding on all, then I suggest that a spirit of doubt can often be the best antidote to ethical fanaticism. Of course, it follows that the principle of "everything must be doubted" must itself be doubted, in order to avoid logical inconsistency. By the way, this continual questioning of all principles—on principle—is a good example of the principle of postmodern irony in action. Needless to add, this latter principle is itself dubitable.

At some risk, I will admit, I always ask my students at the beginning of a course in ethics to monitor me carefully throughout the semester in order to give me the feedback that I need to improve my ethics pedagogy. Am I living up to my own highest ideals as a moral conversationalist? Where is my pedagogical practice in obvious conflict with my ethical principles? In an attempt to make myself look good as the discussion leader, am I making them look bad as the discussion participants? Am I being fair to the authors we are reading, particularly those with whom I basically disagree? Do I subtly, or not so subtly, push a particular ethical agenda on students when it comes to resolving certain professional dilemmas? Do they ever get the message from me that it is *my way* or *no way* whenever we engage in ethical, religious, educational, or political conversations that are controversial? The risk in asking these questions, of course, is that sometimes students will honestly tell me that I have a long way to go before I can ever become a credible moral compass for them. I would expect to hear nothing different from them.

QUESTION: You never bother to mention what place, if any, an understanding of Lawrence Kohlberg's stages of moral development, and William G. Perry, Jr.'s stages of intellectual and ethical development, has in analyzing and working out ethical dilemmas? Is this omission purposeful?

RESPONSE: Yes, the omission is purposeful. I do not believe that either Kohlberg (1984) or Perry (1970) have much to offer to professionals in their study of applied ethics, although I think that their theories are helpful in a vague sort of way. At least for certain people—young, educated, middle-class, white, American males—the developmental theories explain certain general moral tendencies in their reasoning. Without going into a detailed presentation of Kohlberg's and Perry's theories, I will reiterate only briefly what most educators already know. Both thinkers believe that individuals progress through an orderly sequence of predictable stages in their development as moral thinkers.

In Kohlberg's view, adolescent boys, age 10–16, pass through "pre-conventional," "conventional," and "post-conventional" stages of moral development, and these stages are hierarchical, invariant, and universal. The highest moral stage for Kohlberg—the "post-conventional"—is when the individual embraces, and attempts to live out, such principles as justice, autonomy, integrity, and empathy. In Perry's case, late adolescents progress from "dualism," to "relativism," to "commitment." The highest stage for Perry—"commitment"—is when the individual develops a view of morality that is complex, situational, and based on a dedication (or pledge) to something larger than the self. Perry's stages of ethical development are "wavelike," less linear than Kohlberg's, but still presented as universal, even, at times, as absolute.

In my work over three-and-a-half decades with students of all ages, I find moral development theory to be too pat and formulaic, too hierarchical, and excessively linked to age and gender. My students think that the stages too often act as boxes, as self-fulfilling labels, and they strenuously resist being forced to slot themselves at various points along a pre-established, ethical plot-line. I agree with them. Students are quick to recognize that these theories, falsely presented as the products of rigorous scientific research, merely reflect the moral biases of their creators—themselves highly educated, white, middle-class males who studied subjects that they hoped would grow up to value what they did. Thus, developmental theory comes off to most of my students as being far more subjective than scientific; and much more prescriptive than descriptive.

I have learned a few lessons about students as moral thinkers during all my years of teaching applied ethics courses, and one of them is this: Pre-professionals and professionals alike resist easy moral classification. Regardless of personal experience, level of maturity, age, stage, or gender, students come at ethical problem-solving in a variety of ways, both on and off developmental schedule. Unlike Kohlberg and Perry, I believe that a student's background beliefs, social and psychological contexts, formal and informal training, and organizational norms are better predictors than stage theory of how they will go about analyzing and resolving ethical dilemmas.

The main practical weakness of moral stage theory for my purposes as an applied ethics educator is that it offers practitioners no concrete problem-solving procedures, no real world ethical languages for processing their thinking, no strategies for sorting through their ethical priorities, and no evaluative criteria for determining whether their decisions can stand the test of tough public scrutiny. The moral dilemmas that Kohlberg used to test young adolescents' moral reasoning were overly dramatic, impractical, and artificial (Sichel, 1988). Perry's interviews with older adolescents took place in the elite cocoon of Harvard University, absent any real world context beyond the Yard and the counseling office. Moreover, his follow-up studies failed to convince critics that his stages were either universal or desirable (e.g., Shelton, 1989).

Finally, in my opinion, one that I hold with tenuous tenacity, I do not believe that there is some "highest" stage of ethical thinking, residing who-knows-where and authenticated by who-knows-what; one that is beneath or beyond socialization; some ultimate, developmental frame of reference that exists outside the impress of our personal histories, languages, cultures, tastes, talents, and temperaments. In my teaching as an applied ethicist, I know for sure that there are no shortcuts to the hard ethical work that every helping professional must do. Each of us must learn how to unravel and address all the complexities of the moral quandaries that plague us. Moreover, no matter where we are on some imaginary developmental continuum or ladder, we must come to a resolution that is both fitting and justifiable, one with which we and our colleagues can live with integrity.

The primary objective of ethical problem-solving is not to arrive at some imaginary "best" solution, pre-determined by a particular moral agent's progress through a series of changeless developmental stages. Instead, real world problem-solving means to muddle our way through the resolution of ethical dilemmas in the only manner we know how. It is to work as ethical bricoleurs, patching together bits and pieces of moral languages, moral memories, and moral reasonings. It is always to look for the "better" solution (the most defensible one), not the "best" solution, because the latter is impossible to achieve, and, in Kant's words, is often the "enemy of the good." Alas, the "best" solution is nothing more than a figment of the developmental theorist's most normative yearnings.

QUESTION: Could you provide a concise example of a problem-solving brief that combines all three of your moral languages in analyzing a case? In Chapter 6, you talk frequently about blending the three languages, yet you never get to the point where you actually give the reader a paradigm or framework to do this. Once I have learned how to speak and to apply each of the three moral languages, is there a shortcut, problem-solving model—maybe you could call it an integrative, bricolage brief—that combines all three languages?

RESPONSE: I like the phrase "bricolage brief." Yes, I have developed such a brief, and my first attempt to explain it was published in one of the leading journals for student personnel administrators in higher education (Nash, 1997b). The initial feedback from readers was copious, as I received over 100 responses in a week's time. Each year, I continue to receive additional inquiries from people who read that article. I always make it a point, however, to advise readers that my integrative brief makes the most sense only after the user has developed a thorough understanding of each of the three moral languages that I construct in *"Real World" Ethics*. Without this background preparation, the "bricolage brief" is nothing more than a problem-solving tease, more suggestive than substantive.

What follows, then, is my bricolage brief (considerably modified and expanded from my earlier one), accompanied by a series of comments that I address directly to *students,* particularly those who have had some prior training in my ethics scheme or, at least, have carefully read my book. I will attempt to put a fresh face on my commentary on each of the questions in the brief, in order to respond to several issues which students have raised since *"Real World" Ethics* was first published.

1. What are the central moral issues in your dilemma?

Moral issues are those matters in your dilemma that touch on themes of goodness, rightness in conduct, principle and duty, and character. Often they will unsettle you, even make you nervous, because they will provoke you to wonder about your personal and professional responsibility in your case. Most of the time these moral issues will be in dispute, waiting for you (frequently in conjunction with others) to decide how to resolve them. A good first question to ask is this: What is there in my dilemma that seems to be bothering me on *moral* grounds, and why? What is the ethical itch that I cannot easily scratch? It might be an issue of confidentiality, promise-keeping, fairness, truth-telling, or whistle-blowing.

What signals an encounter with *morality* as opposed to legality or politics, for example? Any action you take that has the potential of affecting other human beings for good or for bad puts you squarely in moral territory. In this sense, morality comes before legality, sometimes necessitating an exercise of the latter, sometimes not. Your ultimate ethical decision will have a definite effect on the welfare of the people you serve, and you will not be able to avoid the consequent conflict. Identifying the central moral issues in any dilemma is an exercise in discernment, and the more practice you have in doing this, the better you will get at it.

Be on the lookout for ethical issues at all times. Be ever-ready to distinguish, and even to discuss with others, the moral elements you are able to perceive in a news story (including the way the media cover the news), a work of fiction, a television drama, a film, or better still, in a real world work-related or family-related incident that might otherwise seem ethically innocuous. But learn to do this is such a way that you don't appear to be ethically obsessed or a moral scold.

Moral discernment is a skill that one cultivates mainly through practice. There is nothing mysterious about it, and nobody is born a discernment expert. Try reading something like Randy Cohen's column each week in *The New York Times Magazine,* under the heading of "The Ethicist," to see if you agree or disagree with his take on ethical issues. When you can argue confidently with Cohen, or better still, when you are able to presuppose his questions and answers, you'll know that you've become a discerning moral thinker.

One of the more upsetting experiences I can remember having as an applied ethicist was when a pleasant, but morally undiscerning, high-level educational administrator came to me after sitting in my class for an entire semester to tell me somewhat gloatingly:

> I can honestly say that I have never had to deal with a single ethical issue in 25 years of professional practice. My problems are political and practical, not moral. Am I blind, or in denial, or are you and others in the class just making ethical mountains out of common-sense molehills?

I remember asking him if he thought that all the colleagues, students, and parents with whom he came in contact over the quarter-of-a-century that he administered to others would say the same thing about his professional practice. At that point, he abruptly terminated the conversation and walked away. Even granting him the benefit of the doubt in the best spirit of moral conversation, I would be inclined to think otherwise; particularly because I have had educational administrators tell me that ethical decision-making sometimes consumes upwards of 50% of their workdays. I could now understand why this student had been "between administrative jobs" for over a year when he took my course.

2. What are the conflicts in your case that make it an ethical dilemma?

Remember that not all professional dilemmas are necessarily *moral* in content. Some might be logistical, some technical, and some the result of interpersonal differences. You need to be able to tell the difference, and when you do, you can usually resolve these latter conflicts by applying some good common sense. Moreover, not all dilemmas that contain moral content are necessarily problems that require sustained ethical analysis. Sometimes the best moral action to take in an ethical dilemma is self-evident. Intuitively, you (and others) will know just the right thing to do, because all the other possible choices will seem far less ethically satisfying to you.

I hope that the majority of your ethical dilemmas are of this type, but don't count on it. It is interesting to note that one of the meanings of the word *conflict* is the "emotional disturbance that results from an inability to reconcile initial impulses with moral considerations" (Webster's New World College Dictionary, 1997). Most of your ethical conflicts will produce considerable "emotional disturbance," so be prepared for the hard cases, while hoping always for the easy ones.

The kind of ethical dilemma that I am talking about throughout *"Real World" Ethics,* however, is one that presents you with a conflict between two or more relatively equal moral alternatives. Each of these choices or decisions will appear to be personally and professionally defensible, and this is the hell of it. What makes an ethical dilemma particularly confounding is that even though you scrutinize your case from all sides, you just do not seem to know the right course of action to take. You could go in any number of directions. And there is no way that you will ever know for sure that you took the right path. You will need to consider a variety of factors before making your final decision, not the least off which is assessing the validity of a number of competing moral claims on your conscience.

But, if you have learned well the lessons of ethical discernment, and if you have gained a facility in using the three moral languages, you will be able, ultimately, to choose one alternative over another in the most informed and defensible way. I have found that it helps if you can state your ethical choices in the sharpest terms: For example, "On the one hand, I could tell the *full* truth about this treatment regimen, because" .... and "On the other hand, I could tell a *partial* truth about this treatment regimen, because ...." It is always good to declare your moral options clearly and succinctly, before you begin the arduous work of doing a detailed dilemma-analysis. Sometimes the simple act of stating your choices crisply at the outset is enough to point you in the right direction, because it clarifies the options available to you.

3. Who are the major stakeholders in your dilemma?

The major stakeholders are all those people who have a vested interest in your ethical actions. Obviously, these include your direct constituencies, but they also involve any number of other individuals and groups directly or indirectly affected by your decision. These are your hidden moral constituencies, and we know enough about bad political, religious, educational, media, and business decisions—to mention just a few—to understand that short-visioned and cramped ethical decision-making can be a disaster to forgotten stakeholders. The lesson for all of us should be that we will never be caught making our ethical decisions in an interpersonal vacuum. What we do will always affect others.

Think of the unavoidable ripple effect you will create whenever you engage in ethical decision-making. You may be wrestling with a particular ethical dilemma that appears to be affecting only you and the people with whom you are directly involved. On closer look, however, you become aware that your ethical orbit is larger than you thought—alarmingly larger. Because each of us moves within a circle of stakeholders that is continually expanding, we always need to know who else matters.

What rights and interests do they have? What promises and commitments have you made to them? How can you evaluate the direct and indirect impact that your actions and policies might have on them? Sartre may have said somewhere that "hell is others." But I am here to say unequivocally that "ethics is others," and our interests and activities inevitably overlap with countless, relevant others in our professional orbits. To forget this is truly to create Sartre's "hell" for yourself, especially if your ethical decision-making isn't expansive enough to include the interests of as many of these involved others as possible.

4. What are some foreseeable consequences of the possible choices in your dilemma? What are some foreseeable principles?

This question is calculated, among other things, to get you to consider as many of the foreseeable outcomes as possible in your decision-making. I am not asking you to become crystal-ball gazers, because who can ever accurately predict the future? If the future had a name, it would probably be called "unintended outcomes." Instead, I am asking you to consider, in a systematic yet tentative way, what might be some of the possible consequences emanating from your final ethical decision in your dilemma. There is a group of applied ethicists who actually call themselves "consequentialists," because they believe that our actions are good or bad depending on the consequences. They contend that every ethical decision will unavoidably produce good, bad, or mixed results, and these are what count in ultimately deciding what to do.

Thus, it is our professional responsibility to think long and hard about these potential effects before we actually make an ethical decision. In my opinion, and even though his name is currently enmeshed in controversy because of his position on such topics as abortion, animal rights, and euthanasia, Princeton professor Peter Singer is the single most articulate and persuasive spokesman writing in the world today on behalf of the consequentialist position. His *Practical Ethics* (1993) is an indispensable guide to consequentialist decision-making.

But I also maintain that it is not enough simply to list all the perceived consequences of any decision you might make, and then to do a cost-benefit, comparative analysis of each item on your consequentialist agenda before acting. There is still the annoying, but equally important, matter of moral principles to consider. Non-consequentialists hold that a principle-based decision is far more preferable than one that merely computes good and bad outcomes. Non-consequentialists want you to consider what moral principles are important to you, and whether or not you are acting in a way that is consistent with your principles.

To these thinkers, a principle-based decision, one that is independent of outcomes, is the morally superior one. Rushworth M. Kidder (1995), founder of the Institute for Global Ethics, and a leading non-consequentialist thinker, believes that there are eight moral principles that form a common ground for ethical decision-makers: love, truth, fairness, freedom, unity, tolerance, responsibility, and respect for life. Kidder calls these principles a "fundamental core of shared human values." In my opinion, despite their abstractness, they give us a good place to start in our ethical deliberations.

Michael Davis (1999), whom I introduced earlier, believes that most people in the real world seldom refer to moral principles or formal theories when they engage in ethical problem-solving. I for one strongly disagree. His characterization of professionals as being narrowly pragmatic problem-solvers, deliberately unconstrained by basic First Language beliefs, does not mesh at all with my perception of students through the years. Davis creates a stereotype of professionals as harried, practical people with little inclination or time to think deeply. This is an inaccurate caricature.

In fact, Davis himself, in the subtext of his fine volume, subscribes to the principles of utility, academic freedom, fairness, individual liberty, and accountability. He predicates his entire book on these principles, although never explicitly. In my opinion, his argument is soundest whenever it is presented in a way that is compatible with these guiding values. It is actually Davis's background beliefs and underlying ethical theories that capture the reader's attention from the very first page. These are always in his foreground, even though he wishes the rest of us to push them into the nether regions in our own problem-solving.

The upshot of considering both your consequences *and* your principles while analyzing an ethical dilemma is that you are leaving no moral stone unturned. You are blending both outcomes (warranted inferences about consequences) and fundamental beliefs (frameworks of meaning and guiding principles) in thinking through your case. You will soon learn the truth that no ethical decision can ever be complete without such synergy.

5. What are some viable alternatives to ethical courses of action in your dilemma?

What you see initially as an *ethical* dilemma, upon closer look, might actually be too restrictive. There might be no dilemma at all. Other alternative courses of action may be available to you. There are times when it is perfectly acceptable for you to use your practical imagination when confronted with what looks like a *moral* challenge. Look at all the possible *non-ethical* problem-solving processes open to you as you reflect on your dilemma. To do less is to lock yourself into a lengthy exercise in ethical analysis that could be distracting and unnecessary.

First, you need to check out all your facts, and then list all your viable options. It is illuminating that the Latin root of the word *viable* is "being able to live with." Thus, the question you need to answer is this: "What alternative solutions to my problem am I able to live with?" This is the literal meaning of viability, and it is a good guide for any kind of decision-making, particularly the ethical kind. The caution, of course, is to know the difference between *viability* and *expediency*. Figuring out this distinction can itself pose a moral dilemma, and, alas, if recent history is any judge, few politicians at the highest levels of American government appear to have learned the difference.

Fact-finding often brings us back to the reality of the day-to-day professional world we work in; and these facts often suggest some alternative directions you might be able to follow in your problem-solving. Fact-finding could conceivably prevent your later saying: "Why didn't I know this sooner? I could have saved myself a lot of wasted time and energy, if only I had the data." Exploring viable alternatives might mean sounding out colleagues and superiors on possible courses of action in your case. It might also mean thinking outside the dilemma (either-or) box, at least for awhile. One thing I have come to value highly about human service professionals is that most are excellent fact-finders and viable-alternatives explorers. And most are functional synergists.

6. What are some important background beliefs you should consider in your dilemma?

I have already talked about "zero-level" and First Moral Language beliefs enough in this chapter, and so I will not repeat myself here. My short instruction to you is to think as deeply as you can about those reference points (one of my former students, now an ethics instructor for health care professionals, refers to these as "anchors that sit below the surface," and which we ignore at our peril) that tend to give your life purpose, meaning, and direction. Ask yourself: How does the proposed action mesh with the important beliefs that tend to guide my life? This question, of course, necessitates a parallel question: Just what are the important beliefs that guide my life? If you cannot locate any of these beliefs, it is not because you don't have any. It is because you don't know how to access them; hence, my First Moral Language probes.

Intriguingly, the Old English etymology of the word *belief* is to desire or to love. Thus, without our background beliefs, we are unable to love. We are bereft of convictions. Nothing is real or true anymore. We have nothing to give to others, and they have nothing to give to us. We can neither love nor be loved. We are empty, and so is our professional practice. If, however, we do have beliefs, we are able to desire. We can help others, because we believe that this is both possible and desirable. We can help ourselves, because we believe that we have selves worth helping. We know that our lives have meaning, because we believe they do.

My hope for all of my students is that they don't end up where Leo Tolstoy did at age 50, after he briefly jettisoned all his religious and moral beliefs as improvable. Contemplating the possibility of suicide, he asked: "Why should I live? Why should I wish for anything? Why should I do anything? Is there any meaning in my life which will not be destroyed by the inevitable death awaiting me?" (cited in Yalom, 1980, p. 420).

Happily, Tolstoy went on to find a meaning to his life in an ethically based, New Testament Christianity. He became a believer once again, this time a religious anarchist, and he proudly accepted excommunication from the Russian Orthodox Church.

Think of your *general* background beliefs as those behavior-guiding stories that you tell yourself about the world in order to make sense of it, and in order to function in it with some degree of integrity and sanity. Then think of your *moral* background beliefs as those stories that you tell yourself about your relationships with close others, including your confidantes, intimates, friends, and neighbors, in order to do what is right by them and to avoid doing what is wrong to them. Then think of your *ethical* background beliefs as stories you tell yourself about your professional relationships with your colleagues, clients, patients, or students, in order to benefit them and to avoid harming them. I contend that it is impossible to do the work of human service professionals without our moral stories to guide us. Not only is it impossible to be an effective professional helper without guiding ethical beliefs, it is inconceivable that one can be an effective human being without a story to give life a sense of purpose, to foster community, to inspire moral action, and to explain the unknown.

7. What are some of your initial intuitions and feelings about your dilemma?

Do not be afraid to consult your intuitive stirrings and your feelings as you work your way through your dilemma. Intuitive flashes of insight, and emotional stirrings, can often be powerful guides to moral deliberation, if you learn to trust them—even though you also need to treat them with caution. I once submitted an article to a leading journal in higher education on the productive role that intuitions and feelings can play in helping us to arrive at ethical decisions which are reality-based and multi-layered. The critical feedback to the editor from three pre-publication reviewers was acerbic, in spite of which the article was eventually accepted and published:

- "This is a very dangerous article. Reject it. It is anti-intellectual."
- "Is the author saying that ethical decision-making is all about subjectivity and merely letting our feelings be our guide? I've heard it all now. Throw reason to the winds; just get in touch with your feelings. The answer will automatically come to you. The writer must be kidding."
- [And, perhaps the most biting of all:] "The author must be a devotee of Oprah Winfrey, getting in touch with his inner bliss. He should know that there is no place for New-Age, emotional wallowing in higher-education administration."

Of course, as I continually point out in my teaching, the best approach to ethical decision-making is one that fully integrates feelings, intuition, reason, logic, facts, context, socialization, and professional norms and codes. Obviously, when professionals separate feelings and intuitions from all the other factors that I discuss throughout *"Real World" Ethics*, they run the very real risk of relying too much on their subjective hunches and emotions in trying to solve their ethical dilemmas. I said as much in my article; however, the reviewers completely missed my point. I hope that you do not.

It is my understanding that intuitions and feelings are complex combinations of sentiments, biological responses, and thinking patterns which can signal possibly fruitful directions to take in sorting through the moral complexities in an ethical dilemma. Our feelings and intuitions are actually adaptive responses, and they confer survival benefits on us. This is one of the great findings of socio-biology and evolutionary psychology (Wright, 1994). Think of fight-or-flight responses to presentiments of imminent danger, whether in the wilderness of the forest or in the wilderness of the university. To feel does not mean that you must necessarily surrender to irrationality. In a sense, feeling and intuiting can be understood as alternative ways of thinking, and, thus, surviving. This certainly holds true for ethical survival in the professions. I have often had second thoughts about an impending ethical decision, provoked by a strong emotional or intuitive moment of unease. In several instances, I am glad that I did, because I wisely changed my mind at the last minute.

Respected scholars as diverse as David Hume (1751/1952), who referred to morals as "sentiments," Sidney Callahan (1991), who calls feelings "hot cognitions," and Daniel Goleman (1995), who believes that morality is impossible without feelings of empathy, do not view ethics as narrowly as did my critical reviewers. What the above scholars have in common is the wise insight that ethical judgment, moral character, and the art of living well require emotional maturity, or what Goleman calls "emotional literacy." Absent feelings of empathy, compassion, caring, and love, for example, there can be no ethic worth practicing. Feelings are the basis for how we treat others. At times, our feelings can educate us, push us in the ethically appropriate direction, signal a right or wrong turn. So too can our intuitions. It is time for the academy to catch up with the real world. Our clients think *and* feel, reason *and* intuit, and so do we.

8. What choices would you make if you were to act in character in your ethical dilemma?

Chapter 4, on the language of moral character, and the longest in my book, is also the one that represents a true labor of love for me. When I first started teaching courses in applied ethics some three decades ago, few people like me taught in professional schools, and even fewer bothered to teach an applied ethics course that seriously considered the interplay of such factors as narrative, community, and virtue in ethical problem-solving. Proudly, I can say that the Second Moral Language ranks are growing both inside and outside the academy. One example: Whenever I do consultancies for the healthcare professions, they find my Second Moral Language particularly resonant for their concerns. They understand well something that the social theorist, Amitai Etzioni (cited in Goleman, 1995), once said: "Character is the psychological muscle that moral conduct requires" (p. 285). Or as one young physician declared in a workshop I offered:

> Who I am often speaks more definitively to my patients than what I know. And this is the independent variable that begins the healing process with my patients, notwithstanding all the necessary diagnostic,

surgical, and drug interventions that I make. The dictum, "physician, know thyself," is the prerequisite in medicine nowadays for making a real connection with patients as persons, and not treating them simply as customers to be moved through an HMO at 7-minute intervals.

Acting in character means being consistent: knowing who you are, where you came from, and who you would like to become. It means being acutely aware of the ethical story about your life that you would like to "write" in the best of all possible worlds, of your past and present communities that have been so central in defining you as a moral being, and of those dispositions, qualities, motives, and intentions that define you to yourself as an ethical professional. To act out of character is to betray everything that is precious to you. It is to compromise, to turn away from your "best moral self," to abandon those communities, stories, and qualities of character that nourish and sustain you. Asking questions about moral character is one way to remain true to yourself. In my opinion, professionals go awry whenever they lose sight of all those moral characteristics which make them truly unique and for which they strive.

Some Second Moral Language, in-character questions that you might consider asking yourself as you process your ethical dilemma are these:

- Could I live with myself after I make the decision, even if I can rationally defend it?
- Could my professional community support me enthusiastically and without equivocation?
- If my decision were to receive heavy media coverage, would I blush in shame or beam with pride?
- Could I explain my ethical decision clearly and honorably to those I love (e.g., my children, my confidantes, and closest friends)?
- Would my personal integrity remain intact? And, if not, am I willing to compromise it for the sake of doing the expedient thing, or merely pleasing others?
- Could I defend my decision before a legal jury of my peers, or better, before the church community to which I belong?
- Could I defend my decision before my professional organization's ethics committee?
- Would I be happy and supportive if my colleagues, friends, or family members were to make the same decision if they were in my shoes?

The advantage of asking these types of questions is that they force us to be honest with ourselves. In the words of Michael Rion (1990), "they are devices to challenge our own self-deception" (p. 89). They are a wake-up call for us to remember who we are and what we would like to become. Such questions can be unsettling and irritating, but we need to ask them continually in order to avoid lying to ourselves about our presumed virtuousness as professionals.

9. What does your profession's code of ethics say regarding the relevant moral issues in your dilemma?

I discuss codes of ethics at length in Chapter 4, so I will not go into further detail here. I do want to add something that John Fletcher Moulton, an early twentieth-century English jurist, once implied about codes (cited in Kidder, 1995): Codes of ethics are systematic declarations of professional "manners" which attempt to secure from practitioners "obedience to the unenforceable" (p. 66). Unlike legal statutes, codes of ethics simply *point* the way to the good; they do not *stipulate* the good. They *remind* professionals of the rights and wrongs of practice; they do not (and cannot) by themselves *regulate* that practice. More important, they rely on the goodwill and integrity of professionals to observe the moral *spirit* of the code, because not only is the *letter* of the code subject to multiple interpretations, but the code itself is virtually unenforceable unless the profession unanimously agrees on the precise meaning and application of its prescriptions and proscriptions. This unanimity of agreement rarely occurs in the professions (Lebacqz, 1985).

Moulton realized that it is only when a society's ethics fails that the law is then invoked to fill the moral void. So too with the helping professions. It is interesting to note that, at times, some professions have attempted to wield their codes of ethics like law books in order to keep prospective wayward practitioners in line. This, unfortunately, is an exercise born in despair and destined for futility. Moulton would point out that, whenever this happens, the moral decay in these professions is complete: A kind of quasilegal set of ethical regulations from above is expected to do the work that individual practitioners ought to be doing from below.

Here are some questions to ask:

- Which particular ethical principles and practices in my profession's code might be directly, or even indirectly, applicable to my case, and which are not?
- Which specific principles and procedures appear to be congruent with my own personal code of ethics, and which do not?
- Which codified standards, principles, procedures, and practices seem most open to my personal interpretation, and which do not?
- How is my own evolving moral narrative compatible or incompatible with the overall story that the code is telling me about my profession?

Remember that, in the end, you must always *interpret*, not simply read and enact, the specific prescriptions and proscriptions in your code of ethics. This requires a keen understanding of the complex interplay that exists among all the morally relevant facts in your case-dilemma, the profession's codified principles and practices, and your own background beliefs, feelings and intuitions, personal story, and mode of analysis. On those occasions when there is a conflict between your personal code of ethics and your professional code, then you have an additional dilemma, itself demanding resolution. Nothing will ever be easy.

10. What is your decision in the dilemma, and do you have any afterthoughts?

It is at this point that you need to pull together all the material in your bricolage moral brief into an integrated, defensible statement, clearly elucidating the reasons for your ultimate ethical decision. You will need to find what Strike and Soltis (1998) call a "reflective equilibrium" among your feelings, intuitions, background beliefs, principles, and how you experience yourself as a particular type of moral person. Ethical decision-making, is, only in part, like a legal process. Be thankful that it is. In ethical deliberations, frequent appeals to the law, while helpful, can sometimes lead to an abdication of moral responsibility on the part of both the profession in general and of its individual practitioners.

Objective factors such as rationality, logical thinking, data collection, rule-following, normative precedents, and appeals to professional codes must always be balanced by subjective factors and vice versa. These include feelings, intuitions, background beliefs, and your perception of yourself as a moral agent who embodies certain virtues, represents certain communities of memory, and is living out a particular moral story. The most effective ethical reasoning process, I can only repeat, will avoid the extremes of both moral relativism and moral objectivism. A pure moral relativist believes that ethics exists only in the eye of the beholder. A pure moral objectivist believes that ethics exists only in the eye of God. Despite the possibility of truth in each view, in my opinion, there is no room for "purity" in ethical problem-solving, because dilemmas are usually so complex and challenging that they are always susceptible to interpretation, compromise, and concession.

In truth, no solution to an ethical dilemma will ever be fully adequate or fully self-satisfying. You will soon discover that you could have gone in another direction, made another decision, second-guessed yourself yet one more time, gathered more data, consulted another authority, and re-parsed another codified ethical principle in a different way. The upshot is that you need to continue to do the best you can, let the ethical chips fall where they may, and explain and defend your final decision with what I earlier called "tenuous tenacity." And you need to do all of this with dignity and grace. Finally, be grateful for your nagging afterthoughts. They can be an important check on ethical arrogance, because they continually remind us of how arbitrary and fragile moral decision-making really is. They will keep you humble and open to alternative views.

A BRIEF CLOSING REMARK

If [as Clifford Geertz, the anthropologist, once suggested] we are suspended in webs of significance that we ourselves have spun, then it is only by looking closely at how we are situated in those webs that we can see how we may be trapped there, or falling, or gazing contentedly at the ceiling. (Elliot, 2000, p. 12)

The above epigraph aptly sums up my sentiments for writing *"Real World" Ethics,* including this Epilogue. I want my book, which lays out my particular approach to ethical analysis and problem-solving, to be an open invitation for all of us in the professions to think of ethics as a "web that we ourselves have spun." Ethics is our attempt to spin a web of moral meaning in such a way that it profoundly informs our personal and professional lives. We do the spinning as much with moral languages as we do with anything else, and it is with these languages that we produce ethical "webs of significance."

If a course in applied ethics is to be effective, then students and instructors must understand that there is no relief from the full responsibility each of us bears for the moral languages we choose and use. Thus, all of us must think long and hard about these languages, if only to avoid the "trap" of having these languages choose and use us. While the temptation may frequently be great for us simply to "fall" in line with the dominant moral thinking of the profession, or of society at large, or to "gaze contentedly" at what the profession might stipulate as its ultimate moral "ceiling," I am hoping and asking for us to do much more.

I want us to think of ethical problem-solving as a vigorous, risk-taking, intensely reflective, personal as well as communal, process. I want us to think of it as potentially life-affirming and, when necessary, life-transforming, both for us and for the people we serve. I want us to summon up the courage to speak moral truth to colleagues in our professions, whenever they might be living something less than the ethical truth they publicly profess. This, I suspect, is why so many readers have found my approach to ethical problem solving to be both useful, but also incredibly challenging. I feel similarly, and I, for one, would not want it any other way.

REFERENCES

INDEX

ABOUT THE AUTHOR

REFERENCES

Albom, M. (1997). *Tuesdays with Morrie: An old man, a young man, and life's greatest lesson.* New York: Doubleday.

American Association for Counseling and Development. (1988, March). *Ethical standards.* Alexandria, VA: AACD Governing Council.

Angeles, P. A. (1992). *The HarperCollins dictionary of philosophy.* New York: Harper-Collins.

Aquinas, St. T. (1256/1948). *Introduction to St. Thomas Aquinas* (A. C. Pegis, Ed.). New York: Random House.

Aristotle. (1976). *The ethics of Aristotle: The Nicomachean ethics* (J. A. K. Thomson, Trans.). New York: Penguin.

Aristotle. (1982). *The politics* (T. A. Sinclair, Trans.). New York: Penguin.

Arkes, H. (1986). *First things: An inquiry into the first principles of morals and justice.* Princeton, NJ: Princeton University Press.

Baier, K. (1965). *The moral point of view.* New York: Random House.

Barnes, H. E. (1971). *An existentialist ethics.* New York: Vintage.

Barnes, J. (1982). *Aristotle.* Oxford: Oxford University Press.

Beauchamp, T. L., & Childress, J. F. (1979). *Principles of biomedical ethics* (2nd ed.). New York: Oxford University Press.

Becker, H. (1970). *Sociological work: Method and substance.* Chicago: Aldine.

Bellah, R. N., Madsen, R., Sullivan, W. M., Swidler, A., & Tipton, S. M. (1985). *Habits of the heart: Individualism and commitment in American life.* Berkeley: University of California Press.

Bennett, W. J. (1988). *Our children and our country.* New York: Simon & Schuster.

Bennett, W. J. (1992). *The de-valuing of America: The fight for our culture and our children.* New York: Summit.

Berger, P. L. (1970). *A rumor of angels: Modern society and the rediscovery of the supernatural.* New York: Anchor.

Bernstein, R. J. (1992). *The new constellation: The ethical political horizons of modernity/postmodernity.* Cambridge, MA: MIT Press.

Bloom, A. (1987). *The closing of the American mind.* New York: Simon & Schuster.

Bok, D. C. (1976, October). Can ethics be taught? *Change,* pp. 27–30.

Bok, S. (1978). *Lying: Moral choice in public and private life.* New York: Vintage.

Booth, W. (1988). *The company we keep: An ethics of fiction.* Berkeley: University of California Press.

Broad, C. D. (1930). *Five types of ethical theory.* London: Routledge & Kegan Paul.

Brody, H. (1987). *Stories of sickness.* New Haven, CT: Yale University Press.

Brody, H. (1991). *The healer's power.* New Haven, CT: Yale University Press.

Bromwich, D. (1992). *Politics by other means: Higher education and group thinking.* New Haven, CT: Yale University Press.

Bruffee, K. A. (1993). *Collaborative learning: Higher education, interdependence, and the authority of knowledge.* Baltimore, MD: Johns Hopkins University Press.

Buber, M. (1958). I *and thou* (2nd ed.). (R. G. Smith, Trans.). New York: Charles Scribner's Sons. (Original work published 1923)

Butler, J. (1949). *Five sermons.* New York: Liberal Arts Press.

Callahan, D., & Bok, S. (1979, September). The role of applied ethics in learning. *Change*, pp. 23–27.

Callahan, S. (1991). *In good conscience: Reason and emotion in moral decision making.* San Francisco: HarperCollins.

Carmody, D. L. (1992). *Virtuous woman: Reflections on Christian feminist ethics.* New York: Orbis.

Carr-Saunders, A. M., & Wilson, P. A. (1933). *The professions.* Oxford: Clarendon.

Clouser, K. D., & Gert, B. (1990). A critique of principlism. *Journal of Medicine and Philosophy, 15,* 219–236.

Coles, R. (1989). *The call of stories: Teaching and the moral imagination.* Boston: Houghton Mifflin.

Damon, W. (1988). *The moral child: Nurturing children's natural moral growth.* New York: The Free Press.

Davis, M. (1999). *Ethics and the university.* New York: Routledge.

Drucker, P. (1981, Spring). What is business ethics? *The Public Interest*, pp. 18–36.

Dyck, A. J. (1977). *On human care: An introduction to ethics.* Nashville: Abingdon.

Eck, D. L. (1993). *Encountering God: A spiritual journey from Bozeman to Banaras.* Boston: Beacon.

Eger, M. (1981, Spring). The conflict in moral education. *The Public Interest*, pp. 62–80.

Elliot, C. (2000, March-April). Pursued by happiness and beaten senseless: Prozac and the American dream. *The Hastings Center Report*, pp. 7–12.

Engelhardt, H. T., Jr. (1986). *The foundations of bioethics.* Oxford: Oxford University.

Engelhardt, H. T., Jr. (1991). *Bioethics and secular humanism: The search for a common morality.* Philadelphia: Trinity Press International.

Fetter, J. H. (1995). *Questions and admissions: Reflections on 100,000 admissions decisions at Stanford.* Stanford, CA: Stanford University Press.

Fish, S. (1999). *The trouble with principle.* Cambridge, MA: Harvard University Press.

Flanagan, O., & Jackson, K. (1987, April). Justice, care, and gender: The Kohlberg-Gilligan debate revisited. *Ethics*, pp. 622–637.

Fletcher, J. (1966). *Situation ethics: The new morality.* Philadelphia: Westminster.

Fletcher, J. (1967). *Moral responsibility: Situation ethics at work.* Philadelphia: Westminster.

Fowler, J. (1981). *Stages of faith: The psychology of human development and the quest for meaning.* New York: Harper & Row.

Fox, M. (1990). *The coming of the cosmic Christ.* New York: Harper & Row.

Fox, R. (1957). Training for uncertainty. In R. K. Merton (Ed.), *The student physician* (pp. 207–241). Cambridge, MA: Harvard University Press.

Frankena, W. K. (1973). *Ethics* (2nd ed.). Englewood Cliffs, NJ: Prentice-Hall.

Freidson, E. (1973). *Profession of medicine: A study of the sociology of applied knowledge.* New York: Dodd, Mead.

Freire, P. (1985). *The politics of education: Culture, power and liberation* (D. Macedo, Trans.). Granby, MA: Bergin & Garvey.

Gadamer, H.-G. (1976). *Philosophical hermeneutics* (D. E. Linge, Trans.). Berkeley: University of California Press.

Gaskin, J. C. A. (1984). *The quest for eternity: An outline of the philosophy* of *religion.* Middlesex, England: Penguin.

Gilligan, C. (1982). *In a different voice: Psychological theory and women's development.* Cambridge, MA: Harvard University Press.

Glaser, J. W. (1994). *Three realms of ethics: Individual, institutional, societal.* Kansas City, MO: Sheed & Ward.

Glover, J. (1999). *Humanity: A moral history of the twentieth century.* New Haven, CT: Yale University Press.

Goleman, D. (1995). *Emotional intelligence.* New York: Bantam.

Gomes, P. J. (1996). *The good book: Reading the Bible with mind and heart.* New York: William Morrow.

Greeley, A. M. (1990). *The Catholic myth: The behavior and beliefs of American Catholics.* New York: Charles Scribner's Sons.

Grimshaw, J. (1986). *Philosophy and feminist thinking.* Minneapolis: University of Minnesota Press.

Gustafson, J. (1981). *Ethics from a theocentric perspective: Vol. I. Theology and ethics.* Chicago: University of Chicago Press.

Halberstam, J. (1994). *Everyday ethics: Inspired solutions to real-life dilemmas.* New York: Penguin.

Harding, S. (1987). The curious coincidence of feminine and African moralities: Challenges for feminist theory. In E. F. Kittay & D. T. Meyers (Eds.), *Women and moral theory* (pp. 296–316). Totowa, NJ: Rowman & Littlefield.

Hare, R. M. (1952). *The language of morals.* Oxford: Oxford University Press.

Hare, R. M. (1963). *Freedom and reason.* Oxford: Oxford University Press.

Hart, H. L. A. (1963). *Law, liberty, and morality.* Stanford, CA: Stanford University Press.

Hauerwas, S. (1977). *Truthfulness and tragedy: Further investigations into Christian ethics.* Notre Dame, IN: University of Notre Dame Press.

Hauerwas, S. (1981). *A community of character: Toward a constructive Christian social ethic.* Notre Dame, IN: University of Notre Dame Press.

Hebblethwaite, B. (1988). *The ocean of truth: A defence of objective theism.* Cambridge, England: Cambridge University Press.

Hegel, G. W. E. (1953). *Reason in history* (R. S. Hartman, Trans.). Indianapolis, IN: Bobbs-Merril. (Original work published 1821)

Hirsch, E. D., Jr. (1987). *Cultural literacy: What every American needs to know.* Boston, MA: Houghton Mifflin.

Hobbes, T. (1962). *Leviathan* (M. Oakeshott, Ed.). New York: Macmillan. (Original work published 1651)

Honig, B. (1985). *Last chance for our children.* Reading, MA: Addison-Wesley.

Howe, K. R., & Miramontes, O. B. (1992). *The ethics of special education.* New York: Teachers College Press.

Hudson, W. D. (1970). *Modern moral philosophy.* New York: Doubleday & Company.

Hume, D. (1930). *An enquiry into the principles of morals.* Chicago: Open Court Publishing Company. (Original work published 1748)

Hume, D. (1952). An enquiry concerning human understanding. In *Great books of the Western world* (Vol. 35). Chicago: Encyclopaedia Britannica. (Original work published 1751)

Hunter, J. D. (1991). *Culture wars: The struggle to define America.* New York: Basic Books.

Hunter, J. D. (1994). *Before the shooting begins: Searching for democracy in America's culture war.* New York: The Free Press.

Johnson, P. G. (1997). *God and world religions: Basic beliefs and themes.* Shippensburg, PA: Beidel Printing House.

Jonsen, A. R., & Toulmin, S. (1988). *The abuse of casuistry: A history of moral reasoning.* Berkeley: University of California Press.

Kaminer, W. (1990). *A fearful freedom: Women's flight from equality.* Reading, MA: Addison-Wesley.

Kant, I. (1968). *Critique of pure reason* (N. K. Smith, Trans.). London: Macmillan. (Original work published 1781)

Kant, I. (1991). *The metaphysics of morals* (M. Gregor, Trans.). Cambridge, England: Cambridge University Press. (Original work published 1797)

Kidder, R. M. (1995). *How good people make tough choices.* New York: Morrow.

Kilpatrick, W (1992). *Why Johnny can't tell right from wrong.* New York: Simon & Schuster.

Kirk, R. (1987). *The wise men know what wicked things are written on the sky.* Washington, DC: Regnery Gateway.

Kittay, E. F., & Meyers, D. T. (Eds.). (1987). *Women and moral theory.* Totowa, NJ: Rowman & Littlefield.

Kohlberg, L. (1981). *The philosophy of moral development.* San Francisco: Harper & Row.

Kohlberg, L. (1984). *The psychology of moral stages.* San Francisco: Harper & Row.

Kreeft, P. (1990). *Making choices: Practical wisdom for everyday moral decisions.* Ann Arbor, MI: Servant Publications.

Kreeft, P. (1992). *Back to virtue: Traditional moral wisdom for modern moral confusion.* San Francisco: Ignatius Press.

Kurtz, P. (1988). *Forbidden fruit: The ethics of humanism.* New York: Prometheus.

Lamott, A. (1994). *Bird by bird: Some instructions on writing and life.* New York: Pantheon.

Lawrence-Lightfoot, S. (2000). *Respect: An explanation.* Cambridge, MA: Perseus.

Lebacqz, K. (1985). *Professional ethics: Power and paradox.* Nashville: Abingdon.

Lewis, H. (1990). *A question of values: Six ways we make the personal choices that shape our lives.* San Francisco: Harper & Row.

Lickona, T. (1983). *Raising good children.* New York: Bantam.

Lickona, T. (1991). *Educating for character: How our schools can teach respect and responsibility.* New York: Bantam.

Light, D. (1980). *Becoming psychiatrists: The professional transformation of self.* New York: Norton.

Lilla, M. T. (1981, Spring). Ethos, ethics, and public service. *The Public Interest,* pp. 3–11.

MacIntyre, A. (1984). *After virtue: A study in moral theory* (2nd ed.). Notre Dame, IN: University of Notre Dame Press.

Mackie, J. L. (1977). *Ethics: Inventing right and wrong.* New York: Penguin.

Macklin, R. (1987). *Mortal choices: Ethical dilemmas in modern medicine.* Boston: Houghton Mifflin.

Maguire, D. C. (1978). *The moral choice.* New York: Winston Press.

Maguire, D. C. (1984). *Death by choice.* New York: Image.

Martin, J. R. (1985). *Reclaiming a conversation: The ideal of the educated woman.* New Haven, CT: Yale University Press.

McGrath, E. Z. (1994). *The art of ethics. A psychology of ethical beliefs.* Chicago: Loyola University Press.

Mednick, M. T. (1989). On the politics of psychological constructs: Stop the bandwagon, I want to get off. *American Psychologist, 44*(8), 1118–1123.

Meilaender, G. C. (1984). *The theory and practice of virtue.* Notre Dame, IN: University of Notre Dame Press.

Midgley, M. (1991). *Can't we make moral judgements?* New York: St. Martin's Press.

Mill, J. S. (1957). *Utilitarianism* (O. Piest, Ed.). New York: Macmillan. (Original work published 1861)

Mill, J. S. (1982). *On liberty.* New York: Penguin. (Original work published 1859)

Moran, G. (1989). *Religious education as a second language.* Birmingham, AL: Religious Education Press.

Nash, R. J. (1988, Winter). The revival of virtue in educational thinking: A postliberal appraisal. *Educational Theory,* pp. 27–39.

Nash, R. J. (1991, May-June). Three conceptions of ethics for teacher educators. *Journal of Teacher Education,* pp. 163–172.

Nash, R. J. (1996). Fostering moral conversations in the college classroom. *Journal on Excellence in College Teaching, 7,* 83–106.

Nash, R. J. (1997a). *Answering the "virtuecrats": A moral conversation on character education.* New York: Teachers College Press.

Nash, R. J. (1997b, Fall). Teaching ethics in the student affairs classroom. *NASPA Journal,* pp. 3–19.

Nash, R. J. (1999). *Faith, hype, and clarity: Teaching about religion in American schools and colleges.* New York: Teachers College Press.

Nash, R. J. (2001). *Religious pluralism in the academy: Opening the dialogue.* New York: Peter Lang.

Nash, R. J. (in press). Fostering moral conversations in the college classroom. *Journal on Excellence in College Teaching*

Nash, R. J., & E. R. Ducharme. (1976, May). A futures perspective on preparing educators for the human service society: How to restore a sense of social purpose to teacher education. *Teachers College Record,* pp. 441–471.

National Association of College Admission Counselors. (1989, October 7). *Statement of principles of good practice.* New York: NACAC Delegate Assembly.

Natoli, J. (1997). *A primer to postmodernity.* Malden, MA: Blackwell.

Neuhaus, R. J. (1986). *Virtue: Public and private.* Grand Rapids, MI: Eerdmans.

Nietzsche, F. (1967). *On the genealogy of morals* (W. Kaufmann, Trans.). New York: Vintage. (Original work published in 1887)

Noddings, N. (1984). *Caring: A feminine approach to ethics and moral education.* Berkeley: University of California Press.

Noddings, N. (1989). *Women and evil.* Berkeley: University of California Press.

Nord, W. A. (1995). *Religion and American education.* Chapel Hill: University of North Carolina Press.

Nozick, R. (1989). *The examined life: Philosophical meditations.* New York: Touchstone.

Oakeshott, M. (1950). The idea of a university. *The Listener, 43,* 420–450.

Okin, S. M. (1989). Reason and feeling in thinking about justice. *Ethics, 99,* 229–249.

Oldenquist, A. (1986). *The non-suicidal society.* Bloomington, IN: Indiana University Press.

Oxford English Dictionary (The New Shorter). (1993). (L. Brown, Ed.). London: Oxford University Press.

Palmer, P. (1983). *To know as we are known: A spirituality of education.* New York: Harper & Row.

Perry, W. G. (1970). *Forms of intellectual and ethical development in the college years: A scheme.* New York: Holt, Rinehart, & Winston.

Pincoffs, E. L. (1986). *Quandaries and virtues: Against reductivism in ethics.* Lawrence: University Press of Kansas.

Plato. (1961). *The collected dialogues* (E. Hamilton & H. Cairns, Eds.). Princeton, NJ: Princeton University Press.

Pojman, L. P. (1995). *Ethics: Discovering right and wrong.* Belmont, CA: Wadsworth.

Polanyi, M. (1966). *The tacit dimension.* Garden City, NY: Doubleday.

Pregeant, R. (1988). *Mystery without magic.* Oak Park, IL: Meyer, Stone, and Company.

Purpel, D. E. (1989). *The moral and spiritual crisis in education: A curriculum for justice and compassion in education.* Granby, MA: Bergin & Garvey.

Purpel, D. E. (1999). *Moral outrage in education.* New York: Peter Lang.

Ramsey, P. (1970). *The patient as person.* New Haven, CT: Yale University Press.

Rand, A. (1961). *The virtue of selfishness.* New York: New American Library.

Raths, L., Harmin, M., & Simon, S. (1966). *Values and teaching.* Columbus, OH: Merrill.

Ravitch, D. (1985). *The schools we deserve: Reflections on the educational crises of our time.* New York: Basic Books.

Rawls, J. (1971). *A theory of justice.* Cambridge, MA: Harvard University Press.

Rawls, J. (1993). *Political liberalism.* New York: Columbia University Press.

Rion, M. (1990). *The responsible manager: Practical strategies for ethical decision making.* New York: Harper & Row.

Roof, W. C. (1993). *A generation of seekers: The spiritual journeys of the baby boom generation.* San Francisco: HarperCollins.

Rorty, R. (1989). *Contingency, irony, and solidarity.* Cambridge, England: Cambridge University Press.

Rorty, R. (1999). *Philosophy and social hope.* New York: Penguin.

Ross, W. D. (1930). *The right and the good.* Oxford: Clarendon.

Sandel, M. J. (1982). *Liberalism and the limits of justice.* Cambridge, England: Cambridge University Press.

Scruton, R. (1982). *A dictionary of political thought.* New York: Hill & Wang.

Shelton, C. M. (1989). *Adolescent spirituality: Pastoral ministry for high school and college youth.* New York: Crossroad.

Sichel, B. A. (1988). *Moral education: Character, community, and ideals.* Philadelphia: Temple University Press.

Singer, P. (1993). *Practical ethics* (2nd ed.). Cambridge, England: Cambridge University Press.

Smart, N. (1983). *Worldviews: Crosscultural explorations of human beliefs.* New York: Charles Scribner's Sons.

Smith, B. H. (1988). *Contingencies of value: Alternative perspectives for critical theory.* Cambridge, MA: Harvard University Press.

Smith, H. (1991). *The world's religions.* New York: HarperCollins.

Spong, J. S. (1991). *Rescuing the Bible from fundamentalism: A bishop rethinks the meaning of scripture.* San Francisco: Harper.

Stern, D. (1984). *The interpersonal world of the infant.* New York: Basic Books.

Stevens, E. (1974). *The morals game.* New York: Paulist Press.

Stout, J. (1981). *The flight from authority: Religion, morality, and the quest for autonomy.* Notre Dame, IN: University of Notre Dame Press.

Stout, J. (1988). *Ethics after Babel: The languages of morals and their discontents.* Boston: Beacon.

Strike, K., & Soltis, J. F. (1992). *The ethics of teaching* (2nd ed.). New York: Teachers College Press.

Strike, K. & Soltis, J. F. (1998). *The ethics of teaching* (3rd ed.). New York: Teachers College Press.

Taylor, A. E. (1955). *Aristotle.* New York: Dover.

Taylor, C. (1992). *The ethics of authenticity.* Cambridge, MA: Harvard University Press.

Tournier, P. (1963). *The meaning of gifts.* London: Oxford University Press.

Weiler, K. (1988). *Women teaching for change: Gender, class & power.* New York: Bergin & Garvey.

Welch, D. D. (1994). *Conflicting agendas: Personal morality in institutional settings.* Cleveland, OH: Pilgrim Press.

Welch, S. D. (1990). *A feminist ethic of risk.* Minneapolis, MN: Fortress Press.

Williams, B. (1985). *Ethics and the limits of philosophy.* Cambridge, MA: Harvard University Press.

Wilson, J. Q. (1993). *The moral sense.* New York: The Free Press.

Wittgenstein, L. (1968). *Philosophical investigations.* New York: Macmillan. (Original work published 1953)

Wright, R. (1994). *The moral animal: Evolutionary psychology and everyday life.* New York: Vintage.

Wynne, E. A., & Ryan, K. (1993). *Reclaiming our schools: A handbook on teaching character, academics, and discipline.* New York: Macmillan.

Yalom, I. D. (1980). *Existential psychotherapy.* New York: Basic Books.

INDEX

ABOUT THE AUTHOR

Robert J. Nash is a professor in the College of Education and Social Services, University of Vermont, Burlington, specializing in philosophy of education, ethics, higher education, and religion, spirituality, and education. He holds graduate degrees in English, Theology, Applied Ethics and Liberal Studies, and Educational Philosophy. He holds faculty appointments in teacher education, higher education administration, and interdisciplinary studies. He administers the Interdisciplinary Master's Program, and he teaches ethics courses across three programs in the college, including the doctoral program in Educational Leadership and Policy Studies. He has published more than 100 articles, book chapters, monographs, and essay book reviews in many of the leading journals in education at all levels. He is a member of the editorial board for the *Journal of Religion & Education,* and one of its frequent contributors. Since 1996, he has published six books, among them *Answering the "Virtuecrats": A Moral Conversation on Character Education; Faith, Hype, and Clarity: Teaching About Religion in American Schools and Colleges; Religious Pluralism in the Academy: Opening the Dialogue;* and *Spirituality, Ethics, Religion, and Teaching: A Professor's Journey.* He has done ethics consultancies throughout the country for a number of human service organizations. He has also made a series of major presentations at national conferences and at universities on the topics of ethics, character education, religious pluralism, and moral conversation.